Enchanted America

Enchanted America

*How Intuition and Reason
Divide Our Politics*

J. ERIC OLIVER AND
THOMAS J. WOOD

THE UNIVERSITY OF CHICAGO PRESS   CHICAGO AND LONDON

The University of Chicago Press, Chicago 60637
The University of Chicago Press, Ltd., London
© 2018 by The University of Chicago
Published 2018
Printed in the United States of America

27 26 25 24 23 22 21 20 19 18   1 2 3 4 5

ISBN-13: 978-0-226-57847-7 (cloth)
ISBN-13: 978-0-226-57850-7 (paper)
ISBN-13: 978-0-226-57864-4 (e-book)
DOI: https://doi.org/10.7208/chicago/9780226578644.001.0001

Library of Congress Cataloging-in-Publication Data

Names: Oliver, J. Eric, 1966– author. | Wood, Thomas John, 1944– author.
Title: Enchanted America : how intuition and reason divide our politics / J. Eric Oliver
    and Thomas J. Wood.
Description: Chicago ; London : The University of Chicago Press, 2018. |
    Includes bibliographical references and index.
Identifiers: LCCN 2017060698 | ISBN 9780226578477 (cloth : alk. paper) |
    ISBN 9780226578507 (pbk. : alk. paper) | ISBN 9780226578644 (e-book)
Subjects: LCSH: United States—Politics and government—21st century. | Religion and
    politics—United States. | Right and left (Political science)—United States. |
    Reason—Political aspects. | Intuition—Political aspects.
Classification: LCC JK275.O559 2018 | DDC 320.973—dc23
LC record available at https://lccn.loc.gov/2017060698

♾ This paper meets the requirements of ANSI/NISO Z39.48-1992 (Permanence of Paper).

The fate of our times is characterized by rationalization and intellectualization and, above all, the disenchantment of the world.

MAX WEBER, 1920

Contents

An appendix containing a full description of the surveys and other information can be accessed at press.uchicago.edu /sites /oliver_wood /.

Illustrations

TABLES

Preface

We Americans are a curious people.

We live in a time of unprecedented safety, yet are beset by chronic anxieties about imminent doom. We are highly educated, yet harbor a vast constellation of outlandish and primitive beliefs. We obsess over our children's well-being, yet often refuse to vaccinate them against real diseases. We are awash in news and information, yet subscribe to all sorts of preposterous conspiracy theories. We live in an era of breathtaking scientific achievement, yet cling to ancient myths of angels, demons, and an impending Rapture.

And then there is Donald Trump. In 2016, Trump, a presidential candidate with no governing experience and little knowledge of public policy or world affairs, won the election with over 46 percent of the popular vote. Throughout his campaign, he continuously boasted about himself, denigrated others, and lied about nearly everything else.[1] He refused to release his tax returns. He was repeatedly sued for fraud. He was recorded bragging about sexually assaulting women. He had historically high unfavorable ratings and was shunned by much of the leadership within his own party. Yet not only did Trump capture both the Republican nomination and the presidency; he persuaded tens of millions of self-described conservatives and Christian fundamentalists to rally behind him, despite having no apparent political or moral convictions.

What is going on?

Most people who write about society and politics don't have a particularly good answer. Political commentators regularly dismiss Trump supporters, "anti-vaxxers," fundamentalist Christians, and conspiracy theorists as hoodwinked, deluded, or just plain stupid. Their "irrational" beliefs seem out of step with modern times—superstitions, conspiratorial fantasies, and apocalyptic visions were supposed to have vanished with the Dark Ages. A sensible public is supposed to see through the transparent contrivances of petty demagogues. So when these experts encounter opinions that don't conform to their own "rational" ways of thinking, they either denigrate such views as pathological or relegate them to the error term in their models.

This is a major oversight. One reason so many political experts underestimated the electoral chances of Donald Trump was because they could not comprehend how people would embrace a worldview so foreign to their own. These experts had fallen prey to the assumption that all other people perceive the world as they do.[2] By their logic, any reasonable person would reject Trump as a presidential candidate.[3] And a reasonable person, as they understand it, probably would—just as any "reasonable" person rejects conspiracy theories, appreciates science, and recognizes common facts. But there is another powerful force organizing American politics that has little to do with reason, science, or fact. It is a force with its own powerful logic. It compels fundamentalists to support Donald Trump, it motivates liberals to reject vaccines, and it prompts millions to believe that the US government orchestrated the attacks of 9/11. This force is human Intuition.

Intuitions are the ways we comprehend reality that don't involve deliberate thinking. They are our "gut feelings," the subliminal ways we make quick judgments, the mental processes that guide us in the absence of conscious, purposeful thought.[4] They are how we just "know" that some actions are right, some things are true, or some people are trustworthy. Intuitions comprise our "folk wisdom," the commonsense ways of understanding worldly matters. This book explains how these intuitions operate, and how they are shaping American politics.

Our central argument is that the most important political division in the United States is not simply between liberals and conservatives or between "red" and "blue" states; rather, it is between Rationalists and Intuitionists. Rationalists are people who comprehend reality using nonintuitive sources. They utilize abstract theories, philosophical deductions, and observable facts. They view social and political problems in a dispassionate manner, seeking pragmatic, technical solutions. They exist all over the political spectrum but generally share a common respect for science and reason. They may adhere to different philosophies, but inevitably, they all draw from the same intellectual wells dug by Locke and Kant, Smith and Mill, Keynes and Hayek.

Intuitionists are *enchanted*. Rather than using thoughtful deliberation or detached observations, they rely on their internal feelings as a guide to their external reality. They are quick to embrace superstitions, magical beliefs, or other simplistic explanations for complex events. For Intuitionists, truth is found more in metaphors and myth than in arcane theories or facts. Fervently tribalistic, they mistrust outsiders and suspect unfamiliar cultures. They are the followers of mystics and prophets, faith healers and charismatics, demagogues and provocateurs. Their beliefs are things they just *know* and are not subject to reasoned interrogation.

Most Americans exist somewhere in between these poles, harboring a combination of Rationalist and Intuitionist proclivities. But how close someone is to one side or the other can tell us a lot about their political thinking. Drawing from a rich array of anthropological and psychological studies, we explain how our intuitions function. Then, based on these insights, we develop an Intuitionism scale, a single metric that measures how much people rely on their intuitions when making judgments. Deploying this scale across six nationally representative surveys, we find a remarkable set of results. As Intuitionism rises, a distinctive constellation of opinions and beliefs comes into focus. The higher a person's Intuitionism score, the more likely that person will

- believe in supernatural notions like angels, hidden Bible codes, or the power of prayer;
- believe in paranormal ideas like reincarnation, ghosts, or ESP;
- reject well-established scientific explanations or the advice of medical experts;
- mistrust their fellow citizens, the media, and civic institutions;
- be more easily swayed by emotional appeals and evocative symbols;
- subscribe to conspiracy theories;
- embrace populist characterizations of money, power, and politics;
- hold strongly nationalistic and ethnocentric views;
- endorse alternative medicine and the sanctity of natural foods;
- be intolerant of basic democratic norms and civil liberties.

In politics, Intuitionists are the folks who were most captivated by Donald Trump's populist rhetoric and his nativist accusations. They are the fundamentalist Christians who desperately want to outlaw abortion. They support bans on genetically modified foods, resist vaccinations, and believe that 9/11 was an inside job. They are passionate about protecting gun rights, promoting herbal remedies, or banning physician-assisted suicide. They are fearful of immigrants and stridently nationalistic in their political views. And while they exist all over the political spectrum, they are increasingly found among the political Right.

Which brings us back to our central argument: Americans are divided not simply in how they see the proper role of government but in how they see reality. Fifty years ago, nearly all Americans believed in both God *and* science; today, Americans have become increasingly split between those who believe in only one or the other. And each of these sides is staking an ideological claim: liberals proclaim that they believe in science while rejecting prayer in public schools; meanwhile, many conservatives dismiss climate science while trumpeting the coming Rapture, when the faithful will be assumed into heaven as the world comes to an end. Rationalism has become increasingly relegated to the political Left, while Intuitionists have become *the* dominant force in the conservative movement and Republican Party politics.

This is a major problem for the Republic. Historically, American liberals and conservatives may have disagreed about the proper role and scope of government, but they usually shared a common regard for reason, facts, and the basic ideals of democracy. They shared a common religious tradition as well. They may have drawn different conclusions about policies, but liberals and conservatives shared a common framework for understanding the world. Yet the growing chasm between Rationalists and Intuitionists threatens the consensual basis of American democracy. Intuitionists dislike compromise, generally viewing politics as a bifurcated struggle between good and evil. They are intolerant of dissent and are quick to abridge the civil liberties of those they disagree with. When Intuitionists were dispersed across the political spectrum, their antidemocratic tendencies could be kept in check by their Rationalist counterparts. But as they have come to dominate the conservative movement, their authoritarian impulses are more likely to be realized. *Enchanted America* explains how Intuitionists understand the world, and offers suggestions for counteracting their illiberal influences in American politics.

Introduction

You Believe in Reason, and I Believe in the Bible

At first glance, Lucy Ryan seems like the kind of liberal we might find in San Francisco, California, or Cambridge, Massachusetts. An amiable retired teacher and self-described "former hippie," Lucy loves organic produce and herbal remedies. She mistrusts vaccines and abhors foods containing genetically modified organisms (GMOs). Like many Democrats, she worries about whether billionaires and large corporations have too much political power. And she believes that government should help take care of the sick and the elderly.

But Lucy lives in rural Texas, and like many Texans she often votes for Republican candidates, even those who want substantial cuts in social services. Lucy doesn't usually read the newspaper, but sometimes she watches Fox News, and once she even attended a meeting of a local Tea Party group. Her biggest political concern is abortion, which she regards as murder. She doesn't believe in global warming, but she'll readily admit that she doesn't know much about it. She dislikes Obamacare, although she's not sure what it actually entails. She doesn't voice any other firm political convictions, but she suspects that Barack Obama not only faked his birth certificate but is secretly Muslim. A born-again Christian, Lucy believes that the Rapture is soon to occur, and often interprets current events, especially those regarding Israel, in relation to biblical prophecy. In 2016, she supported Ben Carson for president at first but then voted for Donald Trump.

To people who study democratic politics, Lucy is an enigma. For starters, she violates our idealized notions of what a proper citizen should be.[1] There are whole fields of political theory that assume that citizens aim to be logical and consistent in their beliefs. According to these august speculations, citizens respect facts and keep informed about current events. Their opinions and judgments don't veer wildly into implausible whims or myths but are steadily guided by overarching principles. Even public opinion polls, in their attempts to formulate unbiased and non-leading questions, assume that Americans approach politics in a largely rational manner.

In reality, however, most Americans are more like Lucy. They don't know much about politics or don't really care about being consistent or factually correct.[2] They exhibit little coherence or stability in their opinions: they'll have liberal views about some issues, conservative views on others, and then completely change their mind three months later.[3] They usually think that the most important problem is the one they've heard about most recently.[4] And they harbor lots of outlandish beliefs and oddly conspiratorial views.[5] From the exalted heights of democratic theory, Americans seem like inexplicably bad citizens.[6]

But Lucy is enigmatic not simply for these failings—she is enigmatic because her way of thinking doesn't conform to our current models of public opinion either. Ever since the advent of modern polling, social scientists have crafted some powerful explanations as to why Americans hold the political beliefs they do. Americans may not meet our outsized expectations of good citizenship, but there are some rough patterns to their thinking. For example, their opinions partly depend on the *type* of issue in question— some matters like abortion or gun rights invoke steadier opinions than arcane notions like government finance or foreign affairs.[7] Americans' opinions also depend on how issues get *framed*. Americans are a lot more supportive of "aid to the poor," for example, than they are of "welfare."[8] But more important than anything else, Americans' opinions come mostly from what they *hear*, particularly from political elites and the media. In US politics, coherence comes largely from the top and not the bottom.[9]

Yet Lucy's odd constellation of opinions doesn't really conform to any of these models. For example, it's not clear why she gets so animated by an imaginary threat of GMOs, but worries less about the very real dangers of global warming. Nor is it evident what connects her suspicion of Obama's citizenship with her desire to help the poor. It's unclear how she reconciles her strong Christian beliefs with her enthusiastic support for the mendacious, philandering Donald Trump. And most intriguingly, she seems to blatantly disregard what most elites are telling her. In subjects ranging from health care to vaccines, Lucy holds opinions that directly contradict what most political leaders, scientists, and other experts are saying. And in this she is not alone. Millions of Americans not only dismiss expert opinion but hold views that actively contradict well-established facts. If Americans like Lucy are as ovine as existing research suggests, then how can they hold such transgressive beliefs? What can account for their "truthiness," their willingness to embrace "alternative facts"?

Interestingly, Lucy herself offered a poignant answer. Throughout our conversations, she was remarkably sanguine about her own inconsistencies. She seemed blithely unencumbered by the need for core values to bind her political opinions together. When, for example, we asked how her opposition to Obamacare conflicted with her desire to help the poor, she just shrugged. When we mentioned that the Affordable Care Act expands medical insurance to low-income folks, she shook her head and said that she didn't think it would work. But she really couldn't elaborate on this. Eventually, when she began to sense our frustration at reconciling her contradictory opinions, she paused and offered us a very telling observation: "Do you want to know what the difference is between you and me? You believe in reason, and I believe in the Bible."

Now, when Lucy implied that she doesn't "believe in reason," it doesn't mean that she is generally illogical. She lives mostly in a pragmatic and orderly fashion. Instead, she was saying something much more profound. She was basically telling us that she doesn't comprehend the world in the way we do. Specifically, she doesn't subscribe to a scientific framework for understanding reality. Lucy doesn't ponder abstract theories about how the universe operates. She doesn't come to her judgments through reasoned deductions from general principles. And she's not worried about whether her beliefs hold up to empirical scrutiny. Those criteria have little relevance for her. Rather, Lucy's opinions follow a different path. For her, the world is not a place of facts and cold rationality but one of symbols and emotion. It is a place where meaning is extracted from ancient prophecy, where alternative dimensions collide with the mundane, and where everyday events carry sacred meaning.

Here again, Lucy has plenty of company. Regardless of whether they are devoutly Christian, vaguely spiritual, or dreamily pagan, tens of millions of Americans share a worldview fundamentally different from any expressed on Sunday morning talk shows, in editorial columns, or at academic conferences. Instead of using principles or ideologies to perceive the world, they view it through a kaleidoscope of myths and superstitions. Instead of deliberately pondering through complex problems, they work from feelings and hunches. Instead of seeing institutional cycles or random events, they see plots and conspiracies. Instead of viewing their life as an arbitrary by-product of evolution, they observe an intrinsic purpose from a higher power.[10]

Now, most people who read (and write) books like this one tend to have a different way of looking at the world. We call such folks Rationalists. The Rationalist worldview is anchored by the notion that the best explanations are ones rooted in observable phenomena. For the Rationalist, reality is interpreted through dispassionate systems of knowledge that are subject to empirical verification. And because Rationalist beliefs are constrained by these scientific criteria, it's not too hard for Rationalists to understand how other Rationalists think. They may argue over fundamental premises or whether assertions are factually correct, but even when they disagree, Rationalists still use a common vernacular.

Intuitions are altogether different. Rising from the murky thicket of the unconscious mind, intuitions hum with primordial impulses. Whereas our reason may elevate us above other species, our intuitions draw us back to the animalistic judgments of nature. Because our intuitions so often violate the constitutive rules of logical thought, they often seem mysterious and opaque. How, then, can a Rationalist make sense of the other side?

For starters, let us clarify our terminology. By *intuitions*, we are referring primarily to our inborn mechanisms for making decisions. Although some intuitions arise from practice and expertise, as when a chess grand master "feels" the right move, the intuitions we are discussing are those mental tendencies that are "organized prior to experience."[11] They are the impulses that guide us amid the unfamiliar, how we discern whether foreign foods are safe to eat or what's behind the unexpected noise in the middle of the night. Such intuitions are how children understand the world, relying heavily on feelings and instinctive strategies for deciphering the unknown. And for people with no systematic knowledge sources, they are the primary way of making sense of their reality.

Such intuitions pervade our thinking. Nearly all thoughts and judgments are inexorably linked to emotions and other unconscious mental processes. Although we like to believe that we are the masters of our own thinking, our mental processes are preconsciously hewed by feelings, heuristics, and other cognitive shortcuts. The power of these intuitions is especially potent when it comes to politics.[12] Our opinions about public matters—policing, rights, regulations, war, and welfare—are shaped by our visceral reactions to evocative symbols.[13] With politics, our opinions are often rendered less from the lofty elevations of the prefrontal cortex and more from the inky depths of the gut.

What separates Intuitionists from Rationalists is not whether they use intuitions—intuitive thinking is something that all of us do all the time. Rather, what separates Intuitionists from Rationalists is *how much* they rely on intuitions as the source of their opinions, particularly about public matters. Intuitionists like Lucy make their intuitions the *primary* determinant of their beliefs. For almost any explanation to be accepted, it must comport with their feelings. For Intuitionists, it's their gut that tells them that evolution is wrong, that places where people have died are "cursed," or that calamities are caused by secretive, unseen forces. And it usually takes a lot of careful explanation for them to be convinced otherwise.

Rationalists, by contrast, will subsume their emotions to more dispassionate explanations. They are willing to accept beliefs rooted in abstract deductions that are supported by empirical evidence, even when such beliefs are highly counterintuitive. While they might be highly stubborn in their beliefs, such beliefs are still held up to empirical scrutiny. They will accept that the world is round or that deaths and calamities result from complex, probabilistic factors, not because such accounts feel right, but because they are logically sound.

The labels *Intuitionist* and *Rationalist* are, of course, stylized archetypes. They better represent the poles of a spectrum than discrete categories in themselves. Just as most Americans have some combination of liberal and conservative opinions, so most have a worldview that combines Rationalist and Intuitionist elements. "We are all capable of believing things which we know to be untrue," George Orwell famously observed, but "sooner or later a false belief bumps up against solid reality."[14] In other words, most people will eventually correct their "foolish consistencies" if presented with enough convincing evidence. By the same token, even the coolest Rationalists are still subject to biases and distortions that come from their own inborn psychology. As David Hume asserted, "Reason is, and ought only to be the slave of the passions, and can never pretend to any other office than to serve and obey them."[15] When we are referring to Intuitionism, we are referring more to a proclivity, a tendency toward one way of viewing the world. Nevertheless, our contention is that Americans are differentiated in this proclivity, with some tilting toward the Rationalist side and some toward the Intuitionist one.

Of course, this immediately raises a thorny issue: how exactly can we tell when people are relying on their intuitions versus more deliberative processes? This is a difficult question to answer. Poets, philosophers, and psychologists have struggled for centuries to discern the contours of our inborn psychology. Despite recent advances in genetics and neuroscience, the innate sources of cognition remain an elusive quarry.[16] The brain is a terrifically knotty organ; when it comes to people's opinions, it's very difficult to decipher what comes from instinct and what comes from learning. In fact, when it comes to our intuitions, it's not clear where we even might begin to look.

Here again, though, Lucy gives us a clue. It's hard to have a conversation with Lucy where God, prophecy, natural healing, or some conspiracy theory doesn't come up. But what's also striking about Lucy is how her magical beliefs come from so many different sources. Like many fundamentalist Christians, she believes not only that the end of days is upon us, but that we can dramatically improve our health by ingesting dietary supplements.[17] Like many people who fear vaccines and resist antibiotics, Lucy is quick to see conspiratorial forces running the government.

Such tendencies are common across the American population. People who hold magical beliefs in one domain tend to hold them in others. Survey the American public and you'll find that the same types of people who believe in "natural cures" for cancer are also more likely to believe in hidden biblical codes or that the attacks of 9/11 were an inside job.[18] These interconnections suggest an important possibility: beliefs in conspiracy theories, ESP, end-time prophecy, and alternative medicine all reflect the same intuitive proclivities. Magical thinking, whether it lies in the fantastical longings of a Donald Trump or the apocalyptic screeds of a tent preacher, comes from our inborn psychology. And logically, this makes sense. Humans have always used magical beliefs to deal with the unknown. Every culture has generated myths, legends, and superstitions as a way of comprehending the mysteries in their surroundings. By examining magical thinking, perhaps we can find some clues as to how our intuitions function.

Before proceeding further, however, some clarification is in order. For many readers, the term *magical thinking* may sound pejorative. Most people probably don't consider any of their beliefs, no matter how magical, to be whimsical fancies or infantile musings; rather, these are deeply held truths. So let us be clear about our terminology. When we refer to magical thinking, we are referring to a process that *makes causal attributions to unobservable forces.* For a belief to be magical, it must point to some invisible power, be it luck, God, or the Illuminati, that is making things happen. Of course, simply believing in an unobservable force or forces doesn't make that belief magical—plenty of scientific theories refer to things we can't directly observe (for example, dark matter). Rather, for a belief to be magical, *it must also contradict an alternative explanation that is based on observable phenomena.* Magical thinkers assume not only that hidden powers are behind much of what happens in the world, but that this explanation is more correct than an empirical one.

This scientifically transgressive character is crucial for differentiating magical beliefs from nonmagical ones. By our definition, then, it's not magical to believe that an invisible God created the universe, because we don't have another scientific explanation for *why* the universe exists. A sentient, universe-creating God is simply one of many theories that we cannot currently test (albeit one that is highly implausible, at least as commonly imagined). It is magical, however, to think that simply by praying to this invisible God, we can resurrect the dead, turn water into wine, or cure someone's cancer. These beliefs have no empirical support and violate well-established laws of biology, chemistry, and physics. A belief is *magical* only if it contradicts other ideas that are validated by testing and observation.

It is this scientifically transgressive quality that makes magical beliefs a useful guide into the workings of our intuitions. When people embrace a magical belief, they are, by our definition, choosing a fantastical explanation over an empirically viable one. But there must be some reason for their choice; something must be compelling them to choose magic over science. If we can understand the psychology of magical beliefs, then we might gain a template for how our intuitions function. Luckily for us, social scientists have been studying magical thinking for quite some time. From the remote islands of Melanesia to the austere laboratories of the world's elite universities, researchers have examined how and why we are so drawn to strange beliefs, and how our subconscious minds try to comprehend the unknown. And as we describe in chapter 1, their research can be boiled down to two crucial insights.

First, magical beliefs are forged from our emotions. Like all complex vertebrates, when we face things that are unfamiliar, we feel afraid. Dark places, deep waters, and strange noises all make us anxious because they present us with uncertainty, which in nature is dangerous. Magical beliefs help us impose order on the world and give us the illusion of control.[19] A sacred talisman protects us from danger, an incantation cures a sick child, a golden charm gives us luck. Magical beliefs are a primordial form of "motivated reasoning," a way we can craft beliefs to be in line with our prior feelings and placate our distress.[20] Whereas scientists may search for more complex explanations that make logical sense or that are best supported by empirical fact, magical thinkers look for the most expedient explanation to make them feel better.[21] They take their own emotions as valid signals about the state of reality.

Second, magical beliefs do not operate in a random fashion; rather, they have a "grammar" that constrains their form. One of the most interesting things about magical beliefs is how similar they tend to be. Consider religion. Across a wide array of disparate cultures, religions contain remarkably similar types of images, symbols, and metaphors. Nonsexual births, resurrections, dietary restrictions, and apocalyptic visions can be found in nearly all mythologies and religious traditions.[22] This uniformity is remarkable considering the enormous variation in cultures across the world. It's even perplexing if we consider that once people are freed from the constraints of empirical reality, they could fashion any type of belief that they wanted. For example, someone could believe that her car won't start because invisible, cocaine-snorting mice used its battery to fuel their midnight raves. Of course, to most of us such an idea seems absurd. But why is the idea of invisible, coked-up mice any less plausible than the idea of an invisible, omniscient God who chooses to delineate his commands via a two-thousand-year-old set of texts written by third-generation followers of his only son?

The obvious answer is that most of us were raised in a Christian tradition, not one involving invisible, drug-taking mice. But there is more to it than that. Christianity, like most long-standing religions, has precepts that comport with our inborn psychology. One reason magical beliefs are plausible to their followers is that they draw from the very same innate mental shortcuts underlying all our judgments.[23] These heuristics pervade human cognition, influencing everything from our visual perception to our choice of breakfast cereal. In most instances, they help us make efficient decisions, but often they can distort our perceptions. It is our unconscious heuristics, for example, that lead us to exaggerate our driving skill or overestimate our chances of winning the lottery.[24] These same cognitive biases also govern our magical beliefs. When we encounter the unknown, we unconsciously rely on these instinctive rules to make sense of it all.

This way of thinking is nowhere more visible than with children. Kids are terrific magical thinkers—they see monsters in closets, human intentionality in animals, and karmic justice in the universe. Such imaginings are how they make sense of the unfamiliar.[25] But what is most remarkable is how children fabricate these explanations on their own. No parent who values his sleep is going to suggest to his child that a monster is lurking in the closet. Instead, children's magical fantasies are informed by the same unconscious assumptions that kept their ancestors safe: dark spaces are likely to hold predators; things that look like spiders or snakes are dangerous; objects that touch "yucky" substances should be avoided; and so on.[26] Because they know so little, children must rely heavily on their innate inferences, which often lead them into a world of monsters, fairies, cooties, and imaginary friends. But children's inferences are not unbound either—monsters don't typically live in brightly lit rooms, evil forces don't waffle in ambivalence. Instead, their inferences are constrained by innate cognitive rules, the same ones that bind their magical beliefs into adulthood.

These two insights—that magical beliefs arise from our emotions, and that they follow cognitive "rules"—can tell us a lot about how Intuitionists comprehend both politics and the world at large. Intuitionists put their emotions at the center of their decision making—their feelings provide their first step for interpreting reality. When Intuitionists encounter political news, they give primacy to managing their own emotional response. They may do so by tuning out the bad news—a lot of Americans don't like to think about politics precisely because politics present them with uncomfortable realities. But sometimes these political realities are unavoidable: a terrorist attack dominates the headlines, an election demands a choice, a survey researcher wants an opinion. For Intuitionists, the discomforting weight of their anxiety is so heavy that it drives them to prioritize explanations that placate their fears. And the types of explanations that do this are the ones which accord with their own innate impulses. The very reason people choose supernatural accounts, conspiracy theories, or scandalous rumors over empirical explanations is that the former better comport with their own emotional signals about the world. Intuitionists gravitate to magical beliefs because such explanations both validate their feelings and placate their anxieties.

Consider, for example, how two Americans might respond to a politician bellowing about the US trade deficit with China. One is a Rationalist. She knows a bit about economics and often reads the *Wall Street Journal*. She recognizes the trade deficit as a complicated phenomenon reflecting a mix of labor costs, currency valuations, import restrictions, and other factors. Knowing this, she is less likely to feel alarmed by all the threatening rhetoric. She comprehends trade deficits in a dispassionate way. She may even see the trade deficit with China as indicative of the success of the US economy: because of our superior position, we are getting more of the stuff we want at a cheaper price.

The other person is an Intuitionist. He didn't finish college, never reads the paper, and has spent a lot of time in a church that reinforces the belief that an observant God causes most natural events. Knowing little of macroeconomic theory, this Intuitionist equates a trade deficit with something he understands, such as owing someone else money. From his vantage point, the trade deficit seems ominous, an indicator of American decline. Taking his anxiety as an important signal, he'll seek a compelling explanation that accords with his feelings. Perhaps he'll gravitate toward a conspiracy theory about some secret group orchestrating a bad trade deal to cheat the American people. This explanation will not only validate his anxiety but also align with the other ways he sees the world, particularly his religious beliefs. To the Intuitionist, the conspiracy theory seems more self-evident than some abstract notions of currency valuation and labor flows.

For many Americans, fantastical explanations and magical beliefs feel more plausible precisely because they accord with both their emotions and their common strategies for making naive decisions. In the cacophonous marketplace of ideas, intuitive explanations come with a great starting advantage—they coincide with our natural ways of thinking and feeling. Abstract theories or ideologies, on the other hand, often run contrary to our impulses. This is partly why so many scientific theories or reasoned value systems have often encountered initial resistance. Germ theory, heliocentrism, free trade, due process, individual rights, vaccination, and tolerance of dissent are all ideas that derive from reasoned deductions and dispassionate conjecture. They aren't concepts that come naturally to us, nor are they easily learned. On the other hand, conspiracy theories, apocalyptic narratives, invisible gods, tribalism, and a fear of poisons all accord with our natural inferences. For people uninterested in science, these transgressive narratives can seem so self-evident as to be unquestionable. In other words, when religious conservatives rally behind Donald Trump, when liberals protest GMOs, or when anyone believes that the US government planned the attacks of 9/11, it's not facts, reason, or even abstract principles informing their beliefs. Instead, it's the same unconscious tendencies telling them that praying to Jesus will cure their leukemia, that Aunt Myrtle can see into the future, or that homeopathic remedies can stop a cold.

Intuitions and US Politics

Or at least this is our theory. But as political scientists, our task is to see if this theory accounts for some of the "inexplicable" patterns in American public opinion. Can we find measures of Intuitionist proclivities that would predict not only Americans' magical beliefs but their political views as well? To answer this question, we developed a survey that captures both how much weight people give to their emotions and their appetite for innate heuristics. For example, we asked our survey respondents how averse they are to symbolically harmful gestures, such as stabbing a photograph of their family or touching something that once belonged to an evil person. We asked how often they engage in apprehensive acts like shredding their bills or checking the locks on their doors. We asked them to estimate the likelihood of occurrence of bad events such as recessions, terrorist attacks, or war. In compiling their responses, we created an Intuitionism scale, a measure of how much they prioritize both feelings and symbols when making judgments.

As we describe in chapter 2, the Intuitionism scale is a remarkable predictor of magical beliefs. Across six national surveys and a wide array of notions, the results follow a regular pattern: the higher a participant's Intuitionism score, the more likely that person will believe in supernatural or paranormal phenomena. The Intuitionism scale not only predicts a belief in God or life's purpose, it also predicts a belief in horoscopes or ghosts. It also predicts whether Americans use alternative medicine, and if they are drawn to apocalyptic prophecies. And it predicts explicit measures of intuitive thought, such as whether Americans value "their heart over their head" or "if they accept their own intuitions over the advice of a doctor." In short, this scale is a robust predictor of how much Americans rely on their intuitions when making sense of reality.

And who scores high on the Intuitionism scale? Chapter 3 gives an answer. On average, Intuitionists are less educated and less wealthy, and feel more financially stressed. They are more likely to be female. They are less curious about the world and less interested in pondering deep questions. They tend to come from strict, religiously conservative homes and believe strongly in authoritarian values such as obedient children. They are more likely to identify as orthodox or fundamentalist in their religious beliefs. Although a small percentage of Intuitionists are atheistic or loosely spiritual, an overwhelming majority are regular church attenders. And they are far more likely to identify themselves as conservative.

Which brings us to politics: in chapter 4, we show how the Intuitionism scale predicts not only magical beliefs but a host of political views as well. In fact, Intuitionism is often as important as ideology in determining Americans' political opinions, especially when issues get framed in evocative ways. For example, if we ask respondents about complex technical matters like tax policy, intuitions don't offer much guidance. But when we invoke handy metaphors or emotional considerations, Intuitionism emerges as a major force in differentiating people's opinions. A prime example of this is health care. Intuitionists tend to be more in favor of the specific provisions of the Affordable Care Act, but they are far more likely to oppose "Obamacare." These inconsistencies are evident across politics—on issues ranging from defense spending to GMO policy, Americans are separated as much by their reliance on intuitions as by their ideology.

Typically, intuitions operate below the radar of US politics. American political discourse is mostly Rationalist in tone, at least in the edited media.[27] But sometimes a political figure or political movement arises that is based primarily on intuitive appeals. Donald Trump is one such figure. In chapter 5, we show how Trump's nativism, conspiracy theories, and populist rhetoric all resonate with how many Intuitionists perceive issues of money and power. In their worldview, things are bad because some secret group of "others" is plotting against them. They believe that "the system is stacked against" them, and they'd much rather put their trust in "ordinary people" than "the opinions of experts and intellectuals." Not surprisingly, they also embrace conspiracy theories. These factors, in turn, are highly predictive of support for Donald Trump. Surveys from 2016 show that Trump's anxieties about immigration and crime, his nostalgic nationalism, his appetite for conspiracy theories, and even his opposition to vaccines accorded with the populist views held by Intuitionists within the Republican Party.

Another distinguishing aspect of Trump's campaign was his blatant attacks on Mexicans, immigrants, and Muslims. Here too we see intuitions playing a defining role. Whether they take the form of a sentimental nationalism or a fervent ethnocentrism, intuitions affect the way we comprehend our own social groupings and those who aren't like us. As we describe in chapter 6, social identities are especially important for Intuitionists. Intuitionists are far more likely to affiliate themselves with national or racial categories and to use ethnic stereotypes to judge others. This ethnocentrism also looms much larger in their political views. Whereas Rationalists are less likely to make sweeping generalizations about racial minorities or immigrants, Intuitionists tend to form quick judgments of anyone in these categories and assume that their stereotypes apply to all.

The Intuitionism scale is also a major predictor of people's attitudes about food and health. As we detail in chapter 7, the political movements concerned with vaccines, GMOs, alternative medicine, and natural foods all share the same elements found in both magical beliefs and Trump's conspiratorial populism: they fear contaminants and revere the natural; they see Big Food and Big Pharma as plotting against them; they are drawn more to metaphors about health than actual empirical facts. Where populism often captures intuitive thinking about power and money, the natural health movement crystallizes intuitions about food and medicine. And we see this in our data: the same Intuitionism scale that predicts whether people believe in conspiracy theories, paranormal phenomena, or fundamentalist beliefs also predicts whether they oppose mandatory vaccines, use natural remedies, or believe in alternative medicine.

What does this mean for the future of US politics? We take up this question in chapter 8. As a liberal democracy, the United States was founded to be a Rationalist enterprise. James Madison, Alexander Hamilton, and the Constitution's other framers predicated the American system of government on the assumption of reasoned political deliberation. Indeed, many of the checks and balances in the Constitution were instituted precisely to inhibit the "mischiefs" of our intuitions. Now, for much of their nation's history, Americans' irrational tendencies have been muted by the fact that Intuitionism was dispersed widely across the political spectrum. But in the past few decades, a realignment of the nation's political parties has shifted this balance. As fundamentalist Christians and rural whites migrated to the political Right, the GOP has become a more Intuitionist party. At the same time, the concentration of secular liberals within the Democratic Party has made its leadership more Rationalist in orientation.

This ontological polarization is defining the contours of US politics. Much of America's ideological gap stems not from abstract considerations about the scope of government but rather from differences in worldview. Increasingly, liberals and conservatives are becoming as separated by their ways of perceiving reality as by their governing philosophy. Conservatives are more likely to draw from their intuitions or adopt magical beliefs; liberals are more likely to put their confidence in dispassionate empirical explanations. In other words, liberals and conservatives appear divided not simply because they can't agree on issues like taxes, social spending, or regulation, but because they hold fundamentally different approaches to perceiving reality.

This Intuitionist divide is far more profound than any mere division between red and blue states. For while liberals and conservatives may disagree about certain policy issues, they typically share an underlying respect for rationality and facts. Intuitionists and Rationalists, however, have a fundamentally different worldview. Compromise and deliberation are far less possible when citizens have different ways of perceiving reality. Intuitionism not only precludes the possibility of rational discourse, it also contests the basic principles of democratic governance. Pluralism, compromise, and tolerance of dissent run afoul of the Intuitionist worldview, which tends toward rigid absolutism, deep nationalism, and longing for strong authority. The political ascendancy of Intuitionism poses a deep challenge to American democracy. But to address this challenge, we first need to understand what is causing it. Thus, we need to take a deeper look at how out intuitions function. And a great place to begin is with magical beliefs.

CHAPTER ONE

If There's No Monster in the Closet, Then Why Am I Afraid?

How do we comprehend the world?

If you're reading this book, it's likely that your worldview is informed by empirical observations and logical deductions. You probably believe, for example, that the earth is round. This is not an idea that came naturally to you but is rather something you were taught. And this teaching, in turn, was based on earlier formulations and experiments from scientists and other thinkers.[1] And you probably accept it because of how the roundness of the earth has been demonstrated, through either photos from satellites or other proofs. Many of our beliefs, however, are not based on such deductions. Instead, they come from a different source: our intuitions. Whether we call them gut feelings, instinct, or common sense, our judgments often arise from nondeliberative sources. These visceral notions often serve us well, but they don't always give us an accurate picture of the world. Our intuitions generally tell us that the earth is flat, that vaccines are dangerous, and that attractive people are smarter than the rest of us.[2]

Intuitions also present us with a quandary—it's not clear how they work. Scientific thinking is easy to comprehend, because scientific beliefs are explicit in their logic and assumptions. When a scientist tells you the earth is round, she will point to observable facts and logical deductions to demonstrate this point. Intuitions, by contrast, arise from the opaque depths of the mind. And this murky origin raises a host of difficult questions: What exactly do we mean when we say "go with our gut"? Where does an intuition come from? Who or what defines common sense?

The answers can be found in a seemingly unlikely place: our magical beliefs. Such beliefs are excellent windows on the workings of our intuitive minds because they exist as alternatives to empirical facts. Recall that by our definition, a belief is magical precisely when it invokes an invisible force *and* contradicts an alternative, empirical explanation. When we believe that a drought is a sign of God's displeasure or that a lucky ring will help us win at blackjack, we are doing so despite scientific explanations based in meteorology or conditional probability. This is magical thinking. And why do we choose to adopt such beliefs? Because they coincide with our natural inferences, how we make sense of the world when we don't have a lot of information about it. Magical beliefs are appealing because they reflect our inborn ways of perceiving reality.

In this chapter, we examine a host of anthropological and psychological investigations into the sources of our magical beliefs. Together, this research reveals two important facets of the intuitive mind. First, intuitive thinking is emotional thinking. Our intuitions are motivated often by feelings of apprehension or anxiety. Moreover, these feelings typically serve as clues to the state of the world. If we feel scared, we look for threats; if we are elated, we look for sources of wonder. This emotional primacy of our intuitions is evident in magical beliefs. Myths, superstitions, and other magical notions are accepted not because they provide rational explanations but because of how they make us feel. In providing explanations for why we get sick or what happens when we die, magical beliefs give order to the universe and assuage our fears of the unknown. Our magical beliefs also reflect our feelings—because we feel afraid, we therefore assume that some evil force is out to get us. In short, intuitions both draw from and rationalize our emotional states.

Second, intuitions have a "grammar," a set of rules that constrain their forms. When we are trying to make sense of the unknown, we rely on a suite of innate mental shortcuts to guide our perceptions. Absent any other information, these heuristics help us understand the world. The ideas or notions that seem intuitive conform to these heuristics, while counterintuitive ones violate them. For example, our innate heuristics tell us that something that looks like a turd will be gross, even if in fact that gooey brown mass is a yummy piece of chocolate. This intuitive "grammar" pervades our magical beliefs. For example, nearly all religions will claim that holy people have special powers, that natural phenomena are caused by intentional gods, or that ancient prophesies are always about to come true. These commonalities occur because they all reflect the same innate heuristics, the inborn ways we make judgments when we are otherwise uncertain.

These same mechanisms (that is, emotions and heuristics) also shape our political thinking, especially among people who rely heavily on their intuitions. Such Intuitionists are more likely to base their political opinions on visceral reactions than abstract values. They will take their elations or anxieties as proof that something is right or wrong in the world. They will accept metaphors and symbols as literal embodiments of truth. They will employ gross stereotypes, blatant dichotomies, and crude generalizations. They will assume that a single intentional purpose is behind complex social phenomena. They are highly suspicious of outsiders or "unnatural" contaminants. In short, they view the political world through the same mental framework that animates their beliefs in angels and demons, healing crystals and secret prophecies. But before we get to this in further detail, it is helpful to first explain how our intuitions operate. And there is no better place to start than at a baseball game.

Finding Solace: The Emotional Roots of Magical Thinking

Baseball players and fans are famous for their superstitions. Wade Boggs, one of the greatest hitters of all time, ate fried chicken before each game. Pitcher Turk Wendell always made colossal leaps over foul lines and insisted that umpires roll him the ball when he was on the mound.[3] The New York Yankees spent thousands of dollars to dig out a Red Sox jersey that a treacherous worker had buried under their new stadium. Many players wear twisted rope necklaces containing tiny flecks of titanium that supposedly "realign the body's energy field."[4] Fans have innumerable rites and take all manner of lucky objects to the games help their team win.[5]

Why does baseball, of all sports, attract so many superstitions? A good answer comes from one of the founders of modern anthropology, Bronislaw Malinowski. According to Malinowski, magical thinking is a way we cope with the stress of uncertainty.[6] While studying tribes in the Trobriand Islands, Malinowski observed that magical thinking was mostly prevalent in those instances where uncertainty was great and stakes were high. A good example was fishing. Sometimes the Trobianders fished in lagoons and ponds. This kind of fishing posed few risks and so triggered few superstitions or magical beliefs—when fishing in shallow water, the Trobrianders did not use many special amulets or say a lot of "magic" words. They just fished. But when fishing in deep ocean waters, where the risks are great and the outcomes unpredictable, magical thinking was rampant. Just like American deep-sea fishermen today, the Trobriand ocean fishermen used all kinds of particular superstitions to "ward off" danger.[7]

Malinowski realized that superstitions and other magical beliefs are not signs of mental deficiency or cultural poverty; rather, they are tools for alleviating fear.[8] In other words, the primary function of magical beliefs is to make us feel better. This is clearly the case with baseball. Much like deep-sea fishing, baseball is a game of inescapable uncertainty. It is a game with a high number of probabilistic events, any of which can be decisive. And, as with soldiers, gamblers, or anyone else who deals with meaningful risks, baseball players and fans look for ways to cope. Their superstitions, rituals, and myths are the tools they use. The same logic holds with other magical beliefs. While we may believe that our lucky charm is helping us win the poker game, it's actually doing something altogether different: it's giving us the illusion of control.[9] Religions may not accurately describe the cosmos or the cause of disease, but they can provide emotional comfort or a sense of moral coherence.[10] Conspiracy theories may not be true, but they can rationalize the inexplicable. In short, our magical beliefs are very instrumental, even if their actual functions are often not what they purport to be.

Which leads us to our first insight about intuitions: *intuitive thinking is emotional thinking.* To appreciate this, let us briefly consider exactly how our brains think and feel. Most of the time, our minds operate in a state of rough emotional equilibrium. In this state, they are trying to optimize our energy output by following routinized, unconscious protocols. As our brains continually process the millions of pieces of sensory inputs, they aggregate them into larger perceptions and link them together into still larger recurring neural chains. As long as these neural signals conform to routinized pathways, our "thinking" will continue in a quick, impulsive, and largely unconscious way. This habitual, routinized neural processing is what psychologists often refer to as System 1 thinking.[11]

However, when something unexpected happens, our habitual information patterns get disrupted. Facing such uncertainty, our brains shift gears and move into a different way of thinking. Our attention gets focused, we become more inquisitive, and our thinking becomes more effortful and conscious. In this more animated state, we are trying to comprehend these new neural signals and integrate them into our habitual chains of association. This is what psychologists call System 2 thinking. System 2 thinking is what happens when we're thinking "hard." It's intentional, slow, and taxing. Because such thinking is so effortful, we only move from System 1 to System 2 when motivated to do so.[12]

Uncertainty, surprise, fear, and exhilaration are some of the emotions that trigger the move from System 1 to System 2 thinking. When something upsets our normal patterns of information association, we become emotional.[13] This affective state then *motivates* us to focus our attention on an immediate problem at hand. We can describe this with a simple example. Say you are hiking in a forest, happily strolling along. System 1 is processing the information around you, taking in the sights and smells of the forest, directing you to step unconsciously over rocks and to duck under low-hanging branches. Suddenly, you hear an unexpected growling in the bushes. You freeze and listen. Your heart rate rises and adrenaline starts pumping. You feel alarmed and your brain moves from System 1 to System 2 thinking. You try to identify the source of the noise. At one level, your brain is trying to determine if the noise is a threat. But, more fundamentally, what your brain is really trying to do is to reduce your uncertainty. Apprehension is an uncomfortable state, and it is there for a reason—to motivate your System 2 thinking until the uncertainty is resolved.

Intuitions arise from this shift from System 1 to System 2 thinking. When we encounter something inexplicable yet consequential, we become emotionally activated. As long as the uncertainty persists, we are motivated to find an explanation and restore our emotional equilibrium. We move from a habitual mode of thinking into an effortful one. But what our brains are really trying to do is to restore the emotional equilibrium as quickly as possible. Although we'll shortly explain how our intuitions do this, for now we simply want to stress that intuitions are a type of motivated reasoning, an effort to deal with the emotional consequences of our own indeterminacy. Magical thinking, like all our intuitions, is precisely that attempt to make sense of the incomprehensible, to find a signal in the noise. This in turn leads us to two other important insights into the emotional sources of our intuitions: (1) intuitions are expedient generalizations, and (2) our feelings inform our beliefs.

Intuitions Are Expedient Generalizations

Much of the time, our intuitions serve us well, but sometimes they are completely wrong—our first impressions of a stranger turned out to be completely unfounded, or a restaurant that looked so great from the outside had horrible food. The reason why our intuitions are often incorrect is because they are "lazy."[14] As noted earlier, we utilize our intuitions when we lack information. This uncertainty generates anxiety, and anxiety, like all our emotions, is there to motivate us; specifically, it moves us to resolve whatever is uncertain in our environment. But here is the problem: we will try to assuage our anxiety in the easiest way possible. If we're feeling scared, we don't necessarily want the correct answer, we simply want the quickest answer that will make our fear go away. When thrust into an emotional imbalance, we will look for the quickest explanation that will satisfy our emotional needs.[15] System 2 thinking does this not by maximizing the accuracy of our judgments but by utilizing the habitual thought patterns that permeate our System 1 thinking. In other words, when faced with uncertainty, most people don't become abstract logicians, they become expedient generalizers.

This was the crucial insight of psychologists Daniel Kahneman and Amos Tversky. In many experiments, they demonstrated that people routinely use mental shortcuts, called heuristics, to make decisions when facing uncertainty. Heuristics are rules of judgment, inferential strategies our brains employ to make sense of the world.[16] A simple example is what we might call a popularity heuristic. Say we are in a new town and trying to decide where to eat. We could spend a lot of time comparing menus, prices, reviews, and so on, or we could notice that one restaurant is crowded and the other is not. Using a popularity heuristic, we might decide that the crowded restaurant is the superior one. Or even more likely, we won't even think that hard but just suddenly say, "Hey, that place looks good!"

Heuristics like this pervade our thinking. In everything from picking friends to judging book covers, we use inborn rules of thumb to help promote efficient decision making. Many of these heuristics are unconscious. Consider, for instance, how we see. While we may think intuitively that our eyes are processing our visual field as a whole, this is not happening. Instead, our retinal cells register distinct elements of light refraction, and upside down no less! These are then aggregated as nerve signals travel to our visual cortex. But in this creation of a unified visual field, our brains use many mental shortcuts. Actually, we have blind spots in our visual field that our brains paper over.[17]

This same process of visual aggregation also can make us "see" things that aren't there. A graphic example of this can be seen with a Kanizsa triangle (see figure 1.1). Here, our visual perception creates a differentiation that has no material reality. Our brains take the corner images of the triangle and, based on these strong cues, register the sides. Since we are habituated to see triangles, our visual perception creates them, even when they don't otherwise exist. This is an unconscious heuristic, a way we form a judgment about reality based on a limited amount of information. But it is a judgment that is not fully accurate.

An analogous process happens with our intuitive thinking as well. When our brains link the chains of association that constitute our thoughts, we

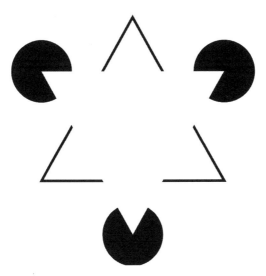

FIGURE 1.1. The Kanizsa triangle. Image by Fibonacci, 15 March 2007; Wikimedia Commons, https://commons.wikimedia.org/wiki/File:Kanizsa_triangle.svg.

inevitably bring up elements to fill in the gaps. When we do this, we often make incorrect assessments or "see" things that aren't there. For example, when we see a compelling advertisement, we assume that a product is good; if someone is overweight or unkempt, we assume that he is lazy; when something bad happens to someone else, we assume that it was her fault, but when something bad happens to us, we blame our circumstances. With nearly all our intuitions, we "fill in the gaps" by making assumptions based on just a few pieces of information. Kahneman and Tversky's central insight was that because System 2 relies so much on these heuristics, it often impedes "rational" thought. Rather than considering a full range of numerical probabilities, we use shortcuts that often lead to erroneous or irrational conclusions.[18]

We can see a vivid example of this in one of our nationally representative surveys.[19] In this study, we ran a version of a classic Kahneman and Tversky experimental question. First, we asked our respondents to ponder the following description:

Steve Foster is shy and uncomfortable speaking in public. He likes to keep his living space organized and free of clutter. He enjoys science fiction movies and riding his bike. He doesn't have a girlfriend.

Then, we asked our respondents the following question:

Which occupation do you think Steve is most likely to have?

A. Stockbroker
B. Fast-food worker
C. Mathematical technician
D. Retail salesperson

If you're a labor economist, you would probably guess that Steve is a fast-food worker or a retail salesperson, two of the largest occupational categories in the United States. But if you are like two-thirds of ordinary Americans, you are likely to say that Steve is a mathematical technician.[20] Despite the fact that this is one of the least common occupations in the country and that the odds are incredibly long that *anyone* would hold this job, most people tend to assume that it is the best answer. Why?

This is an example of how our intuitions are "lazy." Instead of using actual probabilities when thinking about Steve's occupation, we string together inferences based on irrelevant information that nevertheless seems informative. We don't take into account that being shy, neat, and single and enjoying science fiction movies are also traits quite common in the general population; instead, our brains take them as somehow indicative of working in a "nerdy" job. And it is precisely this type of bias in our System 2 thinking that permeates our intuitions. When moving to System 2 thinking, most people simply revert to what their brain does naturally—looking for familiar patterns. For most people, these patterns are not shaped by formal education; they are shaped by innate ways of making judgments.

The impact of heuristics and biases is especially pronounced when it comes to politics. As with most aspects of life, politics often present us with relentless uncertainty. We can never know if politicians are telling the truth, if a policy proposal will be harmful, or if a rival nation will suddenly declare war. Yet democratic citizens are perpetually exposed to such contingencies. For people who avidly follow politics, such issues may be understood as a matter of probabilities or as ideological certainties. But for most citizens, such matters are shrouded in an indeterminate haze, where the consequences of most policies are as bewildering as their details. Still, our democracy requires these fuzzy citizens to make decisions or have opinions about such matters regardless of how much they know.

So what do they do? As with all types of System 2 thinking, they will look for the easiest solution available. When Americans encounter political scandals, financial calamities, or terrorist attacks, they don't become more thoughtful, rational, or deliberative. Rather, they embrace quick heuristics *in order to make themselves feel better.* As with our magical beliefs, many of our political beliefs exist primarily to serve our emotional needs. For a relatively small part of the population, these beliefs take the form of political ideologies. Among this sophisticated minority, ideologies provide a quick palliative for interpreting an uncertain political climate. And this is the type of thinking that political scientists typically focus on.[21] But often, other types of thinking inform our political beliefs. This is why conspiracy theories, ethnic stereotypes, or other gross judgments are so common in political life—they are intuitively compelling. Although we'll examine these in more detail shortly, for now the important thing to consider is that while uncertainty will trigger System 2 thinking, it doesn't necessarily produce more rational thought. Uncertainty may motivate *some* people to become more deliberative, but most people will instead simply shift from one habitual way of thinking to another to make themselves feel better.

Our Feelings Inform Our Beliefs

Another characteristic of System 2 thinking is that it often takes our specific feelings as important sources of information in themselves. Rather than coolly evaluating all information in a similar manner, System 2 thinking weighs information by its emotional resonance. This idea arises from recent work in cognitive science that shows that our feelings are important delimiters of not just *how* we think but *what* we think. In other words, it's not simply that our emotions shift us from System 1 to System 2 thinking, it's that our emotions steer us toward a particular type of System 2 thinking. If something makes us feel bad, we are more likely to generate negative thoughts in general; if something makes us feel good, we tend to think that it must be healthy.

Consider, for example, what happens when you are awakened by a strange noise in the night. If the noise isn't alarming, you might assume that it's the refrigerator turning on or maybe a pinecone hitting the roof. But if the noise startles you, you are likely to generate anxious fantasies. You may assume that the noise is an intruder or a ghost! And this seems logical—we take our feelings as informative that something is wrong. Or, as five-year-old Ethan Oliver put it so clearly, "If there's no monster in the closet, then why am I afraid?" This is an example of how our System 2 thinking is indelibly stamped by our affective states.[22] Emotions not only prompt us into System 2 thinking, they also shape the way we think. In other words, how we think about the world is determined first and foremost by how we feel about it.

Once again, we see this behavior a lot with magical beliefs. When unusual or inexplicable events happen, we make inferences about what might be causing them. But the inferences we draw are indelibly aligned with our feelings at the time. For example, if I'm thinking about a long-lost friend and, at that moment, she happens to call, I'm amazed. And in the grip of this exhilaration, I don't see the coincidence as a probabilistic event. I don't remember all the times I was thinking of her and she didn't happen to call. Instead, I take my feeling of amazement as informative in itself. Because I feel amazed, it must be indicative that indeed this is some fantastic event. I then come up with a rationalizing explanation: I must have ESP!

Our political beliefs are also molded to align with our prior feelings. As political scientists Milton Lodge and Charles Taber describe, citizens understand politics relative to the emotional "tags" they assign to pieces of political information.[23] As we store various bits of political data in our long-term memory, we give them emotional weights. Indeed, such emotional markers are how we learn about the world. Although we may associate learning with dry lessons from the classroom, we usually don't absorb information in an abstract, neutral way. Instead, we assign emotional "tags" to new information.[24] For example, when we learn about history, we associate things like Hitler or racial injustice with feelings of anger or contempt. If we learn about energy policy, we might learn to associate concepts like solar power with positive feelings. When we later encounter an image of Hitler or a solar power plant, they trigger feelings in us. These feelings in turn shape our subsequent political opinions and beliefs.

Politicians use these emotional weights in their political rhetoric. Say a politician wants to gin up opposition to illegal immigration. He could marshal a lot of statistics about the economic and social costs of undocumented workers. Or he can simply announce that "our nation is being flooded with illegal aliens pouring across the Mexican border." The latter is much more evocative. Words like *flooded*, *illegal*, and *aliens* all evoke negative and apprehensive feelings. How many people think of immigration will be "primed" by the feelings these terms evoke.[25] Moreover, such processes are very subtle and mostly unconscious. We probably don't recognize that words like *flooded* and *aliens* are making us feel bad, or that these negative feelings are shaping our thoughts.[26] If we have to explain our beliefs, we can easily come up with a rational-sounding explanation for why we oppose immigration reform. But these beliefs are fundamentally shaped by our moods. Not surprisingly, when concepts like this are framed with threatening metaphors, beliefs and attitudes about immigration become much more hostile.[27] Here again, how we think about an issue is determined by how we feel about it. As Lodge and Taber artfully note, when we articulate our political beliefs, our explanations are "typically more rationalizing than rational."[28]

The question, however, is how exactly we go about this rationalizing. Most research on emotions in public opinion has focused only on the direct effects of emotions. For example, if we think warmly about a candidate, we're more likely to find reasons to vote for her.[29] But our knowledge of political thinking has not advanced much beyond these simple conclusions. Here again is where magical thinking can be illuminating. For in our magical beliefs we see *patterns of cognition* that are also evident in our intuitions. To find out what these patterns are, let us return to the baseball game.

Seeing Patterns: The Grammar of Magical Beliefs

Many baseball players employ lucky items or perform certain rituals before or during games. Often, a certain piece of clothing is worn for good luck—slugger Mark McGuire wore the same cup from high school into the big leagues. Sometimes a particular custom is observed—Joe DiMaggio would always touch second base when running back from playing outfield. But what's most notable about these totems and rituals is how they are usually connected to some aspect of the game. And this is somewhat curious. After all, players could try *anything* to improve their team's fortune. They could rub two pennies together or pray to Shiva. But to most players, such activities probably just don't *seem* right—rubbing pennies together is about my own personal fortune and not about my team; Shiva is a Hindu deity, and they don't play a lot of baseball in India; and so on. Instead, players and fans mostly choose superstitions somehow connected to the game—they don their lucky cap or rub their "magic ball." Is this more effective than rubbing two pennies together or praying to Shiva? No, but the important thing is that they *seem* more effective because they are symbolically linked to baseball.

Which leads us to our second major point: *intuitive thinking follows rules.* Just because we are fabricating explanations for inexplicable events doesn't mean we are suddenly removed from the bounds of cognitive psychology.

Instead of just making ideas from whole cloth, we use existing mental habits and apply them to the very same unknown situations we are seeking to control. In other words, when we are trying to make sense of something unfamiliar or unknown, we don't employ a freewheeling creativity; rather, we use the same cognitive templates that are already in place.

This was the insight of another founder of modern anthropology, James Frazer. In amassing troves of information from nineteenth-century missionaries and explorers, Frazer observed that the world's magical beliefs and religious rituals all contained the same two elements. He called these homeopathic magic and contagious magic. Homeopathic magic is the assumption that things which resemble each other also share certain characteristics. For example, many people believe that stabbing an effigy of their enemy will bring them harm. Contagious magic is the belief that the essence of an object, either good or bad, can be transferred through contact with it. Sacred relics can confer special powers or can heal us; cursed places must be avoided.[30]

In this typology, Frazer presaged the later discoveries of Kahneman and Tversky. For Frazer's "types of magic" are heuristics, inferential strategies that are innate and unconscious. In the many years since Frazer's *The Golden Bough* was first published, anthropologists and psychologists have identified many other heuristics that are pervasive in magical beliefs. And what all these heuristics share is an underlying biological rationale. In other words, the same heuristics common to all religious beliefs are mental properties that helped our ancestors survive. These heuristics also comprise the "grammar" of our intuitions. They constrain our beliefs and determine which ideas are compelling to us and which are not. Although our intuitions draw from lots of heuristics, here we will focus on four of the most common ones:

1. *Representativeness heuristics.* This is the awkward modern term for what Frazer called homeopathic magic, the tendency to assume that things which resemble each other also share certain characteristics. A representativeness heuristic is when we believe that good-looking people are smarter or that wealthier people are more virtuous than others. In many religions, such heuristics often take the form of voodoo dolls, statues of saints, or other effigies. When we believe that a lucky cap helps win games or that statues of the Buddha give special energy, we are using a representativeness heuristic.[31]

From a biological perspective, it's easy to appreciate why representativeness heuristics inform our intuitions. In nature, animals must always

FIGURE 1.2. An assortment of "dangerous" shapes.

assess their surroundings, usually with less than perfect information: Is this food safe to eat? Will this animal attack me? In having to make these judgments for their survival, animals need to make quick and efficient choices. For them, a representativeness heuristic is often the most logical criteria—if something resembles a predator, it is probably dangerous; if something smells good, it is probably healthy to eat.[32]

This biological legacy is something we unconsciously carry today. Absent any other information, our brains judge unfamiliar objects based on what they resemble. And our brains do this partly through our emotions. Things that resemble the objects we like will make us feel good or positive; those that resemble things we dislike we'll try to avoid. For example, people will think that high-quality chocolate tastes worse if it comes in the shape of dog feces than if it comes in a standard bar shape.[33] These heuristics are especially important when our information levels drop. When we have to make decisions and we don't have a lot of facts, we unconsciously rely on representativeness heuristics to aid our choices.

We can see the power of such heuristics in an experiment we ran. In our August 2014 survey, we asked people to consider the following scenario:[34]

> Suppose you are locked in a room with five completely unfamiliar objects like the ones in the picture [see figure 1.2]. You are told two pieces of information: (1) the key to the door is hidden under one of the objects; (2) one of the objects is deadly and needs to be avoided. Which object do you think is the most dangerous? Which object is the least dangerous?

As you can see from figure 1.2, all the objects are abstract shapes. We intentionally created them to be diverse yet nonspecific. Nevertheless, two-thirds of Americans say that object C, the object with five spindly "arms," is the most dangerous. Why was this the case? Well, in the absence of know-ing any other information, respondents were intuitively using a represen-tativeness heuristic: choosing to avoid the object that somewhat resembles a potentially venomous spider. But their choice was usually driven by an unconscious impulse: object C just made them feel creepy.[35]

Representativeness heuristics like this pervade human thinking. In fact, they are an unavoidable by-product of human language and metaphor. Ev-ery time we make a comparison or give a description, we use a representa-tiveness heuristic. When we say it's raining cats and dogs or that our love is like a rose, we are weaving together chains of association. Indeed, even the phrase "chains of association" is itself a metaphor. But metaphors are more than simply tools of poetic expression—they profoundly delimit the ways we think. As the philosopher George Lakoff points out, when we use metaphors to describe something (that is, your arguments are indefensible, his point was on target), we structure our understanding in a particular way (that is, an argument seems like a violent battle).[36]

Such metaphors are the building blocks of our complex beliefs. When we begin to ponder things beyond our immediate sensory environment, we inevitably rely on metaphors. Consider beliefs about whether the earth is round. For most of human history, most cultures have thought that the earth is flat or disk shaped. And intuitively speaking, they have a point: as far as our senses tell us, the earth is flat and the sun sails across our sky. The only way we "know" that the earth is round or that it revolves around the sun is from words. It is only with words that we can begin to develop beliefs about things that we can't directly sense. All our notions about time, soci-ety, or any other abstraction are fundamentally constructed through these symbols.

Such metaphors are particularly strong when it comes to magical be-liefs. We can see this in another survey experiment. In our July 2014 sur-vey, we posed the following scenario:

> Suppose your state had a $500-million lottery and you decided to buy a ticket. A friend tells you he won a $10,000 lottery by rubbing his lottery ticket on a XXX. Would you give it a try?

When we posed this question, we randomly assigned our respondents to one of two groups. Half the sample was told that XXX is a *paper nap-kin*, the other half was told that XXX is a *dollar bill*. Even though both activities seem rather arbitrary, we found that people's willingness to try rubbing a lottery ticket really depends on what they are rubbing it on. When the talisman is a paper napkin, only about 40 percent of Americans say they would give it a try. However, when the talisman is a dollar bill, this percentage rises to 54.[37] Even though there is no objective difference between them, a dollar bill is far more appealing than a paper napkin as a lucky token. This is a representativeness heuristic at work.

As our thoughts become more complex and dependent on symbolic representations, we become even more susceptible to metaphorical distortion. In our thinking, we often use metaphors that have absolutely nothing to do with the essence of the thing they describe. Our metaphors can give things greater relevance or attributions that they may not deserve: when we say a man is "hairy as a gorilla," we are portraying him as animalistic. And when such metaphorical allusions influence our decisions or beliefs, they work as representativeness heuristics and shape our judgments. We believe that the spindly object is dangerous because it evokes the creepy feeling of a spider. We believe that Steven Foster is a mathematician because he is single and neat and likes science fiction.

Representativeness heuristics are especially common in both religious and political beliefs. Religion and politics each draw from our metaphorical tendencies and elaborate them, applying them to all kinds of objects, people, and places. The crucifix is sacred precisely because it evokes the image of Jesus's sacrifice; a horseshoe needs to be hung with the ends pointing up in order to "hold" the good luck; the American flag needs to be respectfully folded in a precise way; and so on. As with the lucky cap at ballgames, magical beliefs gain their intuitive resonance precisely in their affiliation with the desired outcome and the physical object or concept we want to influence.

This last point is essential for deciphering the intuitive sources of our political beliefs. Our lived experiences contribute to only a small portion of our understanding. Most of our beliefs come from things we've read, heard, or learned about rather than things we've directly encountered. When it comes to abstract or remote issues of politics, society, religion, and the economy, our judgments are informed by words and symbols. People who regularly encounter politics have a wide symbolic repertoire to inform their understanding; these sophisticates have had many prior encounters for use in judging these symbols. But for neophytes, metaphors may be the primary way they comprehend the political world. As illustrated above by the scenario of the hidden key, the less you know about something, the more you must rely on metaphors to understand it. Political actors capitalize on this by lacing their messages with metaphors containing strong emotional associations. Like the spindly object in figure 1.2, such metaphors trigger our feelings; these feelings in turn drive our subsequent thoughts and behaviors. As we'll see in later chapters, much political communication revolves around the use (and misuse) of representativeness heuristics.

2. *Contagion heuristics.* Frazer's second type of magic is what he called contagious magic. This is our tendency to judge objects by whom or what they've been in contact with.[38] If an object has touched something harmful or unappealing, we avoid it; if it has contacted something we revere, we give it greater value. Frazer observed that this tendency was common across all religions. It doesn't matter whether it was Africa, Asia, or the Americas—a similar preoccupation with cleanliness dominates religious thinking: pilgrims travel to sacred shrines to purify themselves, holy relics confer blessings to the faithful, and objects that once belonged to saintly people convey good luck. Contagious magic also worked in the opposite direction. Impure or taboo objects were to be avoided; people who had had contact with them were defiled and typically subjected to some type of purification ritual.

Today, psychologists would call this type of thinking, appropriately enough, a contagion heuristic. And it's easy to appreciate both why humans are so sensitive to contagion and why it looms so large in our thinking. As a social species, homo sapiens is particularly vulnerable to infection and illness. One of the ways we evolved to protect ourselves was developing a strong sense of disgust.[39] Our aversion to the smells of things that are unhealthy for us, such as feces or rotting carcasses, is an adaptive trait that protects us from infection and disease. In a world where our ancestors were constantly foraging for food and living in close quarters, avoidance of contamination would have been extremely adaptive.

But this sensitivity to disgust and susceptibility to contagion carries over into other kinds of decision making. Not only do we find images of disease, decay, and human waste unappetizing, we continue to believe that anything that has been in contact with such items is itself impure or disgusting. Psychologist Paul Rozin and his colleagues demonstrate this tendency in a series of evocative experiments. They exposed research subjects to objects that were tangibly clean but had symbolic references to contagions. For example, they would show people a glass with a sterilized cockroach in it, wash the glass, and then ask them to rate the taste of grape juice in the glass. As you might expect, subjects viewed the cockroach-associated grape juice more negatively than grape juice drunk from a cockroach-free glass.[40] Other psychological experiments have had similar results in both positive and negative directions. For example, drinks created by obese children were regarded as tasting worse than those made by kids of normal weight; meanwhile, golfing with a putter that formerly belonged to a pro golfer produced better outcomes than an ordinary putter.[41]

But our contagion fantasies go beyond simply defining harmful or revered objects; they also serve as a mechanism for defining political boundaries and maintaining social coherence. According to anthropologist Mary Douglas, cultures define things as clean or dirty to order the world and bring their members together.[42] If each person in a society decided individually what was right or wrong, chaos would ensue. So instead, human societies define objects as being sacred or profane as a way of explicating moral laws.

The biblical book of Leviticus is a good example of this practice. Here, moral regulations of sexually "disgusting" acts served to bring Israelites together under God's command, assure them of a clean and healthy community, and differentiate them from other groups.[43] In Douglas's view, cleanliness is akin not only to godliness but to social stability as well. The more the members of a society hold the same things in either reverence or disgust, the more predictable and stable their social orderings will be. This is why so many cultures have rituals allowing for individual purification and are so intolerant of moral deviance. In striving for purity, they are really seeking greater social coherence.

These same types of contagion heuristics are evident in contemporary politics. As we'll see in later chapters, in policy issues ranging from immigration reform to vaccines to climate change, our opinions are crucially defined by fears of contagion. Characterizing "illegal immigration" (itself a loaded term) as an "invasion" by "aliens" intentionally invokes associations with infection and disease.[44] Vaccines are viewed as harmful because they introduce impurities into the body.[45] Americans do not support costly restrictions on carbon emissions simply to ameliorate climate change, but they will do so if these emissions are linked to pollutants in the air and water.[46]

But contagion fears go beyond political frames and rhetoric; they also compel us toward imposing our own moral and religious beliefs on others. In US politics, this tendency is most evident in various efforts by fundamentalist Christian groups to give their beliefs a larger role in public affairs. Opposing gay marriage and abortion rights, advocating for prayer in public schools, and invoking the Ten Commandments in judicial decisions are all part of their effort to bind Americans together into a single moral community. This not only helps advance the self-proclaimed mission of fundamentalism (to save other souls), it secures its adherents in its moral universe.[47] The more the state is purified of its sinful or heretical elements, the more secure the magical thinkers will feel, if only because they won't have to reconcile their particular dogma with any other beliefs. Inevitably, a belief system that rests heavily on intuitive metaphors of purity must seek to monopolize the truth, if only to rid itself of ideational contaminants.

3. *Anthropomorphism and theory of mind.* Another heuristic common in magical thinking is anthropomorphism, the tendency to attribute human characteristics to nonhuman objects. Like the other heuristics, anthropomorphism pervades our thinking: we find faces in the moon, we give names to ships, we think our pets feel guilty, we believe that plants and trees empathize with our problems, and so on.[48] But while anthropomorphizing is common to all our judgments, it's particularly strong in our magical beliefs, and probably unavoidable in most of them. Because magical thinking is about making causal attributions, this often means conferring some humanlike intentionality to the agent behind the event. Whether it is a wrathful God sending plagues to punish the sinful or Mother Earth crying over the planet's deforestation, supernatural beings are typically characterized as having human emotions or even a humanlike consciousness.

Anthropomorphism is something that comes both quickly and naturally to us. When we see animals or objects moving in familiar or predictable ways, we automatically give them intentionality. A particularly good example is a simple experiment conducted in the 1940s by Fritz Heider and Marianne Simmel. They showed people a short, animated film clip of some shapes moving in and around a box. One of the triangles begins to repeatedly bump into another, and then the second triangle moves in a reciprocal fashion. When people see the film, they typically think that the shapes are communicating with each other. Our natural tendency is to assume that the triangles' movements arise from some specific intentions rather than view their movements as random.[49]

As with other heuristics, anthropomorphism arises from a biological source. In this case, it is the by-product of our particularly strong capacity to discern other people's intentions or mental states, what psychologists call "theory of mind." Although biologists continue to debate its evolutionary origins, a theory of mind is clearly pronounced in our species by the age of five years. With a theory of mind, we take another person's perspective, to see the world through their eyes. It is central to our capacity for empathy. In a social, linguistic species like ours, this capacity is particularly helpful at facilitating communication. A theory of mind not only allows us to better judge other people's actions and intentions, it also allows us to better respond to other people's needs.[50]

Anthropomorphism stems from our promiscuous tendency toward theory of mind. Instead of limiting our mental theorizing to other humans, we apply it to animals, objects, and pretty much anything else that seems to move on its own. For example, when we say "robots are taking our jobs," we give these machines a humanlike acquisitiveness. When dogs look at us sheepishly after chewing our shoes, we presume they feel guilty, rather than correctly reading this behavior as a display of submission in response to our angry shouts.[51]

Given how prominently anthropomorphizing lurks in our cognition, it's not surprising that it's pervasive in our magical thinking. Recall that all magical beliefs invoke some type of invisible force as the source of something to be explained. While sometimes these forces are impersonal (such as luck or karma), more often they are given a personality. Human gods are rarely dispassionate, inchoate beings of infinite malleability, but rather are entities with feelings, concerns, and motivations. Our disasters rarely seem as though they happen by chance, but often seem to be the will of some invisible other. In fact, sometimes the disasters themselves, as with a "nasty" storm, assume a personality.

As is the case with other heuristics, this is an infantile response. Again, we can see this in our kids. Children are enthusiastic anthropomorphizers. They give personas to toys, cars, furniture, plants, and seemingly any object in their life. The reason they do so is because their social skills often outstrip their understanding of the world. Because they are highly dependent on others for their well-being, children are quick to discern their caregivers' intentionality. Children's willingness to assign a humanlike personality to nonhuman objects thus gets widely applied to any nearby object that is socially relevant.[52] Although most children shed this tendency with maturity, the inclination to revert to this infantile projection remains. As with all the heuristics underlying our magical beliefs, the tendency toward anthropomorphizing the world is an early habit that is hard to dislodge.

Small wonder, then, that anthropomorphism is also pervasive in our politics. From the most abstract philosopher to the most visceral demagogue, political thinkers across the board use humanlike metaphors as a way to connect with their audiences. Consider some examples from political speech: the free market is "an invisible hand," the body politic has a "heart," a nation can have a "spirit," and so on. But, as with other correlates of magical thinking, anthropomorphism is especially prevalent in conspiracy theories and religiously inspired political rhetoric. Conspiracy theories often assign human characteristics to organizations and institutions: the Federal Reserve, the CIA, or the Illuminati are described as acting like a person. Millennialist religions often interpret current events in the same way: catastrophes and cataclysms come from a satanic plan or from divine providence. Populists often ascribe a singular intentionality to political and economic elites.[53] When we see inexplicable events happening in our political environment, we often draw from this anthropomorphizing tendency as a way of making causal explanations. It's far easier to understand a stock market crash or a disease outbreak to be the result of an intentional agent than a systemic or random consequence of some conditional probability.

4. *Availability heuristics: illusory correlations and confirmation biases.* The final heuristics important for both magical and political thinking are the availability heuristics. They represent our tendency to make decisions based on the information that we can most easily recall rather than a full set of possible considerations.[54] For example, if we read about recent shark attacks, we are likely to overestimate the danger of swimming at our local beach. Although availability heuristics may sometimes be protective (a series of recent events may indicate a growing trend), they often lead to distorted judgments or bad outcomes. A tragic example of this happened in the two years after the terrorist attacks of September 11, 2001. During this time, many people were afraid to fly and chose to travel by car instead. But because car travel is more dangerous than air travel, a spike in the number of automobile-related fatalities occurred after 9/11. It is estimated that more people died as a result of avoiding air travel during that period than actually lost their lives during the terrorist attacks themselves.[55]

As with the other heuristics, availability heuristics have a strong biological rationale. In the wild, animals need to be sensitive to the frequency of events as well as the changing conditions in their environment. Their memory systems are oriented around both—animals are highly sensitive to changes in their routine as well as more recent developments.[56] The same process occurs in humans. We disproportionately remember events that occur most often along with those that have occurred most recently.[57] While this is a generally sound ecological strategy, it can create perceptual distortions. In particular, we tend to conflate what we remember with what is important.

In magical thinking, availability heuristics often appear in the form of illusory correlations. These are our tendency to assume that coincidental events are somehow related when in fact they are not. Such correlations form the backbone of many superstitions: fans notice that their favorite football team won the day they forgot to shower, so they stop showering on game days; soldiers often believe that talking about fallen comrades endangers future missions, and so will scowl at any newbie who asks about the dead; a baseball player continues to wear the same pair of lucky socks day after day; and so on. But what is really occurring here is an availability heuristic. When we are trying to determine why something good or bad happened, our brains overvalue information that's immediately available. We tend to assume that recency or proximity equals causality.

This type of heuristic has two important implications for public opinion. First, people use availability heuristics all the time when thinking about public affairs. They tend to rate the most important problems as the ones most recently reported in the news; they overestimate crime and safety issues relative to local reporting; they evaluate incumbents relative to recent events; and they are more likely to believe in global warming during unusually hot weather patterns.[58] Second, availability heuristics shape political thinking for the long term. Namely, people use their prior beliefs to filter information about the world. This is commonly called a confirmation bias. Here, we tend to seek or interpret new information that corroborates our existing expectations.[59]

A confirmation bias also has its roots in human cognition. As mentioned above, human thinking is largely based on habit. We interpret and understand the world relative to ingrained cognitive patterns. Once we acquire this way of thinking, it becomes ossified. We look for information that confirms our prior expectations and disregard those inconvenient facts that don't. Our beliefs are sticky in this way, especially if they involve an ambiguous or uncertain phenomenon. Once we come to "see" the world in a particular way or to believe in something, it becomes very difficult to change our minds. For example, if I think I have ESP, then I'll tend to remember all those coincidences when I was thinking of someone and she called; conversely, I'll tend to discount the even more frequent instances when people phoned and I wasn't thinking about them. Psychologist Leon Festinger famously labeled this cognitive dissonance. When we encounter information that contradicts our existing beliefs, we become extremely stressed. In order to relieve this stress and return ourselves to a homeostatic set point, we try to reconcile our contradictory ideas by reorienting our thinking. In other words, we use our reasoning to perpetuate our preexisting beliefs. In Festinger's view, we typically do this by altering our view of reality to conform to our preexisting beliefs.[60]

While confirmation biases are pervasive in human thought, they are especially important with regard to magical thinking because magical beliefs are, by our definition, transgressive. To hold a magical belief is to reject an alternative explanation for some previous explanation. A confirmation bias can explain how and why people can hold on so tenaciously to their superstitions and illusions; for once they become emotionally invested in a set of magical beliefs, they are highly motivated to look for evidence that supports them. Conversely, alternative explanations are nothing but a source of emotional distress.[61]

Confirmation biases are especially important to consider because most Americans are raised in magical traditions. They are born into religions that emphasize supernatural explanations for the world. Many are raised in charismatic denominations that rely heavily on ecstatic religious experiences that divine God's intention through mystical visions or speaking in tongues.[62] Outside these religious traditions, children have long been raised on a diet of fairy tales populated by witches, monsters, and other magical forces.[63] Our current popular culture is chock-full of vampires, superheroes, magicians, and the like. And then there are the myriad commercial products, like crystals or lucky charms, based on mystical forces.

Once we are exposed to magical beliefs, they become easy ways for us to account for the inexplicable. This is the other important element of magical thinking—its cultural contingency. Few of us have the imaginative power to concoct magical beliefs on our own. Instead, we usually adopt them from our surroundings. Someone suggests that our mother's death is God's will or that this special crystal will cure our indigestion, and suddenly this belief becomes our own.

The same process occurs in our political thinking as well. Few of us have the verve or the imagination to come up with our own explanations for political events. We usually just parrot what we have most recently heard from our favorite news source. But once we adopt political explanations that comport with our prior feelings, it's very difficult to dislodge them.[64] There are few examples of this as good as the "birther" conspiracy. There is no evidence that anyone was thinking that Barack Obama had faked his birth certificate when he was a humble Illinois state assemblyman. Although a few hinted at the idea before Obama became a household name, it was only during the 2008 presidential primary campaign that the idea began to take hold.[65] But why did such an outlandish notion become popular?

"Birtherism" exemplifies both the stickiness of our political beliefs and the power of cognitive dissonance. Many white Republicans faced contradictory impulses when Obama was elected president: they wanted to be loyal Americans and follow presidential leadership, but they felt alienated from Obama because of his name, race, and partisanship. Birtherism provided a convenient way for them to reconcile these conflicting impulses. By believing that Obama was an illegitimate president, Republicans could continue to think of themselves as loyal Americans while working to subvert their leader's agenda. And once they adopted this view, it became very difficult to dislodge. Even after Obama released his birth certificate in 2011, Republicans became even more strongly attached to the birther conspiracy.[66] All Obama accomplished in releasing his birth certificate was to exacerbate the misperception that he was born abroad.

Conclusion

Our superstitions, myths, and religious beliefs provide a window on the inner workings of our intuitive minds. Such magical beliefs are motivated by our reactions to the things we don't understand and can't control. They are chosen more for their potency in rationalizing our feelings than for their accuracy in explaining the world. But for our magical beliefs to be emotionally plausible, they need to coincide with our preexisting cognitive habits. This is why so many of these beliefs share the same forms—they reflect our inborn inferences about how the world works. Once we adopt a magical belief, it gets woven into the fabric of our psyche, becoming ossified and unquestionable. It also can create a template for viewing similar phenomena. And because our magical beliefs act as emotional bulwarks, they affect all our subsequent interactions with the world, especially with other people. Fellow believers are to be trusted and joined in practices of mutual self-reinforcement; heretics are to be ruthlessly shunned, if only because their skepticism is so emotionally threatening. Authoritarian dogma and intolerant persecution are the norm for any culture that organizes itself principally around its magical beliefs.

And this leads us to our Intuitionist theory of politics. Americans' political opinions are distinguished not simply by core values or overarching ideologies but by something even more fundamental—their worldview. How Americans think about politics depends a lot on how much they rely on their intuitions versus explanations grounded by logic, empirical observation, and fact. Intuitionists are people who rely heavily on their intuitions when making judgments. They have a lot of magical beliefs. They interpret the world through their emotions, taking their own apprehensions and fears as indicative that something truly is amiss. To resolve this apprehension, they are drawn to symbols and metaphors. Their reliance on their emotions also gives them a narcissistic worldview. It is their feelings that determine the significance of any event, be it natural or man-made. For Intuitionists, the same God that created the universe is also engrossed with their innermost thoughts and deeds. They are at the apex of history, the protagonists of a great cosmic drama. They view politics from their own feelings and infantile longings rather than from dispassionate analysis of world events. They are less concerned with the technicalities of governance and more animated by the visceral issues that stoke their anxieties. In politics, they are drawn to easy solutions, evocative symbols, and the conspiratorial musings of demagogues. In other words, Americans' political opinions are determined not simply by ideologies or abstract values but by how much they rely on their intuitive processes for comprehending the world. In the following chapters, we put this theory to the test.

CHAPTER TWO

Taking Measure of Our Intuitions

America is a magical land. It is a place where angels watch over us, protecting us from harm and shielding us from evil. It is a place where incantations, prayers, and elixirs heal us from sickness and disease. It is a place where sacred texts hold hidden truths that reveal cosmic mysteries to the faithful; where gifted seers offer visions of interstitial dimensions; and where our spirits convene and harmonize with the supernatural. And, if we are fortunate enough to find them, it is a place filled with special objects that can make our deepest wishes come true.

Yet all is not well in this holy place. Small and secretive forces conspire against us, orchestrating terrible catastrophes to further their nefarious aims. Monstrous beings are omnipresent, drawing us into their dire schemes and delighting in our pain and misfortune. A final confrontation between good and evil is upon us, with catastrophic consequences for the human race. We teeter on the precipice of time, where life as we know it is about to fundamentally change. Meanwhile, scientists, academics, and other experts try to convince us that none of this exists as they simultaneously work to impose their profane agendas on us all.

Or at least this is how many Americans view the world. Consider, for example, some findings from recent surveys:

- More than four in five Americans believe in God; for most of these believers, God is a humanlike force who is keenly interested in our daily actions and has a plan for our lives.[1]
- About two-thirds of Americans believe in angels and heaven, roughly the same percentage that also believes that Jesus of Nazareth was resurrected from the dead.[2]
- Roughly half the population believes in conspiracy theories about a wide range of subjects, including the idea that the 2008 recession was a plot of the Federal

Reserve, and that the Food and Drug Administration is deliberately withholding natural cures for cancer.[3]

- Roughly 40 percent of Americans believe in ghosts or ESP.[4]
- A quarter of Americans believe that the end of days is upon us, in which biblical prophecies about the Rapture and the return of Jesus Christ will be realized.[5]
- Meanwhile, only 43 percent of Americans believe in Darwin's theory of evolution by natural selection—not that much more than the 42 percent who believe the erroneous fact that dinosaurs and humans coexisted.[6]

These statistics not only show the tremendously high levels of magical thinking in America, they also show how many Americans potentially hold an Intuitionist worldview. As we described in chapter 1, when people pray to holy relics or believe that evil spirits lurk in dark places, they are utilizing an inborn suite of judgments to interpret reality. These same intuitions also lead them to have very distinct views about public affairs. Whether these are matters of politics, health, race, or the economy, many Americans draw their opinions from the same intuitive processes that lead them to believe in hidden Bible codes, ghosts, and healing crystals.

But at this point, our Intuitionist theory of US politics is still mostly conjecture. To see if it explains Americans' political attitudes, we need to test it with actual data. In particular, we need to see if people who hold magical beliefs do so because they hold an Intuitionist worldview. This task, however, raises a considerable empirical challenge: how, exactly, should we measure Intuitionist thinking? It's not enough for us to simply measure magical beliefs, because such beliefs by themselves can't validate our hypotheses. After all, many people may hold magical beliefs because they're something they were brought up with. Some may believe in angels or Satan, for example, because they were raised in religions that espoused this idea, and it's never been something they've questioned. Like old pieces of luggage that we never use but can't bear to throw out, our myths, superstitions, and religious views may simply reflect cultural habits rather than heartfelt commitments. We need to make sure that magical beliefs are not simply hollow attitudes but actually represent fundamentally different ways of viewing the world.[7]

In this chapter, we introduce our Intuitionism scale, a single metric that measures the intuitive mechanisms underlying our magical beliefs. This scale is the foundation of all our subsequent empirical analysis. It includes measures of apprehensive behaviors, evaluations of negative events, and a proclivity for symbolic thinking. And while these blunt measures have little to do with specific religious doctrines, they are remarkably predictive of magical beliefs. The higher one scores on the Intuitionism scale, the more likely one is to believe in the supernatural, the paranormal, or simply the wisdom of common sense. As we'll see in later chapters, the same Intuitionism scale also predicts a lot of political beliefs. But before we get to that, let us first describe how we measure an Intuitionist proclivity and its relationship to magical beliefs.

Measuring Intuitions

Intuitions are complex, ephemeral, and unconscious phenomena and so are not easy to gauge. Most of the best work on this subject comes from studies that don't lend themselves to any simple generalizations. For example, anthropologist Tanya Luhrmann's book, *When God Talks Back*, is a terrific examination of an Intuitionist worldview within a specific religious community. But it's unclear how much we could generalize from her ethnographic findings. Other great work comes from psychologists like Paul Rozin and his colleagues, who conduct experiments on what makes people more likely to adopt superstitions or magical beliefs. But here again, we don't know if these findings hold up outside the pristine conditions of the lab.

Since we are primarily interested in explaining the viewpoints of the entire American population, we need a different approach. We need to find a method that can identify the intuitive processes behind our magical beliefs and see how they vary across the entire population. For this purpose, we turn to public opinion surveys.[8] Surveys permit us to tap into the attitudes of a large representative sample that we could then generalize to the nation as a whole. In addition, surveys allow us to create specific measures of intuitive processes and then see how these measures correlate with other types of beliefs. To do this, we utilize three sets of questions.

The first set gauges apprehensions. As we discussed in the previous chapter, magical beliefs originate in the apprehension that arises when we face something meaningful that we can't comprehend. Pressured by these anxieties, we concoct or embrace any explanation that seems plausible in order to restore our equilibrium. But these characteristics make the emotional components of magical beliefs a very difficult phenomenon to measure, especially across a wide population. After all, our moods change across time—in the morning we may feel tranquil, in the afternoon anger, in the evening unease. Whatever emotions get measured at one period may not be necessarily indicative of someone's overall state. Another challenge is that people experience their emotions differently—some people

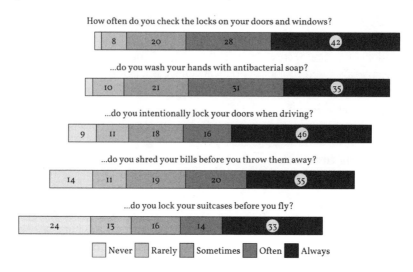

FIGURE 2.1. The distribution of responses in apprehension scale items.

are moody and volatile, highly sensitive to even the slightest trigger; others are stoic and unchanging, immune to all but the most dramatic events. In addition, people experiencing strong negative emotions are unlikely to take a survey voluntarily—if someone is feeling anxious or tense, he is unlikely to concentrate very hard on a bunch of survey questions.

Given these obstacles, how can we take a person's emotional temperature using something as impersonal as an online survey? In our research, we use an indirect approach. We ask people to report on *behaviors* that indicate conditions of greater emotional disequilibria. In other words, we ask if people regularly *act* in ways that demonstrate higher levels of uncertainty or apprehension. Are they overly cautious? Do they worry about disease and death? Do they believe that social disorder, economic collapse, or wars are imminent? If so, then we can probably assume that they are carrying more emotional distress, and might be more susceptible to the emotional palliatives of magical beliefs.

We start with five questions about how often people engage in fearful or overly cautious actions. These actions include regularly checking locks on doors and windows, tearing up old bills, intentionally locking car doors, washing their hands, and locking luggage at airports. As illustrated in figure 2.1, roughly six in ten often or always intentionally lock their car doors or shred their bills; about half regularly check their locks or lock their suitcases. Not surprisingly, these behaviors are highly correlated with one another. In other words, people who regularly lock their bags at the airport also tend to wash their hands after greeting strangers. To measure chronic apprehension, we combine these items into a single *apprehension scale.*[9]

The second way we gauge people's emotional disequilibria is by asking them their perceptions of the future. Many studies have found that when people are anxious, they are more likely to overestimate the likelihood of adverse events.[10] This relates to our discussion in chapter 1—people take their current emotions as informative. If they are feeling afraid, they are more likely to take this feeling as an indication that something bad is imminent. Our assumption is that by asking people to estimate the likelihood of negative events happening in the future, we can use this as a proxy for an underlying apprehensive state.

In our surveys, we do this by asking people to rate the odds (on a scale from 0 to 100) of four negative things that might happen to the country: an economic recession, a disease outbreak, a terrorist attack, or a war with China or Russia. We list the results in figure 2.2. By our measures, Americans look to be somewhat pessimistic about the future: on average,

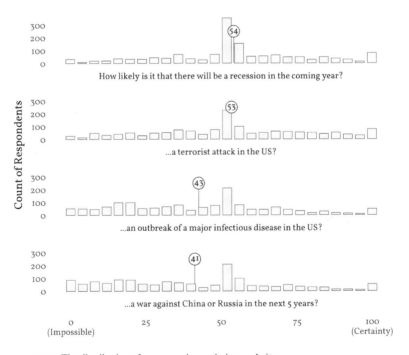

FIGURE 2.2. The distribution of responses in pessimism scale items.

they tend to think there is a relatively high chance of a terrorist attack (50 percent) or a recession (54 percent) in the coming year; they believe that the chances of war with China or Russia in the next five years or a disease outbreak in the next year are closer to 40 percent. Nevertheless, these are remarkably high estimates, on average, of very catastrophic events. As one might expect, these estimates tend to be highly correlated with one another and load highly on a single score that we label a *pessimism scale.*

Together, the apprehension and pessimism scales provide two indirect barometers of Americans' emotional states. Now obviously these are crude measures, but rough as our scales may be, they do tap into distinct dimensions of fearfulness. People who regularly feel the need to check their locks, tear up their bills, or worry about dying may be prudent, but such behaviors also reveal a high level of concern and anxiety. Vigilance like this belies a greater condition of chronic unease, a state we suspect would make someone particularly susceptible to a magical belief. The same findings hold for the pessimism scale. Although none of us can say for certain whether a terrorist strike or a war is imminent, people who believe that such negative events are more likely to occur are probably also living in a state of greater emotional discomfort. If someone really believes that the economy is likely to tip into recession or that war with a major power is inevitable, then that person must be in a negative state. For the apprehensive, magical beliefs might be a very attractive route to tranquility.

The final pillar of magical thinking is an appetite for certain types of inferences, a way of viewing the world through the heuristics informing our naive judgments. Before explaining this further, it is probably most helpful to first present our measures. Below is the sample of survey questions we asked our respondents. We prefaced the questions by saying, "Please try to go through the set of questions as quickly as possible." Then we presented each of the following item sets:

1. On the whole, would you rather . . .
   A. stick your hands in a bowl of cockroaches?
   B. stab a photograph of your family six times?
2. Would you rather spend the night in . . .
   A. a luxurious house where a family had recently been murdered?
   B. a grimy bus station?
3. Would you rather . . .
   A. stand in line for three hours at the DMV?
   B. secretly grind your shoe into an unmarked grave?

4. Would you rather . . .

    A. ride in a speeding car without a seat belt?

    B. yell "I hope I die tomorrow" six times out loud?

5. Would you rather . . .

    A. sleep in laundered pajamas once worn by Charles Manson?

    B. put a nickel in your mouth that you found on the ground?

6. Suppose you wanted to buy a ticket for a $500-million lottery. Would you rather buy your ticket from a nearby gas station that had . . .

    A. never sold a winning ticket but had no lines?

    B. sold two winning tickets in the past three years but had a long line?

To code the survey, we give one point for each of the following answers: 1A, 2B, 3A, 4A, 5B, 6B. They are then added together. If someone scores a 5 or a 6, they should be very susceptible to holding magical beliefs. Let us explain.

These questions are designed to measure people's sensitivity to the types of symbols and metaphors that James Frazer claimed were common to magical beliefs. In each question, we ask people to choose between doing something *symbolic* (such as stabbing a photograph of their family or sleeping in laundered pajamas once worn by Charles Manson) versus doing something *tangibly harmful* (for example, putting a dirty nickel in their mouth, riding in a speeding car without a seat belt) or *unpleasant* (for example, sticking their hand in a bowl of slimy worms or standing in a long line).[11] Here, we don't mean to imply that symbolic actions are costless for us—stabbing a family photograph may make someone feel awful. But magical thinking arises precisely from our willingness to imbue a symbol with this emotional significance—to give ordinary objects sacred power is to make them emotionally potent. In this case, a photograph is more valuable than a simple piece of paper, because it is a venerated totem of our affective bonds.

More important, the power of the metaphors in these questions comes from the common heuristics (those unconscious decision rules) that we described in chapter 1. Charles Manson's pajamas or the house where someone has been murdered is a *contagion heuristic*. Family photos are a *representativeness heuristic*. A gas station with a winning track record is an *availability heuristic*. In short, these questions are about gauging someone's sensitivity to not simply symbols, but their sensitivity to common strategies of judgment that people employ when they face uncertain situations.

When we ask these six questions in our national surveys, one conclusion leaps out (fig. 2.3): many Americans routinely would prefer doing

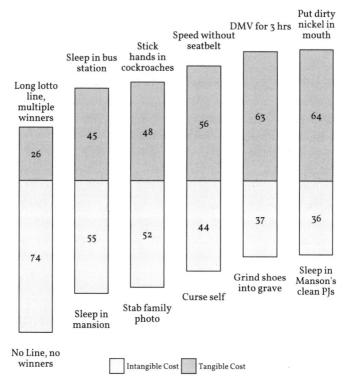

FIGURE 2.3. The distribution of responses in symbolic thinking scale items.

something tangibly harmful to bearing the emotional cost of a symbolic action. For instance, two-thirds would rather stand in line at the DMV for three hours than secretly grind their shoe into an unmarked grave. Nearly the same number would rather put a nickel they found on the ground in their mouth than sleep in laundered pajamas once worn by Charles Manson. Americans nearly split evenly for spending the night in the luxurious house versus sleeping in a bus station. They also split between sticking their hand in a bowl of cockroaches versus stabbing a picture of their family. The only item where tangible costs seem to sway people is buying lottery tickets: only a quarter of the sample would stand in a long line to buy a ticket from a gas station that had recently sold winning tickets versus going to the winless station that had no line.

It is striking how much significance Americans give to these common metaphors and symbols. An unmarked grave is simply a small piece of land; laundered pajamas are physically no different regardless of whether they were worn by Charles Manson or Brad Pitt; all lottery tickets have an equal chance of winning no matter where they are sold. But that's not how many Americans see them: words, photos, gas stations, and even small pieces of land clearly have strong emotional significance. Much of this significance, in turn, is due to the things that words, photos, and small pieces of land are associated with—loved ones, luck, health, and death.

The power of these associations is evident when we compare these responses with those occurring after slight changes to the wording of the same questions given above—in other surveys, we altered the choices to make them less onerous. We find that Americans have no problems with stabbing photographs of flowers, yelling "Tomorrow is just another day," or grinding their heel into old shirts (although most people still don't like wearing someone else's laundered pajamas). In such cases, most people would rather choose these symbolic actions than incur the tangible discomforts listed above. However, when symbolic actions involve contagions (for example, Charles Manson's pajamas or houses where people had been murdered) or evocative symbols (for example, photos of family members or graves), people become more sensitive to these cues.

Adding the responses together, we create a *symbolic thinking scale*.[12] As with the apprehension and pessimism scales above, the symbolic thinking scale has a normal distribution across the population. We have asked the first five items in this battery in five different nationally representative surveys, and the results are remarkably consistent. About 20 percent of Americans are consistently impervious to the questions' metaphorical lures. They will always choose the symbolically costly activity such as cursing themselves or stabbing a picture of their family rather than doing something demonstrably harmful or uncomfortable. About 60 percent of Americans are mixed in their thinking. This group generally splits their answers to the questions above. Sometimes they choose to avoid symbolic costs, and sometimes they avoid tangible costs (such as riding in a speeding car without a seat belt). Interestingly, the symbolic behaviors that semimagical thinkers avoid most are those that might be considered disrespectful or antisocial: stabbing a photo of family members or grinding their shoe on a grave. At the high end of the scale are roughly 20 percent of Americans. This group nearly always chooses to avoid activities with negative symbolic connotations, and instead will consistently select physical discomfort or danger. If there is one exception, it's with playing the lottery at the winless gas station, but even this activity is objectionable to many symbolic thinkers. In short, these are people with a strong sensitivity to metaphors and symbols.

The Intuitionism Scale

With these measures, we now have tools to construct our central measure: the *Intuitionism scale*.[13] This is a very rough and crude gauge of people's Intuitionist dispositions that comes from combining the three scales listed above. People scoring high on the scale have a more Intuitionist world-view—they are more likely to weigh their feelings in making judgments, give a literal interpretation to symbols and metaphors. People scoring low on the scale would be more Rationalist in their orientation, less likely to give weight to their emotions or be swayed by strong metaphors. Figure 2.4 shows the distribution of the population along the Intuitionism scale. For interpretive convenience, we have rescaled the factor score to run from 0 to 1.[14]

On this single scale, Americans are widely aligned along a broad onto-logical continuum. Most reside close to the middle, and this central position may result from any number of sources. Some may be there because they are generally centrist in their symbolic thinking and apprehension scales. Others are in the middle because they have a combination of conflicting views—they may score low in symbolic thinking but high in pessimism and apprehension. However, as one moves away from the center of the scale, the ontological differences become more clearcut. Those well below .4, for example, reject most of the metaphorical costs on the symbolic thinking scale and typically give much lower estimates of bad events. Those scoring

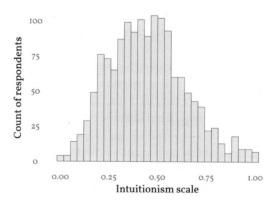

FIGURE 2.4. The distribution of the American population along the Intuitionism scale. Probabilities were extracted from logit models controlling for age, education, and gender. The ribbon charts indicate 95% confidence intervals.

above .7 go in the opposite direction—the higher they move on the scale, the more pessimistic and apprehensive they become.

Before proceeding further, we need to mention two key points. First, the Intuitionism scale is a crude measure. Although we worked through various iterations in refining these subscales, they are neither precise nor specific measures of Intuitionist tendencies. If we could analyze all respondents with hours of individual interviews or subject them to a lengthy battery of questions, we could probably discover a more refined way of differentiating their reliance on intuitive thinking. But we are working within the confines of surveys, where time, and our respondents' attention spans, are limited. This is also a new research methodology and, like all new technologies, is likely to be faulty. We hope that if others find our research interesting, they will discover new ways to improve our measures. But for the time being, this is the tool we are working with.

Second, we should clarify our terminology. At many points in the book we use the term *Intuitionist* or *Rationalist* to describe portions of the population. We want to be clear that these are stylized categories. We conceive of Intuitionism as a continuum of cognitive and emotional tendencies. Some people rely heavily on their intuitions, while others are more immune to intuitive signals. From our measures, most Americans are somewhere in between, exhibiting a mixture of Rationalist and Intuitionist tendencies.

But even though Intuitionism is a broad continuum, it is still easier to communicate our findings if we use discrete labels. Think, for example, about how we discuss ideology. Tally up Americans' actual political beliefs and you won't find the population dividing itself into neat, separate categories; instead, Americans are distributed along an ideological continuum, with most people clustering around the middle. Nevertheless, we still find it useful to use terms like *liberal* and *conservative*, mostly because they make our data easier to report. It is much simpler, for example, to say that "70 percent of conservatives oppose gay marriage" than "as one moves two standard deviations along the ideological scale, opposition to gay marriage increases by .83 points." The same holds for this research. Although the Intuitionist and Rationalist labels are less precise, they make it much easier to communicate our findings. For the rest of this book, when we refer to Intuitionists or Rationalists, we are generally referring to groups at opposite ends of the Intuitionism scale. Most Americans, however, have a combination of Rationalist and Intuitionist tendencies. Nevertheless, with the Intuitionism scale in hand, we turn our attention to its first major test: does it account for people's magical beliefs?

From Intuitions to Magical Beliefs

We start with the most primal source of magical beliefs—the meaning of life. All cultures have some type of myth, legend, or theology that explains or justifies our existence and the events around us, usually invoking some kind of supernatural force. Our tendency to project a larger meaning on our lives coincides with our ability to infer other people's intentions, what psychologists call our theory of mind. Like many cognitive processes, the theory of mind develops in children between the ages of four and five years, roughly the same time they begin to assume that events occur for particular reasons. Around this time, children understand stories from the perspective of their characters rather than just their own viewpoint. At the same time that children adopt this "promiscuous teleology," they begin to think that everything happens for a purpose: rain falls when plants are thirsty, flowers are pretty to make us happy, and so on.[15]

Although such Panglossian logic is a hallmark of juvenile development, it carries well into adulthood.[16] Rather than viewing our existence as a series of random and chance occurrences, we tend to see our lives and the events they contain as occurring for a reason, what some call apophenia.[17] Consider the hypothetical example of Jane. After a long search and many prayers for finding "Mr. Right," Jane meets her future husband at traffic court. Rather than seeing this event as a chance occurrence, Jane assumes that it was the consequence of divine intent—in her mind, God orchestrated her speeding ticket as an answer to her prayers.

This way of thinking is pervasive across the world's religions. In fact, *any* religious belief or mythology that suggests a purpose for our lives or for particular events must inevitably assume the intentionality of a supernatural force. To believe that God has a plan for us is to also assume that God has designs that are apart from our own. This is why certain events can gain so much symbolic potency. If we believe that some larger, invisible force is making all things happen in accordance with some grand plan, then any event, no matter how minuscule, can carry cosmic significance.

But by the cold light of modern science, this way of thinking is quite magical. Few scientific theories suggest any cosmic meaning for either our lives or the major events within them. To most physicists, we are arbitrary accumulations of energy and matter. For biologists, we are simply vehicles of genetic replication, a gene's way of making another gene. For social scientists, the families we are born into, the schools we attend, the jobs we

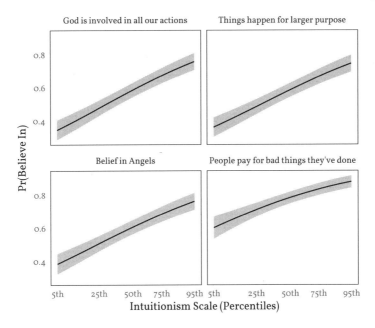

FIGURE 2.5. Supernatural beliefs as predicted by the Intuitionism scale. Probabilities were extracted from logit models controlling for age, education, and gender. The ribbon charts indicate 95% confidence intervals.

acquire, and the people we marry are not an indication of divine will or even fate but the probabilistic outcome of chance, circumstance, and our own efforts.[18]

This, however, is not how most Americans choose to understand their life. In our surveys, about six in ten agree with the statement "Things in my life happen for a particular reason."[19] These views vary by where the respondent scores on the Intuitionism scale. Figure 2.5 depicts predictions from our multivariate models of the average level of belief that "life has a purpose."[20] Intuitionists are far more likely than Rationalists to believe that life has a purpose. For example, our equations predict that less than 40 percent of people scoring at the low end of the Intuitionism scale believe that their life has a purpose, but that over 75 percent of people at the high end do.[21]

Intuitionists also have profoundly different notions of cosmic morality. As with questions about the meaning of life, most people have a deeply ingrained sense that their immoral actions will come with costs. According to Jean Piaget, this type of immanent justice reasoning starts early in childhood and continues into adult life.[22] Whether it is karma, divine retribution, or a desire to feel that there is innate justice in the world, most cultures share the idea that bad actions hold consequences, even if the perpetrators seem to have gotten away scot-free. Somewhere, someone or something is keeping a list and checking it twice. Not surprisingly, this idea is also embraced by a large percentage of Americans: an overwhelming 80 percent believe they will eventually pay for any bad deeds they've committed, even if they don't get caught.[23] However, once again this belief varies by one's place on the Intuitionism scale.[24] Just as Intuitionists are more likely to believe that their life has a purpose, they also believe that any misdeeds will come with consequences. For example, only 60 percent of Rationalists believe in what some people might call karma, compared with 85 percent of Intuitionists.

We find very similar patterns regarding other supernatural beliefs. Take the belief in God. About 85 percent of Americans believe in God, but these beliefs are not always magical. Remember, magical thinking is not simply the belief that unobservable forces shape events, but that these unobservable forces can explain things better than empirical accounts. There are many instances where a belief in God is not magical simply because we have no other explanation for natural phenomena. No one knows, for instance, what preceded the big bang, why life emerged on earth 2 billion years ago, or even what comprises the basis of our universe. Absent empirical explanations, a belief in some superordinate phenomena we could label as God is not a magical explanation but simply an untested hypothesis.

But for most Americans, their conception of God involves more than these remote cosmic initiatives. For them, God is an active, intentional presence in their life, speaking to them in a variety of ways and shaping events occurring to his (with God usually characterized as male) particular will. That is, God is a very humanlike entity. This anthropomorphic conception of the divine tends toward the magical, particularly when God becomes implicated in more daily activities. God is not simply one who dispassionately put the universe in motion but a being that observes and condemns sinful actions and orchestrates particular events according to his whim. In other words, God is a magical being for most Americans.

We can see this in our surveys. Although Americans understand God in many different ways, for the sake of simplicity, we asked respondents to choose among three different ways of interpreting the divine: God as "an observant force involved in all our actions" (60 percent agree); God as "a cosmic force mostly indifferent to our daily lives" (26 percent agree); or

God as something that "doesn't exist" (14 percent agree). These different visions of God vary significantly by a person's position on the Intuitionism scale. Roughly three-quarters of Intuitionists subscribe to the activist, observant view of God, compared with only 35 percent of Rationalists. Although we don't depict it in figure 2.5, we also find that the converse holds as well: Rationalists are seven times more likely than Intuitionists to say that God doesn't exist.[25]

Similar differences occur with other supernatural beliefs. Take one of the most popular ones: angels. Nearly two-thirds of our sample believes in these ethereal guardians, but here too the extent of this belief depends largely on where a respondent resides on the Intuitionism scale. According to our estimates, less than 40 percent of Rationalists believe in angels, compared with nearly 80 percent of Intuitionists. We don't list the figures here, but a nearly identical pattern occurs with Americans' belief in Satan. Roughly 60 percent believe in Satan, although again this varies considerably by the respondent's position on the Intuitionism scale. Less than 30 percent of Rationalists believe in Satan, compared with 80 percent of Intuitionists.

In sum, when it comes to general supernatural beliefs, the Intuitionism scale is a remarkably potent predictor. From general suppositions about the meaning of life to specific ideas of angels, people who score high on our Intuitionism scale are much more likely to believe than people scoring low on the scale. But the predictive power of Intuitionism doesn't stop there. For beyond a general supernaturalism, the thickets of American religious beliefs have some other major branches running through them. One of the most notable is Christian fundamentalism. In the United States, fundamentalism began in the early twentieth century as a movement among some Christian pastors and denominations in reaction to modernist theology. At the time, many Christian theologians were dissatisfied with the growing naturalism of Protestant worship. Fundamentalism was an effort to return to the "fundamentals" of biblical scripture. Since that time, the fundamentalist movement has grown, and today it encompasses hundreds of different Christian denominations and sects.[26]

The immense number of groups that congregate under the fundamentalism banner makes its central precepts harder to describe. After all, each of these denominations features certain ideas and interpretations of the Bible that differentiate it from the others. Southern Baptists, for example, hold many beliefs that are different not only from groups like Seventh-Day Adventists or Pentecostal churches but even among themselves.[27] Yet despite all this doctrinal diversity, contemporary scholars of religion have been able to identify a set of core principles. First, fundamentalists embrace the evangelical notion of salvation through belief in Jesus Christ's atonement and resurrection, typically through a "born-again" conversion experience. Second, fundamentalists emphasize biblical literalism and inerrancy. In their view, the Bible is the key to deciphering God's will. It is not simply a set of divinely inspired texts but a direct set of commands from on high. The Bible is a *sacred* document and revered as such.[28] Third, fundamentalists usually embrace dispensationalism, the idea that God divides time into distinct eras, and that biblical prophecy foretells the Second Coming of Christ. For most fundamentalists, major current events are both the culmination of biblical predictions and the precursor of some greater apocalypse.[29]

At its core, Christian fundamentalism embodies a paradox. On the one hand, it is an emotive way of interpreting the world. For fundamentalists, God is not simply a phenomenon to be learned about but a spiritual force to be felt; God transcends the limits of human reason. Many fundamentalists experience the divine through feelings and visions, not remote deductions. On the other hand, fundamentalists believe that God's will is dictated through the literal interpretation of scripture. Rules of life are crisply delineated in the ancient books of the Bible; God's written word is strict and incontrovertible, never to be questioned or ignored. For fundamentalists, God is both felt in the heart and commanded from the page.

How do fundamentalists address this incongruity? They resolve it primarily by allowing for intuitive interpretations of biblical texts. While the Bible is taken as the literal word of God, biblical language is highly poetic and allegorical: God, Jesus, and the other prophets speak through homily, symbol, and metaphor. Such symbolism allows a great deal of latitude in interpretation. Indeed, it is precisely this ambiguity that contributes to the fantastic plethora of Christian sects. Bound by the inherent vagueness of human language, the Bible requires subjective and emotional explication, which then becomes cemented as sectarian doctrine.[30]

In this combination of emotion and metaphor, fundamentalism relies heavily on intuitive judgments. Fundamentalists prioritize affect over reason, gut feelings over deliberation, the symbolic over the tangible. When one views the world through scripture, which itself is highly stylized and lyrical, one sees through the window of faith and feeling. Fundamentalists take biblical symbols to heart, using their emotional resonance as guides to reality. Yet fundamentalism also emphasizes tradition, rules, and authority. Biblical orthodoxy anchors fundamentalism in the seas of uncertainty and apprehension that modernity brings. It offers both the promise

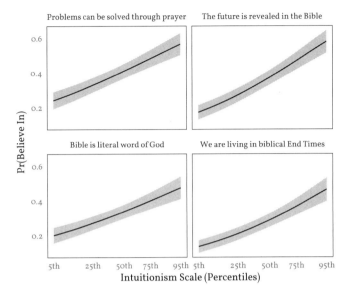

FIGURE 2.6. Fundamentalist beliefs as predicted by the Intuitionism scale. Probabilities were extracted from logit models controlling for age, education, and gender. The ribbon charts indicate 95% confidence intervals.

of emotional stability and the coherence of community bound together in shared purpose.

We can see these beliefs mapped in our data. Throughout our surveys, we asked how much respondents agree with four statements central to the theology of many fundamentalist churches. These include whether respondents believe that we are living in the end of days as foretold in biblical prophecy (33 percent agree); whether "many problems can be solved by prayer" (46 percent agree); whether the Bible is the literal word of God and without error (35 percent agree); and whether "a person can find the future revealed in places like the Bible if only he or she knows how to read the signs" (38 percent agree).[31] Notably, such notions are not limited to fundamentalist churches in the United States. Apocalyptic expectations, doctrinal inerrancy, moral dualism, and sacred words are all found in Islam, Hinduism, and other religions; in fact, these magical elements often differentiate fundamentalist religious epistemologies across the world.[32] Nevertheless, these are distinctive elements within American fundamentalism and represent a highly intuitive worldview.

We see the intuitive power of fundamentalist beliefs in our data (fig. 2.6). As with the more general supernatural beliefs, fundamentalist beliefs

increase dramatically as one moves up the Intuitionism scale. Our equations predict that only about 20 percent of Rationalists agree, on average,
with any of the four fundamentalist statements listed above. Among Intuitionists, however, this percentage more than doubles. For example, our
equations predict that just under 60 percent of Intuitionists believe in hidden Bible codes, compared with only 20 percent of Rationalists. Nearly
50 percent of Intuitionists believe that we are living in end times (the
prophesied precursor to Armageddon, the Rapture, and the Second Coming of Jesus Christ), and that "many problems can be solved by prayer."
Such beliefs are held by only 20 percent of Rationalists.

At this point we want to pause and acknowledge that these are some
of the most striking findings *in this entire book*. Recall the types of items
comprising our Intuitionism scale: stabbing photos, buying lottery tickets,
locking doors, or guessing the likelihood of recessions. These items were
deliberately designed to be devoid of any specific religious doctrine. Nevertheless, such items are extraordinarily predictive of a person's supernatural
and fundamentalist beliefs. If we were to take the 20 percent of Americans
having the strongest supernatural beliefs, they would far outstrip the rest
of the country in their propensity for symbolic thinking, their apprehension
scores, and their levels of pessimism.

But it's not just supernatural beliefs that rise with Intuitionism—
supernatural *experiences* do as well. In our October 2014 survey, we asked
respondents to indicate if they have ever felt the distinct presence of a
supernatural being (such as God) or if they feel they have changed the
outcome of an event through prayer. These supernatural experiences are
quite common among Americans: nearly half report having felt the presence of God, and roughly three in ten say they have changed something
with prayer. And as with their religious beliefs, such experiences vary a
great deal across the Intuitionism scales: about 30 percent of Rationalists
say they have felt God's presence, compared with 68 percent of Intuitionists; 17 percent of Rationalists say they have changed something by prayer,
compared with 44 percent of Intuitionists.[33]

Taking all this together, we see a remarkable pattern: the most common
American supernatural beliefs are highly correlated with our measures of
intuitive thinking. It's not just that measures such as feelings about Charles
Manson's pajamas or checking the locks coincide with a person's supernat-
ural beliefs and experiences, but that they do so in a steady, predictable
fashion. Rationalists have fewer supernatural beliefs and experiences than
Intuitionists across a broad array of measures. These results validate what
Malinowski and Frazer predicted over a century ago: our subscription to

supernatural beliefs is highly related to our tendency to attach emotional weight to our symbols and chronic feelings of anxiety and dread.

Paranormal Beliefs

Of course, Americans' magical beliefs are not limited to the supernatural. They also include a wide array of paranormal beliefs. Some of these include a belief in ghosts (42 percent); reincarnation (25 percent); special mental powers, such as ESP (44 percent); and the power of positive thinking (25 percent).[34] And while paranormal and supernatural beliefs are both magical, paranormal beliefs have some distinct characteristics. They don't necessarily invoke an intentional deity, nor are they usually the central focus of organized religious institutions. Unlike with Christianity, paranormal beliefs are not central to America's national identity; few people would say "America was founded as a *New Age* nation" or "In ESP we trust."

Yet despite these differences, paranormal beliefs also correspond with Intuitionism in a similar manner to supernatural ones (fig. 2.7). Beliefs in ghosts, ESP, reincarnation, and positive thinking all increase along the Intuitionism scale. In two cases, ghosts and positive thinking, the percentages double. For example, less than a quarter of Rationalists believe that you can help someone by sending positive thoughts, compared with nearly half of Intuitionists; similarly, just over 20 percent of Rationalists believe in ghosts, compared with 40 percent of Intuitionists. Beliefs in ESP and past lives also rise along the Intuitionism scale.

What's even more remarkable is the fact that our measures of intuitive thinking relate to paranormal beliefs in the same manner that they relate to supernatural ones. Even though Christian beliefs and New Age beliefs come from different cultural sources (and are often explicitly at odds with each other), they still change across the Intuitionism scale in the same way. Moreover, Intuitionism always works in the same direction. In other words, if you check your locks a lot, think the economy is about to tank, or would prefer not to stab a family photo, you are much more likely to believe in ghosts, ESP, and past lives, just as you are also more likely to believe in angels, God, or end-time prophecy.

As with the supernatural, Americans don't simply have paranormal beliefs; they have paranormal experiences as well. These too change in relation to Intuitionism. In the October 2014 survey, we asked respondents if they have either seen a ghost or changed the outcome of an event by using

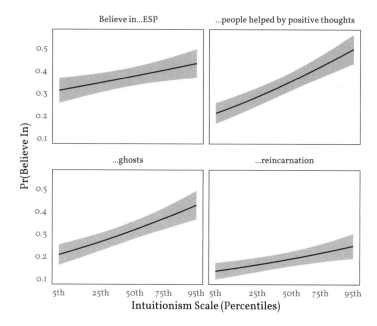

Believe in...ESP   ...people helped by positive thoughts

...ghosts   ...reincarnation

Pr(Believe In)

Intuitionism Scale (Percentiles)

FIGURE 2.7. Paranormal beliefs as predicted by the Intuitionism scale. Probabilities were extracted from logit models controlling for age, education, and gender. The ribbon charts indicate 95% confidence intervals.

a lucky item. About 25 percent of Americans report having seen a ghost, and about 12 percent say they've successfully used a lucky item. These experiences, however, are highly contingent on a person's position on the Intuitionism scale: Intuitionists are twice as likely as Rationalists to say they have seen ghosts or changed their luck using a special item.[35] Our models predict that over one in three Americans at the top of the Intuitionism scale have seen ghosts, whereas only about one in six Rationalists have.

In sum, paranormal beliefs are a more disorganized form of magical thinking in the United States. Unlike supernatural beliefs that are promulgated through religious institutions, paranormal beliefs transmit through the culture in more indirect ways. Few organizations are devoted to promoting belief in ESP or ghosts or promising eternal salvation by believing in positive thinking. Rather, paranormal beliefs spread through forms of popular culture, practitioners of alternative medicine, New Age bookstores, and the like. Nevertheless, they are still firmly magical beliefs, and as such draw adherents from people who prioritize their intuitions. And just like with supernatural and fundamentalist beliefs, paranormal beliefs become much more common as one moves up the Intuitionism scale.

Intuitions and "Folk Science"

Just as Intuitionists are more drawn to supernatural and paranormal beliefs, so they are less inclined toward scientific ones. This is evident in both their support of specific scientific beliefs and their general patterns of thinking. Consider one of the most widely endorsed beliefs in science: Darwin's theory of evolution by natural selection. According to a Pew study, over 98 percent of scientists believe in evolution.[36] But support for evolution is much less common among the American public. Depending on how the question is asked, typically only 35 to 45 percent of Americans believe in evolution. In our surveys, we find that only 44 percent say they believe in evolution, with 30 percent saying they aren't sure and 26 percent saying they don't believe.

But such patterns of belief vary considerably across the Intuitionism scale. For example, our equations predict that over 60 percent of Rationalists believe in Darwin's theory of evolution, but that this number drops to under 40 percent of Intuitionists (fig. 2.8). And these results aren't simply a function of the greater religiosity of Intuitionists. For while fundamentalist Christians score much higher, on average, on the Intuitionism scale, this does not account for why Intuitionists are generally less likely to believe in evolution. If we add a variable that controls for whether the person identifies as "conservative, orthodox, or fundamentalist" in his or her religious beliefs (what we term religious conservatism), the relationship between Intuitionism and belief in evolution attenuates by about a quarter. Thus, clearly religious doctrine may be accounting for some of these results, but not all. If, for example, we examine only respondents who do not identify as a religious conservative, we see that belief in evolutionary theory drops by over twenty-five percentage points as their magical thinking increases.

We find a similar pattern with regard to other nonscientific views. For example, many Christians take a literal reading of the Bible, which would make the earth only six thousand years old. To reconcile this belief with evidence provided by fossils, they often contend that dinosaurs and humans coexisted. This notion flatly contradicts all the scientific evidence that dates the extinction of dinosaurs to over 65 million years ago. Nevertheless, roughly three in ten Americans think that humans and dinosaurs

FIGURE 2.8. Trust and scientific beliefs as predicted by the Intuitionism scale. Probabilities were extracted from logit models controlling for age, education, and gender. Ribbon charts indicate 95% confidence intervals.

coexisted. Much of this belief, however, varies according to a person's Intuitionism. Our equations predict that less than 25 percent of Rationalists think that cavemen ran with stegosaurs, compared with over 40 percent of Intuitionists. Once again, this difference is not contingent on a person's religious beliefs. Adding controls for self-identified fundamentalism does not influence the impact of the Intuitionism scale.

Intuitionism also arises in other nonscientific beliefs. Take the tendency to anthropomorphize nature. Many magical beliefs orient themselves around the notion that nature itself contains spiritual forces. We tapped this notion with a survey question addressing whether Americans agree that "plants and trees can sense what we're feeling." This sentiment has no basis in scientific theory—plants don't have nerve cells or any way of perceiving our emotional states. Nevertheless, 29 percent of Americans agree with this statement. And once again, the likelihood of agreeing depends largely on where a respondent resides on the Intuitionism scale. Our equations predict that nearly 40 percent of Intuitionists think that plants can sense our emotions, compared with just over 20 percent of Rationalists.

Magical thinkers are also less likely to employ basic scientific principles. As we observed in chapter 1, many aspects of scientific thought are counterintuitive. It's not self-evident that microscopic germs make us sick, that time slows as you move faster, or that free trade boosts overall productivity. Such notions arose through scientific approaches to understanding reality: formulating theories, deducing hypotheses, and testing these hypotheses with observation or experimentation. Of the many expressions of scientific thought, one of the most common and counterintuitive is probability theory, which grapples with randomness mathematically. Our minds evolved to seek patterns and make connections between events in the world, not to passively accept haphazard chances.[37] Indeed, this is why magical thinking is so much more common than scientific thinking: it is a natural and intuitive way of understanding the world.

These tendencies are evident in our research. Intuitionists are much more likely to try a superstitious act to influence something random. For example, remember in chapter 1 when we asked respondents whether they would rub their lottery ticket on a dollar bill or a paper napkin for good luck? Intuitionists are about twice as likely as Rationalists to try rubbing their lottery ticket on anything that might bring them luck, but they are especially susceptible when that thing is the more appropriate symbol of money than just a napkin.[38] Rationalists, meanwhile, are less likely to rub their lottery ticket on anything no matter what it is.

Intuitionism is also evident in how people make decisions. One of the central premises behind this research is that public opinion is influenced as much by worldview as by ideology. This extends to basic decision making. We test this premise with a few questions about how people make important decisions. Did respondents think, for example, that "the heart is a better guide than the head" (38 percent agree) or that "when it comes to important questions, scientific facts don't help that much" (16 percent agree)? As with magical beliefs, we see big differences along the Intuitionism scale. Intuitionists are nearly twice as likely as Rationalists to say that the heart is a better guide than the head. Our models predict that only 25 percent of Rationalists go with their heart, compared with 50 percent of Intuitionists. Similarly, only 5 percent of Rationalists agree that scientific facts don't help with important questions, compared with 30 percent of Intuitionists. In short, Intuitionists don't simply have different beliefs, they have different ways of thinking.

Another aspect that differentiates Intuitionists from Rationalists is their trust of other people. In our surveys, we asked two questions commonly used in surveys to gauge interpersonal trust among respondents: (1) Given the chance, do you think most people would try to take advantage of you? (51 percent) / try to be fair? (49 percent); (2) Generally speaking, would you say . . . most people can be trusted? (39 percent) / you can't be too careful in dealing with people? (61 percent). We combined these two items into a dichotomous scale, with the 73 percent of the sample that gave a mistrustful answer to either question a score of one and the 27 percent giving trusting answers to both questions a zero. Intuitionists tend to be far less trusting than Rationalists. Our models predict that only 61 percent of Rationalists are mistrusting, compared with nearly 80 percent of Intuitionists. Given that Intuitionist are the types of people who regularly shred their bills or check their locks, it's not surprising that they would also express higher mistrust of other people. But it does reaffirm yet another way that they differ from Rationalists in their view of the world.[39]

Chickens and Eggs

Anyone familiar with survey research is likely to bring up the question of endogeneity, or what ordinary people might call reverse causality. Perhaps Intuitionists are more likely to have supernatural and paranormal beliefs because the beliefs themselves stress the importance of respecting one's family or revering graves. Perhaps the prognosticators of supernatural beliefs (priests, ministers, and so on) promote greater anxiety in their followers. Perhaps believing in ghosts and ESP makes someone more pessimistic or apprehensive.

These are valid concerns. Endogeneity is a common problem in survey research, and ours is no exception. With our limited survey data, we have no way of knowing exactly when or where people acquire their beliefs. All we do know is that when we put our measures of symbolic thinking, apprehension, and pessimism into a single scale, they are highly correlated with a wide array of magical beliefs. The Intuitionism scale is designed to capture psychological processes that, in theory, come before our magical beliefs, but we can't expect that we are precisely measuring such deep-seated tendencies with our questions. Surveys are cultural artifacts—they still depend on language, concepts, and symbols. We can't say for certain whether we are truly measuring innate cognitive and emotional processes.

That said, we do think the Intuitionism scale is measuring something that comes before the magical beliefs that the scale is predicting. Few religions, for example, have precepts against wearing the clothes of mass murderers, buying lottery tickets from winning gas stations, or even sleeping in homes where someone had died. Few New Age gurus make predictions about Ebola, recessions, or war with China. Science has little to say about regularly checking one's locks, shredding one's bills, or grinding one's heels in unmarked graves.

However, what most magical belief systems do (and science does not) is take symbols, words, and metaphors literally. For many Roman Catholics, the Communion wafer is the body of Christ; for many fundamentalist Christians, the Bible is the literal word of God. People who believe in ghosts often have supernatural experiences as well. The power of our magical beliefs lies in the believers' willingness to steep these words and symbols with emotional significance. Crucifixes, the Torah, crystals, images, and even incantations are important to magical thinkers precisely because of their emotional resonance. And it is this willingness to endow any kind of symbol or image with emotional power that is a hallmark of intuitive thinking.

In addition, we should expect some endogeneity within our measures. This arises from one of the most important arguments in our book: magical beliefs not only draw from our intuitions for their power but also reinforce our tendency to use our intuitions as guides for our decision making. Some of this behavior may be habitual. If you believe that an invisible God is monitoring your behavior and sending natural disasters to punish you for your sins, it probably bolsters your tendency to anthropomorphize the world. If you think that masturbation defiles the purity of the soul, you are likely to be sensitive to other types of contagion metaphors. People accustomed to using their intuitions to explain the world are likely to use them more often, just as people who use scientific beliefs are more likely to think scientifically as well.

The reverse direction of causality applies to emotions as well. Intuitionists may feel more apprehensive and pessimistic because of what their magical beliefs are telling them. Many religious proselytizers have a keen interest in disrupting the emotional stability of their followers—a sanguine flock is less likely to keep coming back for the reassurances of weekly services. Preachers, priests, shamans, and other spiritual profiteers pull their followers into ever-tighter adherence by stoking their fears. Consider three common tenets of fundamentalist Christianity: an invisible, omniscient God is always watching us and keeping track of our sins; Satan is constantly tempting souls into damnation; and a time of great tribulation is soon to be upon us, during which the true believers will be brought into heaven and the rest left in apocalyptic squalor. This is not a cheerful or uplifting vision of the cosmos. It is one of constant observation, threat, and imminent danger. Not surprisingly, those who hear weekly sermons about fire and damnation would feel more pessimistic about the future and apprehensive about the present. This is how, to borrow from Marx, the "opiate of the masses" keeps its followers hooked: stoke the people's fears with threats of damnation and resolve their anxieties with regular doses of promised salvation.

But even if we accept that the direction of causality between intuitions and magical beliefs is a two-way street, it is still possible that our findings result from omitted variables. In other words, could it be that Intuitionists are more likely to believe in God, fundamentalism, ESP, or conspiracy theories simply because of other unmeasured factors like education, age, income, or race? Could our magical thinking scales be picking up differences in upbringing or authoritarianism? Although we'll discuss these questions further in chapter 3, we want to partially address them here. All the figures presented thus far are based on logistic regression equations. These statistics basically mark the change in magical beliefs along the Intuitionism scale while accounting for the effects of education, age, gender, and in a few cases whether someone identifies as a religious conservative. All the equations are presented in the online appendix.

Although we'll explore some of these findings in further detail in chapter 3, for now we just want to focus on three characteristics of our fully specified models. The first is size—the Intuitionism scale is a very *powerful* measure of magical beliefs. Across all different types of magical beliefs, this scale almost always garners the largest coefficients. In other words, the Intuitionism scale is not only better at predicting magical beliefs than factors such as education, income, and gender are, it often exceeds predictors such as a person's religious identification.[40]

The Intuitionism scale is also a very *distinctive* measure. Even when we take people's education, gender, and current religious identification into account, the Intuitionism scale remains a very potent and consistent predictor. Although fundamentalists, women, and the less educated all score slightly higher in their Intuitionism scores (something we'll describe in chapter 3), this does not affect the relationship between Intuitionism and magical beliefs. The predictive power of the Intuitionism scale is independent of all these other influences.

Finally, the Intuitionism scale is a very *consistent* measure. This scale is only one of two variables in all our estimates to generate a consistent relationship with all the magical beliefs. The only other consistent predictor is education. Income and gender also predict magical beliefs, but in ways that aren't always statistically significant. Measures of fundamentalist self-identification correspond to the supernatural beliefs, but they don't predict beliefs in the paranormal. But the Intuitionism scale does. In sum, the scale predicts magical beliefs, not because it is a stand-in for other factors but because it captures the innate decision-making processes underlying how many people perceive the world.

Conclusion

This book's central premise is that intuitions are an important force organizing US politics. In chapter 1, we described how magical beliefs can serve as a guide for describing how our intuitions function. Magical beliefs tend to have similar elements—they draw from feelings of apprehension and anxiety, and they resolve these feelings by weaving narratives that rely on innate judgment strategies, that is, heuristics. Rather using abstract principles to inform their beliefs, magical thinkers are motivated by emotions and guided by cognitive heuristics. We believe that these same processes inform intuitive judgments of many other phenomena. Intuitionists are people who give their apprehensions a lot of weight in making decisions and are highly sensitive to certain types of symbols and metaphors, particularly those referencing the innate heuristics we use to make decisions when we have little information.

In this chapter, we put these insights to their first test. Not only did we come up with measures of these Intuitionist tendencies, the measures are also terrific at predicting people's magical beliefs. Consider, once again, just a few examples from the chapter. Among Intuitionists, those people at the high end of the Intuitionism scale, 78 percent believe in an observant God, 45 percent believe that the Bible is the inerrant word of God, 44 percent believe in ghosts, and 47 percent believe that the heart is a better guide than the head. These numbers are roughly twice as high as they are among Rationalists, the people at the low end of the Intuitionism scale. And these differences don't stop with supernatural or paranormal beliefs. Intuitionists are twice as likely to say they don't need the advice of experts and five times as likely to say that scientific facts don't help with important decisions.

Of course, these categories are not absolute predictors. Even at the low end of the Intuitionism scale, some magical thinking exists: 20 percent of Rationalists still believe in ghosts, and 22 percent believe in the power of prayer. Conversely, not all Intuitionists are consistent magical thinkers—for example, two-thirds don't believe in reincarnation, and over 40 percent don't believe in the power of prayer. Being an Intuitionist or a Rationalist does not absolutely predict any single magical belief, just as being liberal or conservative does not absolutely predict any single policy opinion. Rather, the Intuitionism scale simply shows a proclivity toward beliefs that do or don't reflect our intuitions. More important, Intuitionism doesn't happen in a cultural vacuum, but is orchestrated through a set of cultural practices and institutions. As we start delving into the politics of intuitions, some of these specific sets of beliefs will become more significant. But before we delve into Intuitionist politics in more detail, let us first identify who, exactly, these Intuitionists are.

CHAPTER THREE

Who Is an Intuitionist?

We are all Intuitionists, at least in the beginning. When we are born, we have nothing but our innate predilections for making sense of things. Our fears and apprehensions are at the ready, primed to protect us from harm. Our brains relentlessly seek patterns in our environment, finding humanlike intentionality in animals and objects and making connections between proximate events. In childhood, these proclivities generate a lot of magical beliefs: a bump in the night is caused by a ghost, a stomachache is punishment for being naughty, and so on. Such tendencies continue into adulthood. Many of our inferences are based more on feelings and quick heuristics than dispassionate, logical deductions. Because it is so natural, magical thinking is something we all inevitably do. But not everyone does it to the same degree. Even as adults, some people continue to rely on their intuition as their primary guide to the world. They not only hold lots of magical beliefs, they give priority to their feelings as barometers of truth. And this is important in politics, for when Intuitionists begin to organize themselves around their worldview, they can become an independent political force.

In this chapter, we examine who these Intuitionists are. Throughout our research, we fielded dozens of survey questions about why people may be more likely to rely on their intuitions when making judgments. These ranged from extensive measures of personality to how often they were spanked as a child. In the end, we found a set of core traits that differentiate where people reside on the Intuitionism scale. Intuitionists tend to be less educated, poorer, and under greater financial stress. They are more likely to be female. They tend to belong to conservative religious traditions and attend church often. They were raised in strict homes and themselves emphasize disciplined, obedient children. They are less inquisitive about the world and are easily disgusted. And most important for our inquiry, they are more likely to identify as politically conservative.

For the rest of this chapter, we examine all these factors in more detail.[1] Although we offer some accounts for why each one is important, our story here is more descriptive than causal. Our findings come from multivariate regression models where we examine the effects of each variable while accounting for the effects of other variables as well. In other words, when we look at the differences in Intuitionism by education, we are also holding constant the effects of income, age, gender, religiosity, and other factors. This approach allows us to isolate the particular impact of each factor, but it does not let us specify causal factors. For example, women are more likely to be Intuitionists than men. This may be because women have higher empathy levels, but our data simply don't allow us to examine all other possible reasons. What we can do, however, is broadly describe the factors that differentiate Americans' location on the Intuitionist scale, and suggest some likely reasons why. And as we'll see in subsequent chapters, these findings also hold some major implications for US politics. But before we get to this, let us draw a better picture of Enchanted America.

Education

If there is one force that shapes our worldview, it's our formal education. Schooling reduces our uncertainty by providing us with explanations for how nature, society, politics, and even our own minds function. It provides us with explanations for the world that go beyond our five senses: we learn that our body is composed of cells, that the universe is expanding, that our minds are dominated by unconscious impulses, and so forth. Education also hones our reasoning abilities, teaching us to think analytically. It trains us in probabilities and logic, deduction and critical analysis, and other scientific ways of understanding the world. The more we learn, the more we find alternatives to magical thinking, thereby liberating us from our reliance on inborn intuition.

Given all this, we should expect to see big differences in Intuitionism as predicted by education level. And this is indeed what we find, especially if we don't take any other factors into account. For example, a simple comparison of means shows that Americans with only a high school education score seven points higher on the Intuitionism scale than those with advanced degrees, and four points higher than those with some college education. From these simple statistics, education seems to have a linear effect on Intuitionism — the more schooling people have, the less Intuitionist they become.

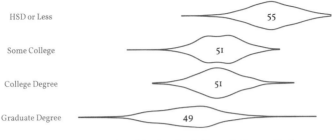

HSD or Less   55

Some College   51

College Degree   51

Graduate Degree   49

Intuitionism Scale (Sample Percentiles)

FIGURE 3.1. Intuitionism as predicted by education level. Labels indicate the percentile of the mean respondent. Density plots indicate bootstrapped distributions of the mean group percentile, controlling for income, gender, authoritarianism, upbringing, church attendance, and religious conservatism.

But this effect changes somewhat once we take other factors into account. As illustrated in figure 3.1, results from our nonparametric resampling analysis show a gap between Americans with only a high school diploma or less and those with a college education.[2] The figure depicts a distribution of the cases along each education category. The width of each category's shape indicates the predicted number of cases, while its length shows its predicted spread along the Intuitionism scale. Our models predict that on average, Americans with either some college education or a college degree score four points lower than those with no college education. Even more interesting, however, is the distribution. Americans with graduate degrees may be more Rationalist on average, but even here we see a wide range of Intuitionism scores. Conversely, Americans with no college education not only have higher average Intuitionism scores but are more tightly concentrated in their Intuitionist tendencies.

These patterns are also evident when we look at specific magical beliefs. As we would expect, the less educated someone is, the more likely he or she is to believe in magical phenomena. For instance, among Americans with no college at all, 51 percent believe in ghosts, 32 percent believe in past lives, and 46 percent believe in hidden Bible codes. By contrast, among Americans with advanced degrees, 25 percent believe in ghosts, 16 percent believe in past lives, and 27 percent believe in hidden Bible codes. When it comes to magical beliefs, education really makes a big difference, especially among those with advanced degrees.

These findings are striking in two regards. First, education is a major influence on people's worldview. People with a college education, and especially an advanced degree, are less likely to hold an Intuitionist perspective. An educated public tends to be a more Rationalist public. That noted, even with all their education, lots of college graduates have magical beliefs, including angels (66 percent), ghosts (43 percent), and hidden Bible codes (37 percent). By itself, a college education doesn't dissuade all Americans from magical thinking. This is partly a testament to the simple power of our own intuitive proclivities. Our susceptibility to certain heuristics and apprehensions runs deep. Even the most educated among us may still be motivated by strong feelings of apprehension, or swayed by metaphors and symbols.[3] Although education may offer more Rationalist ways of perceiving the world, it can't diminish our innate mental tendencies entirely, because they are so deeply rooted in our minds.

Income

Intuitionism also changes by socioeconomic standing. There are several reasons for this. One is simply stress. For many Americans, the strain of living in poverty greatly exacerbates many mental health issues, including feelings of anxiety, depression, and unease.[4] Under such conditions of psychological duress, emotional pressure may be great and the proclivities toward Intuitionism all the stronger. Remember, Intuitionism is partly about extrapolating from one's feelings—if those feelings are strong, then their pressure is all the greater. Conversely, we would expect the affluent, in the comfort of their financial security, to feel less compelled to seek intuitive interpretations of world events.

Intuitionism may also be higher among the poor because of their social marginalization. Many of our intuitions contradict dominant explanations for natural phenomena, particularly in a liberal, industrialized democracy like the United States. Conspiracy theories, horoscopes, Bible codes, and healing by prayer are not ideas generally promoted by scientific communities or political elites. Such magical beliefs are transgressive, and to adopt them is to reject or resist messages coming from hegemonic cultural and political institutions. And this is where social class comes in. Someone at the bottom rung of society may be more mistrustful of its institutions and the messages of its elites, particularly scientific explanations for what happens in the world. The poor may rely more on their intuitions, not simply because these are so appealing, but because Rationalist explanations are not trusted.

To test this, we look at two sets of statistics. The first part of figure 3.2

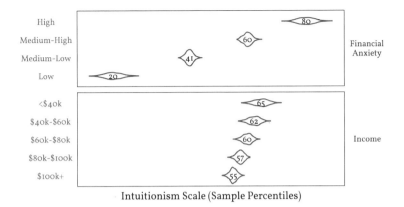

High   ⟨80⟩

Medium-High   ⟨60⟩   Financial
                                                                Anxiety
Medium-Low   ⟨41⟩

Low   ⟨20⟩

<$40k   ⟨65⟩

$40k-$60k   ⟨62⟩

$60k-$80k   ⟨60⟩   Income

$80k-$100k   ⟨57⟩

$100k+   ⟨55⟩

Intuitionism Scale (Sample Percentiles)

FIGURE 3.2. Intuitionism as predicted by income and financial anxiety levels. Labels indicate the percentile of the mean respondent. Density plots indicate bootstrapped distributions of the mean group percentile, controlling for education, gender, authoritarianism, upbringing, church attendance, and religious conservatism.

depicts the predicted distribution of the Intuitionism score across five income categories. As with education, there are few changes in the Intuitionism scale as we move from the poor to the middle class. Looking at just average scores across a nine-category income scale, we find that Americans with a household income under $40,000 a year have an average Intuitionism score of .56, which is not different from people with annual incomes between $40,000 and $60,000. Intuitionism drops by three points, on average, among people making between $60,000 and $80,000 a year, and the distribution also becomes wider. In other words, in this middle-income group there is a wider range of Intuitionism scores. However, Intuitionism declines significantly for those earning $80,000 or above per year. For this group, the average Intuitionism score is .47, a full nine points lower than the poorest groups.

Much of this asymptotic trend appears to be caused by the factors we mentioned above. Consider the effects of financial stress. In our March 2016 survey, we asked respondents how frequently they feel "anxious about having enough money" or that "things are spiraling out of control." We also asked whether they think their finances would get better or worse in the coming year.[5] We then combined these three items into a single financial anxiety scale.[6] As we would expect, poor people express more financial worries than wealthier ones, and the amount of financial insecurity steadily decreases as income rises.[7] However, once we take financial worries into account, the relationship between income and Intuitionism disappears. When the financial anxiety scale is included in a multivariate equation, the predicted differences in income along the Intuitionism scale vanish.[8] In other words, the main reason that both poor and middle-class people are more Intuitionist is not because of income per se but because of their greater financial anxiety.

We see evidence supporting the marginalization hypothesis as well. This comes out mostly in comparing different types of magical beliefs. Poor Americans are far more likely than affluent ones to embrace unusual or less popular magical beliefs. But the gaps between the rich and the poor narrow considerably when it comes to popular supernatural beliefs. For example, 57 percent of the wealthiest Americans believe in an intentional God, a figure not much below the 62 percent of the poorest Americans. Income gaps are the largest for those beliefs that are more socially transgressive, such as ESP or end-time prophecy. Only 11 percent of the wealthy believe in ESP, and only 22 percent believe in end-time prophecy; among the poorest, these numbers are 33 and 40 percent, respectively. And as we'll see in chapter 5, poor Americans express other attitudes that reflect political and social marginalization: they are far more likely to believe in conspiracy theories or agree that "politics is ultimately a struggle between good and evil."[9] With such high levels of political alienation, it's not surprising that poor people find transgressive magical beliefs more acceptable, particularly if those beliefs involve conspiracy theories or folk wisdom.

In sum, both poor and middle-class Americans are far more Intuitionist in their worldview than those at the top of the economic ladder. This is largely attributable to feelings of financial stress. Americans with the fewest financial worries have an average Intuitionism score fifteen points lower than those with the most worries. Poor Americans are also much more likely to embrace unconventional magical beliefs, like end-time prophecy or ESP, reflecting their greater distrust of mainstream cultural institutions. What is most interesting, however, is how prevalent stress is among America's middle classes. While poor Americans exhibit the most stress, they are by no means the only group in the United States who feel financial anxiety. Many middle-class Americans also feel financial pressure, and this emotional state can lead them toward a more intuitive worldview.

Gender

Another factor that may differentiate Intuitionists is their gender. Many studies report that women have more magical beliefs than men.[10] We find similar gender differences in our data. Our models predict that men, on average, score about two points lower than women on the Intuitionism scale. These differences are evident in specific beliefs as well. For example, women are 10 percent more likely than men to believe in angels, past lives, or ESP, and 17 percent more likely to believe in ghosts. There are not, however, large gender differences in all the supernatural items; rather, women are drawn more to magical beliefs involving intentional entities than impersonal cosmic forces.

Why are women more attracted to these particular magical beliefs? Although we don't have the means to determine whether such gender differences are rooted in genes or socialization patterns, one possible explanation is that men and women have contrasting emotional styles. Psychologists have long noted that women score consistently higher in empathetic concern, sensitivity to personal distress, perspective taking, and fantasy projection—all crucial aspects of empathy.[11] These empathetic tendencies are also correlated with the same types of magical beliefs that are more popular among women. In the August 2014 survey, we administered a battery of questions using the Interpersonal Reactivity Index, a method of gauging four types of empathy. Not only do women score, on average, much higher on the empathy scales than men, such differences in empathy are related to differences in magical beliefs. For example, women who believe in ghosts score about 20 percent higher on the empathy scales than men; they also score about 10 percent higher than other women who do not believe in ghosts. From our data, it appears that not only are women more empathetic than men, but that this propensity is at least partially responsible for their stronger Intuitionism scores.

Upbringing and Authoritarianism

In the 1950s, when Freudian psychoanalytic theory was in academic fashion, scholars focused a lot of attention on how childhood experiences shaped adult beliefs. One of the most noteworthy examples was Adorno and colleagues' *The Authoritarian Personality*.[12] Like us, the authors of this pathbreaking book were motivated by why people in developed countries were drawn to inexplicable beliefs. In their case, they wanted to explain the appeal of fascism. According to *The Authoritarian Personality*, these fascistic tendencies emerged from childhood experiences—people raised in overly strict, punitive, and hierarchical households were unable to develop a fully integrated ego. Their childhood trauma left them suffering from chronic anxiety and emotional instability. This neurotic personality gave way to a constellation of authoritarian attitudes, including a high submission to convention and authority, a deep scorn of social deviance, and rigid beliefs about power and tradition. Authoritarians also held many superstitions and mystical beliefs.

The approach of *The Authoritarian Personality* overlaps quite a bit with our theories of intuitive politics. As with magical thinking, authoritarianism is a nonrational way of viewing the world. It is based more on gut feelings, albeit rather dark ones, than on general principles. Like Intuitionists, authoritarians hold Manichaean notions of good and evil, believe strongly in rigid gender roles and immanent justice, and are intolerant of ambiguity and abstract thinking.[13] Even more striking is the importance of anxiety. Just like magical beliefs, authoritarianism appears to be largely triggered by feelings of threat. There is strong evidence that authoritarianism is a latent predisposition that gets activated in stressful circumstances.[14]

But researchers have always been bedeviled by a chronic problem: how does one gauge an authoritarian personality (assuming such a thing exists)? The original scales developed by Adorno and colleagues were savaged for problems of response bias. Later scholars developed a number of different scales in an attempt to correct for this, but they have been subject to further criticisms.[15] In particular, it was never clear whether researchers were measuring personality tendencies or simply adherence to preexisting value systems.[16] This work continues today. For example, the most common measure is the Authoritarian Child Rearing (ACR) scale, which is based on child-rearing values. Respondents are typically asked to choose between pairs of competing qualities in children: independence versus respect for elders; obedience versus self-reliance; curiosity versus good manners. People who choose respect, obedience, and good manners are characterized as more authoritarian, while those who value independence, self-reliance, and curiosity are said to be less authoritarian.

These child-rearing scales have considerable predictive punch. Political scientists Stanley Feldman and Karen Stenner report that these measures are strongly related to nationalist and ethnocentric attitudes; political scientists Marc Hetherington and Jonathan Weiler find that they are a better predictor than ideology of many political opinions (we'll come back to this in chapter 4).[17] And these child-rearing scores are big predictors of the Intuitionism scale as well. Consider the predicted Intuitionist

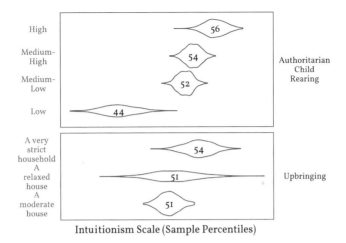

Intuitionism Scale (Sample Percentiles)

FIGURE 3.3. Intuitionism as predicted by the Authoritarian Child Rearing Scale and upbringing. Labels indicate the percentile of the mean respondent. Density plots indicate bootstrapped distributions of the mean group percentile, controlling for education, income, gender, church attendance, and religion conservatism.

score along a four-point ACR scale, as illustrated in figure 3.3. Our models predict that those having the least strict views about child rearing score thirteen points lower on the Intuitionism scale than those having the most authoritarian views. This is one of the largest differences from any variable in our model.

Now, one immediate concern is whether the ACR scale is capturing a distinct personality type rather than a particular value system. There are many reasons for suspecting that socially learned values may be at work. For example, the ACR scale is highly correlated with the same fundamentalist beliefs we described in chapter 2. Over half the strong authoritarians are Christian fundamentalists, nearly twice their rate in the general population.[18] Moreover, the ACR scale does not predict magical beliefs across the board; for instance, authoritarians are *less* likely to hold paranormal beliefs.[19] Many authoritarians may be Intuitionists not because they are magical thinkers but because they are Christian fundamentalists.

One reason why fundamentalists have such high ACR scores may be due to church doctrine. Many of the fundamentalist theologians who espouse supernatural interpretations of scripture are often the same ones who advocate strict child-rearing practices.[20] For example, Rev. James Dobson's best-selling book, *Dare to Discipline*, explicitly links its fundamentalist beliefs to having obedient and well-mannered children. And upon reflection, this connection between strict child rearing and fundamentalism is not at all surprising. Many fundamentalist sects demand submission and obedience to the strict will of God. It's no surprise, then, that obedience and respect are regarded as desirable traits among people who see them as pathways to salvation.

That noted, it's also important to recognize that not all authoritarians are fundamentalists. Indeed, 45 percent of strong authoritarians do not hold fundamentalist beliefs. And some of this difference may have to do with another factor emphasized by the original authors of *The Authoritarian Personality*: childhood experience. By their account, being raised in an overly harsh or punitive social environment contributes to authoritarianism. These same factors might also contribute to magical thinking. Our research suggests that this is plausible. In our surveys, we asked respondents to describe their childhood in very general terms. Did they grow up in a

- very strict house where all rules had to be followed (31 percent);
- moderate house where only some rules were strictly enforced (59 percent);
- relaxed house where my parents largely let me alone (10 percent).

Not surprisingly, these items are correlated with ACR scores. Authoritarians are far more likely to report being raised in strict homes; for example, 42 percent of people raised in strict homes are strong authoritarians, compared with only 23 percent of people from relaxed homes. More important, however, is that the type of home you were raised in is also a big predictor of your Intuitionism score. People from strict homes score four points higher on our Intuitionism scale than people from either moderate or relaxed homes, even when we take their ACR scores into account.

Although it is beyond the scope of our study to put each of our respondents "on the couch," both childhood experiences and attitudes about child rearing are strong predictors of Intuitionism. People who were raised in strict homes or who value obedient, respectful children are more likely to be Intuitionists. What is less clear is what, exactly, these measures about childhood are tapping into. Undoubtedly, they partly reflect the nature of religious beliefs—people from stricter homes are more likely to have been raised in conservative religious practices and identify as fundamentalist. But even as we take people's religious beliefs into account, as our models do, we still find that ACR and upbringing scores are powerful predictors of Intuitionism. Perhaps this relates to a personality type, as scholars of authoritarianism suggest, or some other latent cultural values. Perhaps a strict view of childhood reflects some emotional imbalance, as the Freudians would suggest. Or perhaps both the ACR scale and the Intuitionism scale are tapping into the same phenomena. With our limited data, we do not know for sure. What we do know is that if you want to predict whether someone is an Intuitionist, then asking him about his childhood experiences or child-rearing values is a good way to find out.

Personality

Freudian theories of childhood neuroses aren't the only models of personality. Over the past century, psychologists have developed scores of different ways for conceptualizing and measuring natural-born differences in how we think and feel. From Myers-Briggs typologies to contemporary cognitive neuroscience, many theoretical schemes attempt to account for our innate predispositions. None of these are entirely comprehensive, and each carries its own theoretical or methodological limitations.[21] Rather than try to parse through all these theories here, we focus on two that might have the greatest impact in explaining people's different propensities toward Intuitionism: disgust sensitivity and need for cognition.

One of the most intriguing dimensions of personality is the notion of disgust sensitivity. Disgust, it turns out, is an emotion that has evolved well beyond its early role as a protector from contaminants and poisons. Over the past three decades, psychologists have discovered that disgust is particularly important for our moral and social judgments. Disgust helps people make judgments about things that they often cannot think through. In a series of innovative experiments, psychologists Paul Rozin, Jonathan Haidt, and Clark McCauley presented morally ambiguous scenarios to people, such as one involving consensual protected sex between adult siblings. They found that these scenarios generated disgust feelings, and that these feelings, not rational or philosophical reasons, were the primary drivers of people's judgments.[22] As with our other emotions, feelings of disgust are often informative. Other experiments show that we'll give very different interpretations to the same situations depending on whether something is making us feel disgusted; for example, we'll make much harsher judgments about deviant behavior if we are in a dirty room instead of a clean one.[23]

Disgust sensitivity may be an important part of our intuitions. Intuitive thinking is partly about making judgments based on emotional cues. Disgust is a common emotion, and people whose disgust reflexes are easily triggered are likely to be sensitive to other types of threats as well. In addition, one of the central heuristics in many magical beliefs is assumptions of contagion, the tendency to assume that contact with holy or taboo things will transfer their essence.[24] This contagion heuristic arises from the same evolutionary imperatives as disgust—to protect us from dangerous substances.

We too find that disgust sensitivity is strongly related to magical thinking and beliefs. Drawing from the innovative disgust sensitivity scale developed by Rozin and colleagues, we asked respondents in our August 2014 survey eight questions about their feelings regarding potentially disgusting actions such as touching a corpse, seeing a cockroach at a friend's house, smelling urine at a bus stop, or hearing another couple having sex.[25] We added and scaled all these items to create a disgust sensitivity scale. Similarly to other research, we find that disgust sensitivity is higher among women, younger people, and the less educated.[26]

Most important, disgust sensitivity is also correlated with the Intuitionism scale. From our August 2014 survey, we calculated a model predicting people's Intuitionism scores based on their disgust sensitivity.[27] The two measures are strongly correlated. People who are most easily disgusted or put off by insects, sexual noises, and contaminants score about eighteen points higher on the Intuitionism scale than people not so easily disgusted. This difference far exceeded those based on education, income, or ideology. People high in disgust sensitivity are more likely to hold some magical beliefs too. They are more likely to believe in an intentional god or think their life has specific meaning. They are also more likely to believe in conspiracy theories. Although we cannot determine from these survey questions if the answers to the disgust sensitivity questions are really a function of some inborn personality or some other unmeasured factors, we can say that people who score high in Intuitionism find more revulsion in unsavory actions.

Another personality factor that might relate to Intuitionism is what psychologists call the need for cognition (NFC). This is a dimension of personality involved in effortful thinking. People who are high in NFC are inquisitive thinkers. They like to solve puzzles, ponder the origins of the universe, or enjoy philosophical discussions. Moreover, this seems to be an inborn trait. Following the work of John Cacioppo and Richard Petty, psychologists have identified stable differences in people's tendency to engage in deliberative cognitive thinking.[28] Some people are born who really enjoy thinking about abstract or challenging questions, while others do not. Most important, people who exhibit a low need for cognition are quick to use stereotypes or make snap judgments rather than pay close attention to various contingencies and other arguments.[29]

Intuitionists are not people we'd expect to have a strong need for cognition. A big part of intuitive thinking is looking for the most expedient answer to a question. People who are high in NFC are those who actually like to entertain alternative hypotheses, and hence should be more skeptical about simple or implausible explanations. And this is what our data show. In the August 2014 survey, we employed a variant of the Need for Cognition Scale developed by Cacioppo and Petty. Respondents were asked about how well certain statements describe them, such as "I enjoy complicated games like crossword puzzles and Scrabble," or "I find it exciting to learn about new things."[30] People who score low on items related to intellectual curiosity had much higher Intuitionism scores. Our models predict that people with the lowest need for cognition score fifteen points higher on the Intuitionism scale than people with the highest NFC scores. In other words, people who like to ask questions, figure out how things work, or solve puzzles tend to be closer to the Rationalist end of the spectrum; people who are less compelled to do such things tend to be far more Intuitionist in their worldview.

Of course, with both these measures of personality we need to acknowledge a major caveat—personality is a multidimensional phenomenon. These are limited measures; it's hard to know, with a few survey questions, how well we are tapping into a distinct personality dimension. It's also plausible that Intuitionism itself may simply be a certain personality type as well. In other words, some people may have personalities that are simply more apprehensive, pessimistic, and sensitive to symbols and metaphors. If this is the case, then our Intuitionism scale may in itself be a measure of a certain personality type. Or it might even be that disgust sensitivity and need for cognition are themselves part of an Intuitionist worldview. At this early stage in our research, it's difficult to say. Either way, these findings do give us a somewhat fuller picture of the types of people who are Intuitionists.

Religion

Another factor likely to differentiate Intuitionists from Rationalists is their current religious practices and beliefs. Despite recent declines in religious affiliations, Americans are among the most religious people in the industrialized world. Over 75 percent have a religious affiliation; an over-whelming number of these are Christian.[31] Religious institutions are vital for shaping Americans' beliefs: they promote specific doctrines about God and the supernatural, they interpret current social and political events, and they bring together groups of like-minded people who share their own be-liefs and ways of thinking with one another. Given the importance of orga-nized religion in American life, we should expect to see vital differences in the Intuitionism scale along religious lines.

But America's religious vibrancy also presents us with a considerable empirical challenge: Americans belong to a staggeringly high number of different religious denominations, especially among the scores of differ-ent Protestant groups. Quakers and Unitarians, for example, have a very different conception of the divine than do Baptists and Pentecostals. And even within these religious denominations, there exists a wide range of theologies and spiritual practices. So how can we expediently summarize Americans' religious practices amid this fantastic diversity?

In our analysis, we opt for a very simple measurement strategy based on three questions. First, do our respondents consider themselves "funda-mentalist, orthodox, or conservative" in their religious beliefs? Just under 30 percent of our sample answered yes to this question. Henceforth, we will call this group "religious conservatives." We then asked them which denom-ination they belonged to. Based on their answers to both these questions, we created seven general categories: Catholic, Protestant (which includes all Christian denominations except Catholics), conservative Catholic, fun-damentalist Protestant, Jew, Orthodox Jew, and those with no religious faith. We created as separate variables Mormons, Hindus, Buddhists, Mus-lims, and those from other non-Christian sects; but because of their small numbers, we do not include them in our analysis here. Finally, we asked our respondents how often they attend religious services (outside weddings and funerals), grouping their answers into four categories: Never, Seldom, Weekly, and More Than Weekly.

Americans' religious practices are significant determinants of whether or not they are Intuitionists (fig. 3.4). Let us start by looking at both de-nominations and religious conservatism in conjunction. Americans with no religious faith have the lowest Intuitionism score—their average score is only .44 and is tightly clustered around this point. Among those profess-ing a religious faith, the only group similarly low in Intuitionism is non-Orthodox Jews; they too have an average .42 Intuitionism score. Such Ra-tionalism is also reflected in more specific beliefs. For example, among

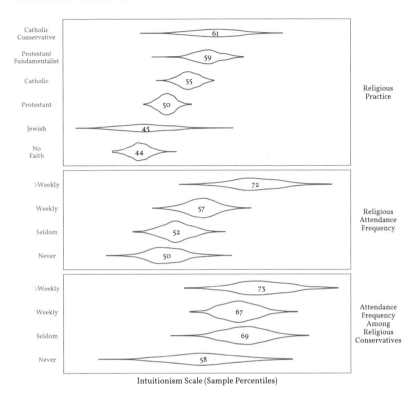

FIGURE 3.4. Intuitionism as predicted by religious faith and church attendance. Labels indicate the percentile of the mean respondent. Density plots indicate bootstrapped distributions of the mean group percentile, controlling for education, income, gender, authoritarianism, and upbringing.

people with no religious faith, only 14 percent believe in an observant God and 16 percent believe in horoscopes, levels well below those in the general population. No other groups in America come close to these two categories in their low rates of magical thinking.

Among Christians, the biggest differences in Intuitionism are between religious conservatives and nonconservatives. The highest average levels of Intuitionism are among conservative Catholics and Protestants. Conservative Catholics have the highest average Intuitionism score of .61, although they are also widely distributed along the scale. Conservative Protestants are just a tad lower on average (at .59), although they tend to be more highly clustered around this point. Behind these groups are nonconservative Catholics, who have an average Intuitionism score of .56, and they tend to be highly concentrated around this point. The least Intuitionist Christians are nonconservative Protestants. They have an average Intuitionist score of .51 and are tightly grouped around this point as well.

Not surprisingly, we also see similar denominational differences in Americans' supernatural beliefs. For example, among conservative Protestants, 46 percent believe in end-time prophecy, 78 percent believe in an observant God, and 62 percent believe in the power of prayer, rates nearly twice as high as nonconservative Protestants.[32] Similarly, conservative Catholics are twice as likely to believe in the power of prayer compared with ordinary Catholics. They are also much more likely to believe in an observant God or end-time prophecy.[33] In sum, American Christians who belong to more conservative or fundamentalist denominations, or think of themselves as religiously conservative, are far more Intuitionist than both their mainstream brethren and especially Jews or Americans having no religious affiliation.

Another way that religion reinforces Intuitionist thinking is through church participation. It's one thing to call oneself Catholic or Methodist, but it's another to attend church services regularly. Frequent church attendance signifies not only a commitment to religious beliefs but also the importance of those beliefs in a person's life. If someone is attending church every week, that person is constantly reinstilling the emotional and cognitive links between self and belief. This faith is perpetually reaffirmed in both the church services themselves and the community of fellow believers. If someone's church has a particularly strong magical tradition, then the types of intuitive thinking common to magical beliefs will also be reaffirmed.

As expected, we also find a great divide in the Intuitionism scale based on church attendance, although much of this is predicated on individuals' religious beliefs. Among those with conservative religious beliefs, church attendance does not have a significant relationship with Intuitionism except among those who never attend. For this group, there are no significant differences in the Intuitionism scores between those who attend church weekly and those who seldom attend (they cluster around the .67 level). For religious conservatives who never attend church, however, the average Intuitionism score drops to .59. For Americans who aren't conservative in their religious identity, we see the mirror image. Among this group, small differences exist between non-attenders (a .47 score) and those who go weekly (a .53 score). A big change happens among those who attend church more than once a week. Among these devotees, the average Intuitionism score is .66, similar in magnitude to that of their conservative brethren.

Although observant Christians are stronger Intuitionists, it's not clear whether church attendance is causing higher Intuitionism, or whether Intuitionists themselves feel more compelled to go to church more often. In all likelihood, both effects are happening at the same time. As we noted earlier, many Christian denominations really emphasize an intuitive way of looking at the world. God is known not simply from scripture but from felt experience. At the same time, people who hold a more Intuitionist worldview may also find validation in the work of church teachings. Either way, church attendance remains one of the most potent predictors of magical thinking, especially among the two-thirds of Americans who are not religiously conservative.

Taken together, we see the power of religious practice in reinforcing an Intuitionist worldview, especially among those churches that are conservative or fundamentalist in their doctrine. Conservative Christians are especially strong Intuitionists. As we've noted before, this is evident in their theology. Many fundamentalist beliefs are made up of not just vague notions of distant angels or God but strong notions about biblical inerrancy and end-time prophecy. They also are more likely to promote narratives that point to hidden evil forces or reject scientific explanations. If we group conservative Catholics together with fundamentalist Protestants, we would estimate that roughly *30 percent of the adult American population* is in a religious context promoting an Intuitionist worldview. As one moves further away in both belief and church attendance, this changes. Among the 23 percent of Americans who are Jewish or profess no religious faith, Intuitionism is far less strong. And as we'll see, these strong differences in religion have profound implications for US politics.

Politics

There is one other major factor distinguishing American Intuitionists and Rationalists that is both connected to and yet distinct from personality, religion, and upbringing—political identity. Although future chapters will examine this in greater detail, for now we want to highlight important political differences between Rationalists and Intuitionists. First, conservatives are much more Intuitionist than liberals (fig. 3.5). As one moves from left to right along the ideological spectrum, Intuitionism scores

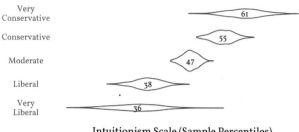

Intuitionism Scale (Sample Percentiles)

FIGURE 3.5. Intuitionism as predicted by ideology. Labels indicate the percentile of the mean respondent. Density plots indicate bootstrapped distributions of the mean group percentile, controlling for income, gender, authoritarianism, upbringing, church attendance, and religion conservatism.

steadily increase.[34] For example, people who identify as strongly liberal have an average Intuitionism score that is six points *below* the national average. People who identify as strongly conservative, by contrast, have an Intuitionism score that is six points *above* the national average and fully twelve points higher than that for strong liberals. Now, some of these differences can be ascribed to religion—as we would expect, religious conservatives are also more likely to identify as politically conservative. But even if we control for religiosity, we still find that conservatives have higher Intuitionism scores than liberals.

Given the greater alignment between ideology and partisanship in recent years, we also see Intuitionist differences between Democrats and Republicans. A graphic illustration of this trend is illustrated in figure 3.6, which lists the percentage of Americans by three characteristics: their ideology, their partisan identification, and whether they score in the lowest, middle, or highest third on the Intuitionism scale.[35] As we'd expect, Americans who identify as liberal (in the left-hand panel) are overwhelmingly likely to identify as Democrat. And this partisan leaning occurs regardless of whether they are in the lowest or highest third on the Intuitionism scale. In a mirror image, conservatives (the right-hand panel) are overwhelmingly Republican regardless of their Intuitionism score. Moderates tend to lean slightly toward the Democrats, although a very large proportion claims no party affiliation. What is more interesting is how these factors divide by Intuitionism. If ideology was unrelated to ontology, we would see liberals and conservatives looking like moderates in their distributions, that is, roughly the same totals in the lower, middle, and upper thirds of the Intuitionism scale. Instead, we see that liberals (and by this we also mean mostly liberal Democrats) are disproportionately in the bottom third of the Intuitionism scale. Conservatives, meanwhile, show the mirror image. Nearly half of conservatives score in the upper third of the Intuitionism scale.

It is worth pausing for a moment to reflect on these differences. Recall that our measures of Intuitionism are based on sets of behaviors that have nothing to do with politics. Intuitionists are not simply apprehensive people who are drawn to metaphors, but people who translate these tendencies into a number of beliefs that defy basic scientific logic. And this way of thinking is becoming increasingly aligned with one's ideological self-description. Only a tiny fraction of Americans calling themselves very conservative do not hold a least some magical beliefs; an overwhelming majority of strong conservatives are also very strong magical thinkers.[36] To be very conservative in America is, almost certainly, to be someone who has a strong Intuitionist worldview.

These differences are important for US politics. Not only are liberals disproportionately Democrat in their party identification, they are disproportionately Rationalist in their worldview. Where liberals do hold higher levels of magical beliefs, they tend to be non-Christian ones like horoscopes or reincarnation. Conservatives, meanwhile, are not only more likely to be Republican, they are more likely to be strongly Intuitionist. The Rationalist conservatives who attend talks at the Cato Institute or subscribe to *Reason*

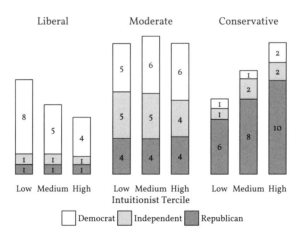

FIGURE 3.6. Distribution of the American population by partisan identity, ideological identity, and terciles of the Intuitionism scale.

magazine are a small minority on the political Right. Indeed, it's the rare American who identifies as a strong conservative who doesn't hold a lot of Christian magical beliefs. Conservatism and magical thinking, especially within religious fundamentalism, are increasingly becoming aligned. And as we'll see in chapter 4, this alignment between Intuitionism and ideology is behind much of the polarization in US politics.

CHAPTER FOUR

Intuitionists and Ideologues

U S politics are paradoxical.

On the one hand, the United States appears to be a nation riven by ideology. Its citizens are segregated in distinctly "red" or "blue" states. Most vote exclusively for liberal Democrats or conservative Republicans. They get political information from the slanted perspectives of Fox News or MSNBC and isolate themselves among like-minded Facebook friends and Twitter feeds. They socialize only with their political kin, choosing friends, neighbors, and even romantic partners by their political views. Liberals and conservatives in America even name their children differently.[1] "Liberals and conservatives dress differently, decorate their rooms differently, read different books, take different vacations and drink different alcoholic beverages," observes psychologist Jonathan Haidt and political scientist Sam Abrams. "As the differences between supporters of the two parties became ever more pervasive and ever more visible to the naked eye, it became easier to spot members of the other team and then dislike them for the way they live."[2] Americans, it seems, are irrevocably divided along ideological lines.

On the other hand, public opinion surveys show that most American citizens are not very ideological. Ideological polarization is largely an elite phenomenon, occurring mostly among political activists and members of Congress.[3] The vast majority of ordinary Americans do not have firm, principled convictions about politics.[4] In fact, about a quarter of Americans claim no ideology at all.[5] And among the remaining 75 percent who identify as liberal, moderate, or conservative, most are unsteady in their political views.[6] For many, politics remain "little more than a sideshow in the circus of life," something far removed from daily concerns and only begrudgingly accepted when necessary.[7]

If Americans aren't very ideological, then why does the country seem so divided? The answer can partly be found in the Intuitionism scale. As we've seen in the past two chapters, Americans are highly divided by how much they follow their intuitions when trying to make sense of the world. When faced with the unavoidable realities of their existence, some listen to their emotions and seek the most expedient beliefs. This Intuitionism is heavily concentrated on the political Right. Many Americans identify as conservative, not because they have firm ideological commitments, but because they identify as a religious conservative, and folks identifying as such tend to hold an Intuitionist worldview. Meanwhile, liberals are far more likely to be Rationalists.

In this chapter, we examine what these differences in Intuitionism mean for American public opinion. We offer two major conclusions. First, Intuitionism is a major reason why liberals are so divided from conservatives, and why conservatives are often divided among themselves. When looking at the "core values" underlying American ideology, liberals are quite united; they are similarly skeptical of laissez-faire economics as well as a Christian-oriented moral order. Conservatives, on the other hand, are quite separated by these two values. Many are stout traditionalists but are not enthusiastic about the free market; many others are just the opposite. Moreover, the conservative values of moral traditionalism are more often rooted in their Intuitionism than in their commitment to abstract values. In other words, liberals and conservatives aren't divided simply because of some philosophical differences concerning the proper scope or function of government; rather, they are also divided by how they come to their judgments about the world.

Second, Intuitionism not only amplifies America's ideological divisions, it exerts its own power on public opinion. Where people reside on the Intuitionism scale can be an important predictor of their political views, depending on the types of issues and the framing of the survey questions. On policies ranging from abortion to defense spending, Americans who hold an Intuitionist perspective have opinions that are very different from their Rationalist counterparts, regardless of their own ideology. Just as a reliance on intuitions can lead people to believe in God, ghosts, and ESP, so intuitions will also lead people to have distinct beliefs about Obamacare, gun rights, and foods containing genetically modified organisms (GMOs). In fact, when it comes to Americans' political beliefs, the effects of intuitions are often as important as those of ideology.

Deciphering Ideologies

Why do Americans hold the political opinions that they do? According to most political pundits, the answer is ideology. Americans oppose tax increases or support gun rights, we are told, because they are conservative; they favor carbon taxes or abortion rights because they are liberal. By itself, however, ideology is not a very accurate or clear explanation for American public opinion. Most Americans are not very ideological—they can't articulate coherent theories about politics, much less translate these theories into consistent opinions. Regardless of whether they are political commentators or ordinary citizens, most citizens (and many political commentators) are quite fuzzy about what being liberal or conservative means. So before proceeding further, let us, at least be clear about our terms.

When political scientists study ideologies, they are typically referring to *belief systems*.[8] Belief systems are systematic frameworks for understanding the world, tools we crafted for comprehending social and political events. They function as interpretive guides, shaping people's behaviors and opinions and binding them together as a group. What makes an ideology a belief *system* is that it is a framework of ideas that generally derives from overarching principles; these principles, in turn, link all subsequent propositions together.[9] Whether they are communist, libertarian, or conservative, ideologies all originate in some foundational assertions that are timeless and universal.

When American political scientists want to identify how "liberal" or "conservative" someone is, they look to see how much that person utilizes a single belief system when coming to his or her opinions. They usually evaluate this by two criteria: first, the coherence of opinions around some abstract, bedrock principles; and second, the stability of these opinions over time.[10] For example, if someone subscribes to the notion that limited government is the best for society, then the authenticity of his or her conservative beliefs should be evident across a wide range of social and political issues. This individual should oppose not only government regulation of business but also restrictions on abortions or an expansively militaristic foreign policy. Moreover, these opinions should be unchanging. As a conservative, opposition to government spending should be as fervent in times of prosperity as during economic crises.

However, when it comes to ideology in the real world, some complications become immediately apparent. For starters, not all ideologues share the same bedrock principles. Take the example of American conservatism. For some, conservatism is based on a reverence for the status quo. As columnist David Brooks notes, "Conservatism stands for intellectual humility, a belief in steady, incremental change, a preference for reform rather than revolution, a respect for hierarchy, precedence, balance and order, and a tone of voice that is prudent, measured and responsible."[11] For others, the guiding truth of conservatism is found in the Bible.[12] Still others orient their conservatism around property rights. Among these free market conservatives, the overarching principle is that "which governs best governs least," particularly in relation to individual liberty.[13] Finally, there are conservatives who put individualism at the center of their governing philosophy. From this viewpoint, welfare programs create cycles of dependence on government aid and rob individuals of their own capacity for self-reliance.[14]

Although conservative leaders often work hard at weaving these different strands together, it is easy to appreciate the tensions that pull them apart.[15] Consider the contradiction between traditionalism and free market capitalism. America has a long history of slavery, racial segregation, and sexual discrimination, precepts that blatantly violate the values of liberty, individualism, and free labor in a market economy. Meanwhile, many biblical tenets are directly at odds with the economic inequality and finance that come with capitalism.[16] Amid all these tensions and contradictions, American conservatism looks less like a single belief system based on a unified doctrine than an amalgamation of different views linked together through political convenience and electoral strategy.

Such tensions also are evident in the views of ordinary citizens. In our January 2015 survey, we asked respondents a series of eight questions meant to gauge their adherence to four underlying values behind American conservatism.[17] These are denoted in table 4.1. Putting all these variables together into a factor analysis, we find that they cohere along two underlying dimensions. The first, which we call *moral traditionalism*, includes both a reference for the status quo and an enthusiasm for putting Christian values at the center of public life. In other words, most people who endorse status quo values also want Christianity to be the guiding influence on US politics. The second, *free market conservatism*, not only prioritizes laissez-faire economic policies but also views government as unnecessary to the general welfare. Here, we see that rugged individualism goes in lockstep with notions of limited government intervention in the economy. And this is highly consistent with a fact that political scientists have long recognized:

TABLE 4.1 **Factor loadings on conservative values**

	Moral traditionalism	Free market conservatism
Traditional ways better	0.700	0.05
People better off in old days	0.658	0.09
Christian religion should be a bigger part of public life	0.811	0.152
Government policies based only on scientific evidence	−0.719	−0.12
Best government policy to leave the economy alone	0.408	0.533
Too many costly regulations	0.133	0.706
Government should let volunteers provide social welfare	0.095	0.773
Government should provide minimum standard of living	−0.002	−0.785

American public opinion tends to be divided between economic and moral issues.[18]

What is more surprising, however, is that conservatives themselves are highly differentiated between these values (fig. 4.1). When we examine the correlation between the moral traditionalism and free market conservatism scales, we find very different patterns depending on how respondents identify themselves. Among liberals, these two dimensions are correlated.[19] In other words, if you identify as liberal, your moral traditionalism scores will be predictive of your free market conservatism scores, and vice versa. But for conservatives, these two dimensions are not correlated at all. Many conservatives who score high on the moral traditionalism scale also score low on the free market conservatism scale, while others score just the opposite. The two central values that undergird America's ideological divisions are in sync on the Left but unaligned on the Right.

One reason for this incongruity is that being a conservative means very different things to different people. For some, it refers to their political beliefs; for others, it refers to their religious convictions or their "traditional values."[20] These differences then bleed into politics. As political scientists Christopher Ellis and James Stimson note, "Millions of Americans who know that they are religious conservatives or that they approve of a 'conservative' approach to child rearing and family life are simultaneously confused by what 'conservative' means in politics."[21] Stimson and Ellis call these folks "symbolic conservatives." They are people who may identify as conservative but are not really bound by any abstract philosophical convictions.

But if abstract philosophical convictions aren't the source of their political convictions, then what is shaping the views of these "symbolic conservatives"? Part of the answer is intuition. As we saw in chapter 3, conservatives

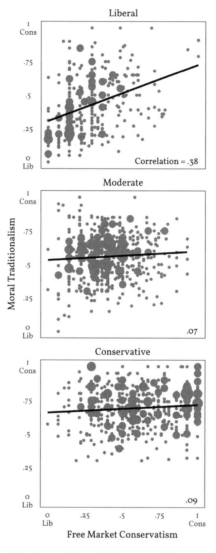

FIGURE 4.1. Moral traditionalism and free market conservatism as predicted by ideological identity.

are far more likely than liberals to be Intuitionists. Partly this is because so many of them are conservative Christians. And it is precisely the conflation of ideology, intuition, and religion that is causing much of the confusion about the role of ideology in US politics. We can see this with a simple illustration. Figure 4.2 depicts the relationship between Intuitionism and four supernatural beliefs (in angels, an intentional God, biblical inerrancy, and hidden Bible codes) separately for each ideological group depending on whether each respondent identifies as liberal, moderate, or conservative. The general linear models that are depicted here also control for education, age, and whether the respondent considers him- or herself "conservative, fundamentalist, or orthodox" in religious beliefs.

The figure shows two important characteristics about the relationship between supernatural beliefs, ideology, and Intuitionism. First, the *slope* of the predicted relationship for each belief is largely the same across ideo-logical groups. Just as we saw in chapter 3, as one moves up the Intuition-ism scale, supernatural beliefs increase, and this occurs in the same fash-ion regardless of whether the person is liberal, moderate, or conservative. Second, *the average height* of the line grows as one moves from liberal to conservative. This means that even when we take Intuitionism into ac-count, conservatives are still more likely than liberals to hold supernatural beliefs. For example, our equations predict that roughly 70 percent of con-servative Rationalists believe in angels, compared with only 40 percent of liberal Rationalists. When it comes to supernatural beliefs, Americans are differentiated by both Intuitionism and ideology.

It is worth reflecting on these patterns for a moment. These religious questions have no political content—they are exclusively about supernat-ural beliefs, and rather extraordinary ones at that. Even when we account

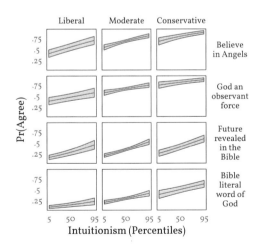

FIGURE 4.2. Supernatural and fundamentalist beliefs as predicted by Intuitionism and ideol-ogy. Estimates include controls for age, education, and religious conservatism. Ribbons indicate 95% confidence intervals.

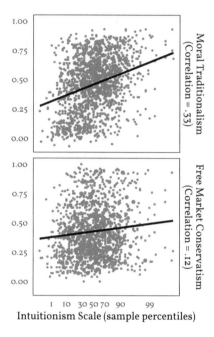

FIGURE 4.3. A scatter plot between both moral traditionalism and free market conservatism scores and the Intuitionism scale.

for people's education, age, and their own religious identity, we still find that conservatives are more likely to believe in hidden Bible codes or angels. The conflation of ideology and religious beliefs is one of the reasons why conservatives hold such different core values.

Once again, this suggests that the ideological differences reflect not simply abstract principles but a gap in worldview. We can see this illustrated with a simple graph. Figure 4.3 depicts a scatter plot between both moral traditionalism and free market conservatism scores and the Intuitionism scale. This figure plots the position of each of our respondents across the two sets of scales. The Intuitionism and moral traditionalism scales are significantly correlated. In other words, the higher a person scores on the moral traditionalism scale, the higher that person's Intuitionism score tends to be. By contrast, the free market conservatism with Intuitionism scales are unrelated—the Intuitionism scale is not a predictor of one's views on the market, and vice versa. This suggests that the tensions within conservatism are not simply disagreement over what the fundamental principles should be; they also relate to profound differences in worldview. Much of what looks like a "bedrock" value of conservatism is grounded not on abstract philosophical commitments but an Intuitionist worldview. Conservatives are divided not simply between those who advocate for free markets and those who advocate for moral traditions, but between those who base their conservatism on abstract values and those for whom conservatism reflects their strong Intuitionist orientation.

This conflation of ideology and Intuitionism is essential for understanding contemporary US politics. Much of what looks like an ideological division is not simply due to a difference in principled understandings about the proper role of government and the sanctity of moral traditions. Conservatives themselves disagree on these things. Rather, much of the split between liberals and conservatives is an ontological divide masking itself as an ideological one. Because of their greater religiosity, conservatives are far more likely to hold an Intuitionist worldview. Liberals, by contrast, are more likely to be Rationalists. This distinguishes many conservatives from liberals in matters that have nothing to do with political principles. And this very reliance on intuitions also produces some very distinct political opinions as well.

Intuitions and Public Opinion

Public opinion research in the United States is a largely Rationalist enterprise. In designing polls, we usually assume that Americans derive their opinions from reasoned deductions rather than intuitive hunches. Consider, for example, how most survey questions get worded. The standard method for asking people about issues is to formulate questions in a non-leading manner. The logic behind this approach appears sound—in order to get as unbiased a reading of public opinion as possible, survey researchers typically strive to make their questions as objective as possible. However, there are two problems with this approach.

First, it assumes that the public views all political issues from the same perspective, regardless of the content of the issue. In other words, when pollsters ask people's opinions on a laundry list of political items, they typically presume that people make judgments about abortion or immigration policy from the same dispassionate framework they use when thinking about fiscal policy or industrial regulation. In reality, not all issues are alike—*how* people think about politics depends on *what* they are thinking about.[22] Some types of concerns are what political scientists call "easy issues."[23] These are political matters that demand no prerequisites for forming opinions. This could be because they require little factual knowledge or invoke clear signals in how they are framed. Abortion and gay marriage, for example, are easy issues because they reference values rather than facts. Other issues are called "hard." Typically, these are complex technical matters that require some factual knowledge. Fiscal policy and foreign policy, for instance, rarely have obvious answers and usually require a sophisticated understanding of economics, history, and international relations. Not surprisingly, Americans are much more likely to offer opinions on easy issues than hard ones.[24] Nevertheless, pollsters still ask about these issues in the same way, even if citizens have very different ways of understanding them.

Second, in trying to be objective barometers of opinion, survey developers use questions that typically strip away many of the common cues and heuristics that ordinary citizens utilize to make sense of politics. In the real world, political discourse is rarely situated around a dispassionate reasoning about policy and issues; rather, it is usually presented in a manner that reflects the speaker's interests or agendas. Political actors constantly jockey to frame issues in a way that is most advantageous to their side. When ordinary people encounter political issues in the real world, they are operating amid a swirl of different slogans, sound bites, and emotional cues, most of which are meant to appeal to their intuitive judgment. And this has an effect—public opinion is highly sensitive to how particular issues get framed.[25] Nevertheless, in an attempt to measure "real" opinion, most survey developers denude all questions of the mechanisms that ordinary citizens utilize to interpret the political world, leaving us with an incomplete portrait of American public opinion.

However, if we take intuitions into account, both as an explanatory variable and in how we word our survey questions, we get a different picture of what animates Americans' political beliefs. Let us start by looking at some issues that are probably the most Rationalist in their orientation—those about taxation. Intuitions are the least helpful for fiscal issues, precisely because they involve a lot of competing considerations and complicated facts.[26] Say, for example, that we ask someone's opinions about tax policy. A meaningful analysis on his or her part would involve a range of considerations, from the nature of the current economy to the role of state spending in bolstering growth. Yet most citizens probably don't want to exert this type of mental effort.[27] So instead, they may look for signals from political elites to discern what a trusted leader or commentator says the right position is. But for many Americans who don't follow politics very closely, even this may be too demanding. When faced with a survey question, they may simply shrug and not even bother forming an opinion. In this instance of a hard issue, public opinion will be dominated largely by the minority of the population that has firm ideological convictions, while the rest will give seemingly random answers in response.

We see this in our survey data. Consider three questions about fiscal policy that we asked in our surveys:

1. Would you prefer a "flat tax" of 18 percent on all Americans, no matter their income level? (40 percent prefer this over a progressive income tax)
2. Now that the economy is doing better, it is time to increase taxes on the wealthy to reduce our deficit. (26 percent disagree)
3. Should the federal government increase the minimum wage to $13.50 an hour? (35 percent say no)

Although each of these questions is straightforward enough, they all represent a rather complex set of considerations. Should the government set the wages of low-income workers? Should we increase taxes on the wealthy to reduce the deficit? Is a flat tax the best way to raise revenue? In each instance, the answer depends on a host of technical considerations about the impact of government both in the economy and as a mechanism for resolving social inequities. In such instances, we should expect that ideology would be a big predictor of people's beliefs but that Intuitionism would not.

And this is what we find. When we compare people's answers to these three questions, we see the same trend. Across all three questions, conservatives are three times as likely as liberals and over twice as likely as moderates to give conservative answers. For example, 58 percent of conservatives prefer a flat tax, versus only 28 percent of moderates and 19 percent of liberals. A similar pattern holds for the other two questions as well— conservatives are two to three times more likely than liberals to oppose increasing the minimum wage or raising taxes on the wealthy.

What we don't see are any large differences along the Intuitionism scale. To illustrate this point, we divided up the sample between self-described liberals, moderates, and conservatives and estimated the effects of Intuitionism on fiscal policy using a general linear model, depicted in figure 4.4. Each panel depicts the predicted differences in opinion along the Intuitionism scale for each ideological group while controlling for factors like education, age, income, and gender. As is clearly evident, there are large

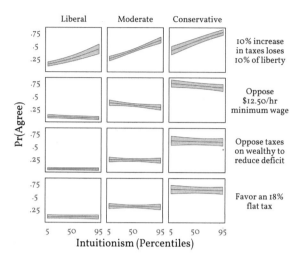

FIGURE 4.4. Opinions on fiscal policy as predicted by Intuitionism and ideology. Estimates include controls for age, income, and education. Ribbons indicate 95% confidence intervals.

differences between liberals, moderates, and conservatives; meanwhile, only small differences exist between Rationalists and Intuitionists. On the whole, Intuitionists show slightly more liberal policy preferences than Rationalists. For instance, only 63 percent of conservative Intuitionists prefer a flat tax, compared with 75 percent of conservative Rationalists.[28] But such differences are small compared with the tremendous differences across ideological lines. When it comes to fiscal policy, ideology seems to be a far more potent predictor than intuition.

But in the world of politics, not all fiscal policy is presented so dryly. Successful politicians know that few voters have the patience or the attention span to focus on the nitty-gritty of taxes and macroeconomic policy. So when they do speak about fiscal issues, they often speak in metaphorical terms. In other words, they strive to make tax policy "easy." And if our surveys about fiscal policy contain questions worded in a way that invokes people's intuitions, we see a very different pattern of responses. When we ask about opinions on taxes with the statement "Every time we raise our taxes 10 percent, we lose 10 percent of our liberty," which frames tax policy as a metaphor for liberty, we find that ideology no longer remains the sole or even the most important determinant of policy opinion; rather, Intuitionism does. Yes, conservatives are still more likely than liberals to equate taxes with liberty, but these differences pale in comparison with those between Rationalists and Intuitionists. Take liberals, for example. Only 16 percent of liberal Rationalists agree that increasing taxes costs us liberty, compared with 45 percent of liberal Intuitionists. Conservatives, no big fan of taxes, also show large divides on this question. Only 45 percent of conservative Rationalists equate liberty with taxes, compared with over 75 percent of conservative Intuitionists. In short, by equating taxes with liberty, a "hard" issue becomes an "easy" issue.

We see a similar pattern with another hard issue, health care. Of political issues in recent times, few are more technical and complicated than health care reform. The 2010 Affordable Care Act (ACA), also known as Obamacare, is over nine hundred pages long and contains many complicated provisions about insurance and financing. At one level, it's a classic hard issue, and it looks like one in our data. When we ask people their opinions about specific provisions of the ACA, we see the predictable ideological differences.[29] If we group opinions about all these provisions together in a single item, as illustrated in figure 4.5, we find that roughly a third of conservatives oppose the ACA, compared with only 15 percent of moderates and 10 percent of liberals.[30] In addition, Intuitionists have slightly more liberal views about the ACA provisions than Rationalists, especially those on the political Right. Our models predict that only 25 percent of conservative Intuitionists are opposed to the ACA's provisions, compared with 42 percent of conservative Rationalists. Nevertheless, these differences pale in comparison with ideology, where conservatives are three times as likely as liberals to oppose the ACA. As with other hard issues, opinions about the specific provisions of the ACA are largely defined along ideological lines.

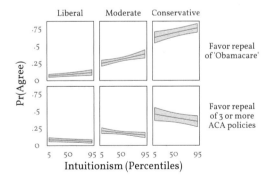

FIGURE 4.5. Opinions on health care as predicted by Intuitionism and ideology. Estimates include controls for age, income, and education. Ribbons indicate 95% confidence intervals.

However, if we ask about health care in a different way, we can see the impact of more intuitive thinking. Later in the same survey, we asked the same respondents a different question about the ACA:

In 2010, the government passed the Affordable Care Act (that is, Obamacare). The current Congress should

1. Give the law more time to take effect (38%);
2. Repeal only parts of the act (25%);
3. Repeal the entire act (37%).

With the Obamacare question, we find two striking differences from the earlier questions. First, people's opinions about the *concept* of Obamacare are very different from their opinions about the *specific provisions* of the ACA. While only 20 percent of the sample was opposed to at least three provisions of the ACA, 37 percent wanted to repeal the entire act rather than just a few specific provisions. Americans are much more opposed to Obamacare as an entity than to what the ACA actually does.

Second, when asking about the concept of Obamacare, we find that ideology and Intuitionism work together in shaping people's opinions. As respondents become more conservative, they become more hostile to Obamacare as a whole—moderates are twice as likely as liberals, and conservatives twice as likely as moderates. And among moderates and conservatives, Intuitionists are even more hostile to Obamacare than Rationalists. This contrasts sharply with the trends about the specific provisions in Obamacare.[31] For instance, our models predict that 75 percent of conservative Intuitionists oppose Obamacare, while only 30 percent oppose what it actually does. The very idea of Obamacare seems to trigger some adverse feelings among Intuitionists, particularly those on the political Right. This suggests that people use very different frameworks when viewing health care: when thinking about specific policy details, ideology is most important; when thinking about symbolic labels, intuitions can exacerbate these ideological commitments.

Intuitions about politics not only get invoked depending on how issues get framed—they can also be invoked by the very issues themselves. Issues that might invoke intuitive responses include those of security and safety. These types of issues tend to be associated with the political Right. For example, a Pew survey finds that 75 percent of conservative Republicans think it's more important to protect gun rights than allow gun control, while only 25 percent of liberal Democrats think so.[32] And historically, Repub-

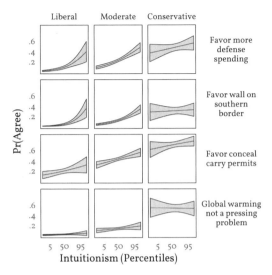

FIGURE 4.6. Opinions on security and threats as predicted by Intuitionism and ideology. Estimates include controls for age, income, and education. Ribbons indicate 95% confidence intervals.

licans have been more enthusiastic than Democrats about defense spending.[33] At one level, these are "hard" issues that typically invoke ideological responses. But at another level, they could also invoke intuitive concerns over safety. Remember, Intuitionists place a high priority on their apprehensions, so issues that touch on these apprehensions may resonate more strongly with them.

And indeed, this is what we find in our data. Figure 4.6 lists differences by Intuitionism and ideology in response to questions about gun rights (the percentage favoring "open-carry" laws), defense spending (the percentage favoring an increase in defense spending), global warming (the percentage saying that global warming is a minor problem or not a problem at all), and building a border wall (the percentage thinking that it is a good idea).[34] In three instances, a similar pattern is evident: both ideology and Intuitionism are important predictors of opinion. Given their historically partisan nature, it's not surprising that each of these issues evokes strong differences between conservatives and liberals. Compared with conservatives, liberals are less in favor of open-carry laws, increases in defense expenditures, or a border wall; they are also more likely to believe that climate change is a major crisis.

But within these ideological boundaries, we also see differences between Intuitionists and Rationalists. For example, Intuitionist liberals have more "conservative" attitudes about defense spending, the border wall, and gun rights than their Rationalist counterparts. The same holds with moderates as well. Among political moderates, support for increased defense spending and open-carry laws doubles as one moves from one side of the Intuitionism scale to the other. And even among conservatives, we see similar patterns (albeit of a smaller magnitude). The only exception is with attitudes about global warming—here, Intuitionism has no influence. Although conservatives are far more likely to deny that climate change is a major threat, there are no differences within any ideological group along the Intuitionism scale.

These findings reveal some interesting dynamics in the intuitive sources of Americans' public opinion. First, they show that ideology alone doesn't determine people's opinions, even with issues that are highly partisan. Although ideology is very important in differentiating opinions on these "hard" issues, intuitions also shape opinions, particularly when the issues at hand tap into concerns about safety or security. Second, intuitions don't get invoked by all potential threats. For instance, Intuitionists aren't any more concerned than Rationalists about threats of climate change. It may be because global warming is based largely on a scientific worldview they often reject. But it may also be that global warming simply doesn't carry the visceral threat that physical threats by criminals or foreign powers do. This latter possibility is particularly evident among those on the political Left. When it comes to safety issues or notions of rule breaking, liberal Intuitionists have much more conservative opinions.[35]

Intuitionism also amplifies the effects of ideology when it comes to "moral" issues. We asked respondents about three types: abortion, opposition to marijuana legalization, and physician-assisted suicide.[36] The results are depicted in figure 4.7. For all three issues, opinion tracks ideology. As one moves from liberal to moderate to conservative, opposition to all three issues increases. But a similar dynamic also happens within each ideological group. As one moves from low to high on the Intuitionism scale, opposition to these three issues increases as well. For example, among moderates the percentage opposed to abortion under all circumstances rises from 27 percent of Rationalists to 55 percent of Intuitionists. Nor are these patterns simply the result of religious differences.[37] Our models account for whether respondents identify as a religious conservative. Yet even when taking the measure of religiosity into account, Intuitionists still have more conservative views.[38] What is even more remarkable is the consistency of these responses across these issues. Whether it's abortion rights, marijuana legalization, or the right to die, the same pattern emerges: Americans who rely more on their intuitions also hold much more conservative attitudes.

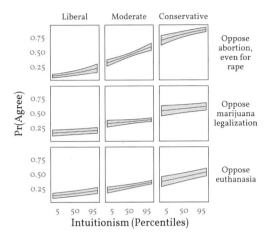

FIGURE 4.7. Opinions on "moral issues" as predicted by Intuitionism and ideology. Estimates include controls for age, income, religious conservatism, and education. Ribbons indicate 95% confidence intervals.

And it's not just with "moral" issues that Intuitionism has an effect. Other types of policy issues also evoke intuitive concerns. We can see this in four items relating to issues of health and science: opposition to vaccines, subsidizing homeschooling, banning foods containing genetically modified organisms (GMOs), and believing that eliminating gluten will make someone healthier.[39] For these four issues, we find a pattern remarkably similar to the "easy" moral issues listed above, as illustrated in figure 4.8. Regardless of their ideology, Intuitionists are far more likely to be against vaccine mandates and GMOs, to support tax breaks for homeschoolers, and to think that eliminating gluten will make someone healthier. For example, our models predict that nearly 80 percent of liberal Intuitionists support banning GMOs, compared with only 57 percent of liberal Rationalists. This difference of twenty-three percentage points is also evident among conservatives—here again, our models predict that 62 percent of conservative Intuitionists support banning GMOs, compared with only 38 percent of conservative Rationalists. A similar pattern is also evident for homeschooling, mandatory vaccines, and ideas about eliminating gluten.

What is remarkable about these questions is that they look very similar to opinions about "moral issues" but have little direct relevance to modern theology. Although some church groups wish to shield their children from secular influences by homeschooling, the other three issues have nothing to do with biblical scripture or fundamentalist ideals.[40] Rather, Intuitionists

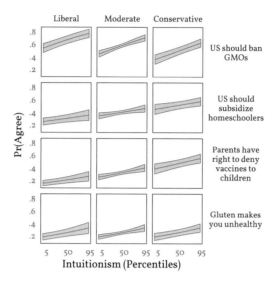

FIGURE 4.8. Opinions on health and education as predicted by Intuitionism and ideology. Estimates include controls for age, income, and education. Ribbons indicate 95% confidence intervals.

hold particular opinions on these issues because such issues speak to their innate decision-making processes. Vaccines and GMOs are human attempts to contaminate the natural order, to inject or ingest something that is artificially engineered. They evoke strong concerns with contamination, a common heuristic in many magical beliefs. Conversely, the idea that eliminating gluten will provide health benefits also holds intuitive appeal: most Americans have little idea what gluten actually is (proteins found in rye, wheat, and barley), and many think that gluten is "unnatural."[41] Once again, the idea of eliminating a strange-sounding substance from one's food probably holds a lot of resonance for Intuitionists, especially after their being exposed to gluten-free products.

Taking all this together, we see a definite pattern. When either political language or political issues evoke intuitive concerns, major differences emerge by ontology. Intuitionists not only have more conservative opinions on issues like abortion and Obamacare, but they have stronger opinions about vaccines, gluten-free foods, and alternative medicine. All these issues tap into intuitive thinkers' proclivities to draw from heuristics and metaphors in understanding the world: life is sacred, euthanasia is dangerous, "nature" is good, politics are driven by evil forces, and so on. Unlike opinions about taxation or the specific provisions of the ACA, these are not views derived from abstract theories about optimal levels of state intervention or social welfare. They are gut reactions, and they reverberate into the larger discourse of US politics.

Conclusion

Intuitive politics are not the sole property of any particular group in America. As we've noted throughout this book, we all rely on our intuitions when we face any pressing uncertainty. Nevertheless, when it comes to most political issues, Intuitionists often have more conservative attitudes. Why is this the case? Partly, it may have to do with people's responses to apprehensive feelings. Conservatism typically offers a defensive posture toward the world, whether it is with upholding traditions or seeking protection from outside threats. This is more consistent with an Intuitionist worldview. Intuitionists view politics in terms of feeling and metaphor. As such, they will be quick to emphasize recent events, be apprehensive of contagion, anthropomorphize institutions, and assume that things that look similar share core traits. Because Intuitionists are so sensitive to both deviant symbols and their apprehensions, they may be more likely to embrace conservative positions.

But another reason that Intuitionists tend to have more conservative attitudes is religion. With well over a third of the adult population describing themselves as fundamentalist or evangelical in their outlook or holding strongly supernatural beliefs, the power of conservative theology in shaping Americans' worldview is formidable. And even though our models crudely control for our respondents' religious conservatism, they cannot fully account for the power of churches to reinforce an Intuitionist perspective. By offering narratives that rely so heavily on scriptural inerrancy, prophecy, and divine intentionality, fundamentalist churches instill a worldview that is often hostile to rationality and grounded in instinct or gut feelings.

Either way, it's clear from our data that the American ideological divide is not simply based on philosophical differences over the scope of government; it is also a reflection of a different worldview. Liberals, moderates, and conservatives may be separated in their opinions on fiscal policy, immigration policy, and health care, but we need to keep in mind that these are precisely the types of "hard" issues for which many Americans actually have no real considered opinions. Ideology is a big predictor of these issues because the minority of Americans who are true ideologues either have informed opinions on these matters or can at least follow cues from co-ideologues as to what their opinions should be. However, for many issues in US politics, ideology is not the sole predictor of people's opinion; intuitions also have an effect. This is especially the case when it comes to "moral" issues like abortion rights or banning GMOs, where we see very large differences by people's Intuitionism scores. Whether they identify as liberal, moderate, or conservative, Intuitionists have very different views from Rationalists on these issues.

These findings are partly why we conclude that US politics are so irrevocably divided between Intuitionists and Rationalists. Liberals and conservatives may disagree about the proper role of government regulation, taxation, or other policies, but their debates are still bound within a similar set of reasoned deductions about how the world operates. As a result, the possibility for persuasion, dialogue, and reconciliation remains. The same cannot be said about Intuitionists and Rationalists. For the former, reason alone is not a sufficient basis for making decisions; gut feelings, intuitions, and faith are. To the Intuitionist, truth is felt, not deduced. As a result, Intuitionists comprehend politics in a manner similar to how they understand God—through emotions, symbols, and metaphors. When people embrace beliefs that are unfalsifiable, they become immune to rational discourse. And such intuitive thinkers are becoming more prevalent on the political Right.

It bears repeating that most Americans are somewhere in the middle of all this. Just as most tend to congregate in the middle of the ideological scale, so too do most tend to exhibit a mixture of Intuitionist and Rationalist tendencies. These folks are "ontological moderates"—they may rely on their intuitions for understanding certain types of issues but take a very scientific approach to others. Adding to the noise is the fact that ideology and Intuitionism tend to blend into each other. There are still plenty of liberal Americans who have strong Intuitionist tendencies, just as there are many Rationalist conservatives. All this creates a very complex mixture of elements that shape US politics. And this complexity is nowhere more evident than with our next examples of how intuitions manifest themselves in US politics: conspiracy theories and the populism of Donald Trump's presidential campaign.

CHAPTER FIVE

Truthers and *Trumpenvolk*

I'm a very instinctual person, but my instinct turns out to be right. —President Donald Trump, March 22, 2017

On the morning of September 11, 2001, a small band of suicide terrorists commandeered four American airliners. They smashed two of the planes into the World Trade Center, causing both towers to collapse. They slammed another into the side of the Pentagon. And one crashed in a field in rural Pennsylvania after several passengers heroically fought back for control of the plane. In total, nearly three thousand people were killed in the day's carnage. The nineteen terrorists were foreign nationals mostly from Saudi Arabia and recruited and funded by Al Qaeda, a radical Islamic terrorist organization headed by the scion of a wealthy Saudi family, Osama bin Laden.

Or at least this is the official account of the US government's 9/11 Commission. Many Americans, however, see the attacks of 9/11 very differently. Instead of a terrorist assault, they believe that 9/11 was a secret government plot orchestrated by the Bush administration (at the behest of Israel, oil companies, and other groups) to provoke ordinary Americans into supporting a war in the Middle East. Proponents of this theory point to various "inconsistencies" in the official account: the symmetrical collapse of the twin towers, the irregularities in cockpit recordings, the unusual debris trails of United Airlines Flight 93, and so on. Rather than being a terrorist attack from the outside, 9/11 was, in their view, an inside job.

It's unclear which is more remarkable about the "truther" conspiracy theories: the very idea that government officials are capable of secretly carrying out such an intricate and dastardly plot, or the fact that roughly one in five Americans agrees with it.[1] The "truther" conspiracy theory is not simply the belief of a lunatic fringe but a notion endorsed by tens of millions of Americans. And it's not just "truther" conspiracy theories that enjoy such wide support. Large percentages of Americans believe that Barack Obama faked his Hawaiian birth certificate; that the Food and Drug Administration is deliberately preventing the release of "natural" cures for cancer because of secret pressure from pharmaceutical companies; or that the 2008 recession was part of a concealed plot to strengthen the control of the Federal Reserve Board over the world economy. At any given time, at least half the American public endorses a major conspiracy theory.[2]

Enter Donald Trump. In 2016, the real estate developer-cum-reality television star captured the Republican presidential nomination with a stridently populist campaign. Even more remarkable was the path of Trump's success. He seemingly broke every rule of campaign politics: he called Mexican immigrants rapists and murderers; he demeaned women, Muslims, and the disabled; he spewed puerile insults at his opponents and made outlandish boasts about himself; he told Republicans that the Bush administration had lied; and he avoided any coherent policy proposals. He was denounced by many stalwarts in his own party, including George H. W. Bush, Mitt Romney, Lindsey Graham, and the editorial board of *National Review*. Nevertheless, he managed to win over 13 million votes in the Republican primary and capture the party's nomination.

Then, even more improbably, he went on to win the national election. Trump's success in November was more complicated than in the primary. First, he lost the popular vote by close to 3 million votes. Nevertheless, thanks to asymmetries in the electoral college, he was able to win the election largely from a combination of significantly lower voter turnout in Democratic urban areas and much higher support from many rural counties, particularly in traditionally Democratic states like Pennsylvania, Michigan, and Wisconsin. Although many factors determine national election results (levels of partisanship, the state of the economy, the length of incumbent party rule, the popularity of candidates, and so on), Trump's victory largely came from his ability to convince less educated, rural white voters in the Midwest that he represented their interests.

This brings us back to conspiracy theories. One of the most notable aspects of Donald Trump's campaign was not simply his populist rhetoric but his liberal use of conspiracy theories and promotion of untrue claims. Trump was a vocal proponent of conspiracy theories, whether they are about Barack Obama's birthplace, the 9/11 attack, the links between vaccines and autism, or how Ted Cruz's father had a role in the Kennedy assassination. He also enjoyed a lot of support from radio host and fellow conspiracy theories defender Alex Jones and his website, infowars.com. Not surprisingly, Trump's voters are big believers in conspiracy theories too. If conspiracy theorists could ever have a political candidate, he would be Donald Trump.

But the connection between "conspiracism" (that is, the extent one subscribes to conspiracy theories) and Trump's populism goes much deeper than these political connections. For both populism and conspiracism are intuitive ways of explaining politics, especially with regard to issues of money and power. Populists and "conspiracists" are against not just the political classes and the financial elite but journalists, scientists, lawyers, doctors, and anyone else claiming expertise.[3] Most important, populism and conspiracy theories both proudly express a "folk politics," commonsense explanations for how the world operates. Rather than viewing questions of "who governs" or "who wins" as a matter of historical or systematic forces, Intuitionists view these as questions of secret power, conspiracy, and deceit.

In this chapter, we examine how conspiracy theories, populist rhetoric, and Donald Trump were so attractive to Intuitionists. In reviewing survey data from the spring and fall of 2016, we see that Trump's supporters were notable not just for their strong support of conspiracy theories and populism but also for their high Intuitionism scores. Intuitionists are quick to embrace conspiracy narratives and are highly suspicious of any claims to expertise. Trump's success, then, partly resided in his ability to connect with voters in a way that seemed authentic, precisely because he was articulating the very folk politics that Intuitionists use to understand the world. His populist rhetoric, emotional outbursts, and quick assumption of conspiracy theories all spoke to their feelings. The *Trumpenvolk* weren't looking for reasoned analysis of the nation's political problems; they were looking for validation of their apprehensions. And Donald Trump was the candidate who provided that.

Populism and Conspiracy Theories

What causes economic recessions, unemployment, infectious diseases, mass shootings, and other distinctive social events? The answer depends on whom you ask. Rationalists, like social scientists and policy experts, generally try to understand such phenomena in systematic ways based on deduction and observation. Their beliefs are typically based on overarching theories about the nature of markets, the power of incentives, the importance of history, and the quirks of the human mind. They test and update their theories by making observations and analyzing data. And as with so many scientific approaches, this empiricism often leads to counterintuitive explanations: trade deficits can be a sign of success; progressive income taxes are actually "fairer" than a flat tax rate; flying is safer than driving; swimming pools are more dangerous than handguns; and so on.[4]

But people who aren't trained in the social sciences often comprehend matters of power and money differently. Unacquainted with scientific tools, they employ commonsense or "folk" beliefs. They compare political and economic events relative to things that they know. For example, they may understand budgetary or trade issues as being similar to their household finances. By this reckoning, trade deficits and government debt are categorically bad, because for most people, spending more than they earn will get them in trouble. By the same intuitive reasoning, a single tax rate seems "fairer," and guns seem more dangerous than swimming pools.

Such folk knowledge is particularly strong when it comes to politics. The political world is complicated—policy decisions and government actions rarely stem from a single coherent source and often reflect many obscure influences. While a small portion of citizens may rely on abstract principles and detailed information to shape their views, most aren't so philosophically minded. Instead of looking to complicated explanations, they comprehend politics relative to things that are familiar or that simply "feel" right. Take, for example, the Syrian refugee crisis of 2016. Most Americans probably wanted to help these people in need, but their exaggerated fears of terrorist attacks caused them to oversimplify the threat that refugees actually pose. Instead of acting on their compassion, they understood the issue through the lens of an inflated threat. This is an example of folk politics at work.

Although many kinds of political narratives express these intuitive folk politics, for this chapter we focus on two exemplars: populism and conspiracy theories. Both share many important characteristics. Both target elites as *the* central problem with contemporary politics. Populists typically characterize governing officials as distorting the will of the masses; most conspiracy theories view political leaders as either orchestrating or complicit in nefarious plots. Both generally run counter to traditional descriptions of politics, existing largely outside the dominant venues of political communication. By exploiting alternative media outlets, they can advance unorthodox explanations that often defy logic or systematic observation. Finally, populism and conspiracism share many intuitive tendencies with magical thinking: they draw from feelings of apprehension and utilize common heuristics to provide alternative explanations. But before elaborating this any further, let us clarify what these two prosaic concepts mean.

Populism

Populism is a promiscuous term. Internationally, it gets applied to everything from rightist anti-immigration movements in Europe to leftist anti-imperialist movements in Latin America to anticorruption efforts in Asia. In the United States, it has most recently been used to describe Bernie Sanders, a socialist senator from Vermont whose central concern is the billionaire class, *and* Donald Trump, a (putative) billionaire real estate magnate from New York whose central concern is immigration. In fact, seemingly anyone who criticizes political incumbents or the wealthy gets called a populist. In 2016, Senator Ted Cruz, neurosurgeon Ben Carson, and former Hewlett Packard executive Carly Fiorina all were given the populist label.[5] Such a wide usage begs the obvious question: what exactly is populism?

Thanks to a deep trove of comparative research, we now have a good answer. Populist movements throughout history and across the globe share distinctive traits. First and foremost is the fact that populism is not really an ideology but more of a rhetorical style. There is little theorizing among populists about what promotes the common good or properly regulates the market. Instead, populism orients itself around a simplistic description of politics as *a conflict ultimately between a virtuous "people" and a small group of nefarious, parasitic elites.* By the populist reckoning, *all* politics boil down to a struggle between "the people" and "the powerful." Of course, in democracies nearly all politicians seek to align themselves with "the people," which is partly why the populist label gets so widely applied. But populists do more than depict themselves as part of the majority—they make populist rhetoric the center of their campaign. Collectivism and anti-elitism are the sine qua non of their politics. They strive to challenge the dominant elitist order and give voice to the collective will.[6]

To this end, populist candidates employ a simplistic style. Populist language is one of broad generalities. All elites, whether they are Wall Street bankers, career politicians, scientists, or academics, are painted with the same thick brush. They all share a singular intentionality and the same set of goals: to deprive "the people" of their rightful sovereignty. Similarly, the people too are portrayed as a single unified entity. Usually, they are defined relative to a shared nation or culture—the people are those who speak the same language or hold the same citizenship. But often, populists define the people by who they are not. By this reckoning, the people are all those who aren't among the rich and powerful, but who also aren't foreign, from a minority group, or any type of social deviant. In short, the populist not only rails against elites but also conjures a singular people, united in some primordial, organic way.[7]

Populist rhetoric also has some tonal peculiarities. First, it is typically simplistic and Manichaean, describing all conflicts in bifurcated terms: good versus evil, the powerful versus the people, winners versus losers, and so on. In addition, populist rhetoric is typically restorative, looking back to a time when things were better for ordinary people. Trump's Make America Great Again slogan epitomizes this nostalgic longing.[8] Populism is also apprehensive, continually suspicious of any claims to economic, political, or cultural privilege. For populists, the good is found in the common wisdom of the people rather than the pretensions of the experts. Finally, populists often employ mannerisms that are outlandish and indelicate.[9] To those in the political mainstream, the populist often seems oafish or boorish, like "a drunken guest at a dinner party."[10] But this very brashness contributes to an aura of authenticity, distinguishing the populist from the "typical politician." The populist hones his or her bona fides precisely by ruffling the feathers of polite society. Vulgar or indelicate behavior is not a problem for the populist but a token of credibility.

But most important is the apprehensive nature of populism. The populist candidate doesn't applaud the status quo. Instead, he or she must both stoke and validate voters' anxieties. The populist depicts a world in chaos, where the nefarious elites have led the people astray and where doom is impendent: the economy is typically imploding, foreign adversaries are gaining strength, and the cherished goodness of the people is about to disappear. As Trump said, "If we don't get tough, and if we don't get smart, and fast, we're not going to have our country anymore. There will be nothing, absolutely nothing, left."[11]

By stoking voters' anxieties, the populist then paves the way for other heuristics common in intuitive reasoning. Indeed, populism employs many of the same mental shortcuts readily found in other magical beliefs. Populists use representativeness heuristics when they portray all members of a type as the same: all billionaires have identical political interests, all scientists are scornful of common wisdom, all ordinary people are good, and so on. Populists also use contagion heuristics. In their rhetoric, the people are often depicted as pure, tainted only by the influx of foreign or deviant elements. Most important, populists tend to anthropomorphize political institutions and social groups. They depict "elites," "the people," or "foreigners" as having a singular intentionality. These groups behave not as diverse collections of individuals but more like a single individual, with a oneness of purpose and thought.[12]

In its anxieties and its heuristics, populism exemplifies the politics of intuition. By implicating a "billionaire class" or "establishment politicians" as singularly evil beings with extraordinary powers, they invoke a causal explanation for politics that is far different from the ones usually offered by social scientists. They don't, for example, portray people in positions of wealth and power as having a variety of interests—by the populist reckoning, liberal financier George Soros is of the same mind as conservative David Koch; congressional Republicans and Democrats ultimately have the same political interests in "protecting the establishment." The messy pluralism of real politics is ignored by the populist, who conveys otherworldly competences and nefarious intentions upon the powerful. The people, by contrast, are endowed with a magical wholeness, a uniform moral goodness belying the pathologies, conflicts, and social indifferences that social scientists see as dividing the "common folk." Populist orientation is rife with the same intuitive elements that animate other mythologies, religions, and folktales.

It is also these magical qualities that ultimately differentiate populism and socialism. Although both movements locate politics as a struggle between the masses and the powerful, they differ in their magical character. Populists place political virtue in the hands of a mythic "people," usually defined by ethnicity or nationality. Socialists, by contrast, define politics primarily in economic terms where political virtue lies with the working classes, whose labor adds all "real value" to the economy. Moreover, socialism often locates itself within an empirical framework—Marxism is, among many other things, an attempt at a scientific theory of human social organization. Socialists often draw from theories of capital accumulation and labor exploitation as the rationale for their politics; most populists, meanwhile, don't have an overarching theory beyond the idea that all elites and outsiders are bad and the people are good. Whereas socialist rhetoric itself often veers into the magical, populism and socialism draw from fundamentally different frameworks for describing politics.[13]

Conspiracy Theories

One area where populists often become even more magical in their thinking is in their penchant for conspiracy theories. Like *populism*, the term *conspiracy theory* is contentious. Many people who endorse conspiracy theories don't think of them as "conspiracy theories" in the pejorative sense, but instead regard them as truths. Let us first be clear by what we mean. We define a conspiracy theory as any *narrative about hidden, malevolent groups secretly perpetuating political plots and social calamities to further their own nefarious goals.* This definition does not preclude the fact that conspiracies sometimes do occur: Richard Nixon did try to cover up the Watergate burglary, executives at Enron did intentionally manipulate energy prices, and so on. But most popular conspiracy theories about things like water fluoridation, fake moon landings, or Barack Obama's birthplace have little empirical support.

Instead, conspiracy theories are similar to other types of magical beliefs, drawing from shards of facts and circumstance to weave fantastical narratives about extraordinary events. Like most religions, conspiracy theories tend to assume that unseen or obscure forces are behind what is happening in the world; that is, if something unusual happens, it is because some clandestine group is intentionally willing it to occur. And like many religions, conspiracy theories interpret politics and history as an ongoing struggle between good and evil. For the conspiracy theorist, the major events of our time are typically the final acts in some ultimate conflict. Also like many religions, conspiracy theories usually suggest that mainstream accounts of political events are a ruse to distract the public from the hidden real sources of power.[14] By this account, experts, political leaders, and scientists are merely dupes for darker satanic forces. Conspiracy theories often aim to interpret hidden symbols as clues about the "true" nature of the world, much like religions.

But the most important thing that conspiracy theories share with religion is that they both attempt to order an ambiguous reality. For all their ominous overtones, conspiracy theories provide an explanation for why things are happening. Rather than puzzle through random events or the impersonal machinations of larger socioeconomic forces, conspiracy theories explain events though definitive narratives with great dramatic license. The terrorist attack, disease outbreak, or economic recession is the result of a small group of evildoers who often possess extraordinary powers, seeking to exert their will. Conspiracy theorists often put themselves at the center of the drama—only by unearthing and publicizing this hidden plot can they heroically thwart the nefarious aims of the secret cadre. As with the apocalyptic visions common to many religions, the conspiracy theory not only explains what happens but gives meaning to the life of the explainer, making him or her an integral part of a greater story. This is also why trying to talk conspiracists out of their beliefs is like trying to convince true believers that their religion is false—because it's instrumental to their emotional balance, it's held as firmly as a life raft.

Populism and conspiracy theories often go hand in hand. From the antimonarchical pamphlets of the 1780s to the McCarthyist Red Scares of the 1950s, populist political movements in American history have been associated with fears of conspiracies.[15] For instance, the Anti-Masonic Party of the early nineteenth century was a populist third party based on a conspiracy theory about elite powers secreted in Masonic lodges.[16] Then in the late nineteenth century, the populist movement emerged. According to historian Richard Hofstadter, it was rife with a "paranoid style" of politics.[17] Today, conspiracy theories are common in populist movements worldwide. A particularly notable example is in Venezuela, where in 2014 president Nicolas Maduro launched a formal government inquiry into whether his populist predecessor, Hugo Chavez, was secretly poisoned by the United States.[18] Such conspiracy theories are so common in populist movements that many scholars view these as one of the *primary* forms of populist discourse, how ordinary people understand power structures.[19]

Yet for all the ink that has been spilled about both conspiracy theories and populism, we actually have little empirical evidence concerning their relationship in the contemporary United States. Most studies have relied on historical documents or subjective interpretation of texts. Despite the great deal of public speculation, there are few empirical studies on the extent of populism and conspiracism in the American public. So while we have many theoretical reasons for thinking that they are linked in contemporary life, the empirical proof is lacking nonetheless. So to see whether these claims about populism and conspiracy theories are valid, let us return to our survey data.

The Populist Divide in the 2016 Presidential Primaries

The primary elections of 2016 offered an extraordinary opportunity to examine this validity. On the Democratic side was the improbable popularity of Bernie Sanders, a seventy-four-year-old Jewish, socialist senator from Vermont. Running a campaign that focused primarily on economic inequality and the excesses of the "billionaire class," Sanders won primaries and caucuses in over twenty states and garnered roughly 44 percent of the Democratic vote, nearly surpassing heavily favored former secretary of state Hillary Clinton.[20] The Republican side included several candidates who had never held elected office, including Donald Trump, Carly Fiorina, and Ben Carson. In the first six months of the primary campaign, Carson and Trump consistently led in the polls, getting the support of well over half the Republican voters. By the end of the primary, Carson had faded, but Trump managed to displace a large field of formidable Republican candidates, including former Florida governor Jeb Bush, Ohio governor John Kasich, New Jersey governor Chris Christie, and senators Ted Cruz and Marco Rubio. Trump did this by running a campaign that focused on the corruption of the political establishment, putative threats from immigrants, trade deals, Muslim terrorists, and his self-proclaimed authenticity as a political outsider.

During the primary electoral season (late February and early March), we gauged the populist and conspiratorial attitudes of the American public with a nationally representative survey of 1,063 citizens. Given all the rhetoric about 2016 being "the year of the populist," we wanted to measure the extent of the public's populist sentiment as well as its support for conspiracy theories. Starting with populism, we asked twelve survey questions that together capture three dimensions underlying populist rhetoric. These factor scores are listed in table 5.1.

The first dimension is *political populism*, the extent that people feel alienated from economic and political elites. In our survey, it was captured in five statements that are widely endorsed by the American public:

1. People like me don't have much say in what government does. (66 percent agree)
2. Politics usually boil down to a struggle between the people and the powerful. (74 percent agree)
3. It doesn't really matter who you vote for because the rich control both political parties. (58 percent agree)
4. People at the top get there from some unfair advantage (38 percent agree)
5. The system is stacked against people like me. (39 percent agree)

Responses to these questions all "load" highly on a single dimension that we measure with a political populism factor score.[21] Taking these highly correlated answers together, we can say that over half of Americans express some type of alienation from their political system.

The second dimension is *cultural populism*. This is the extent that people feel mistrustful or suspicious of expertise, primarily in fields of science,

TABLE 5.1 **Factor loadings on populism measures**

	Political populism	Cultural populism	National affiliation
People like me don't have much say in what government does.	0.589		
Politics usually boils down to a struggle between the people and the powerful.	0.628		
The system is stacked against people like me.	0.660		
It doesn't really matter who you vote for because the rich control both political parties.	0.692		
People at the top usually get there from some unfair advantage.	0.506		
I'd rather put my trust in the wisdom of ordinary people than the opinions of experts and intellectuals.		0.603	
When it comes to really important questions, scientific facts don't help very much.		0.729	
Ordinary people can really use the help of experts for understanding complicated things like health and science.		0.667	
Politics is ultimately a struggle between good and evil.		0.510	
I generally consider myself to be like most other Americans.			0.729
How important is being an American to who you are?			0.666
I trust the collective judgments of the American people.			0.0622

culture, and medicine. We tap into this sentiment with four questions that are also commonly endorsed by the American population:

1. Ordinary people are perfectly capable of deciding for themselves what is true and what is not.[22] (48 percent agree)
2. I'd rather put my trust in the wisdom of ordinary people than the opinions of experts and intellectuals. (32 percent agree)
3. When it comes to really important questions, scientific facts don't help very much. (11 percent agree)
4. Politics are ultimately a struggle between good and evil. (40 percent agree)

Once again, all these items load highly on a single dimension and can be combined, via principal component analysis, into a single cultural populism factor score. While sentiments of cultural populism are not quite as prevalent as political populism, they are still common in nearly half the population.

The third dimension is what we call *national affiliation*. Unlike the first two dimensions, which are about people's alienation from elites, national affiliation taps into identification with "the people." As with the other dimensions, we find strong sentiments of national affiliation in the American public. Over two-thirds of Americans say they generally consider themselves "to be like most other Americans." Over half say they "trust the collective judgments of the American people" even for complex political issues. And 44 percent say that being an American is extremely important (the highest increment on a seven-point scale) to their sense of self. In the principal component analysis, these items all load strongly into a third factor score.

Taken separately, each of these scales suggests a strong populist sentiment lurking in the American electorate. A majority of Americans express strong feelings of nationalism and feel that the political system tilts too strongly toward the rich; in addition, a solid plurality also suspect scientists, doctors, and other experts. But by themselves, none of these dimensions represents all of populism. Those scoring high in political populism may be cynical about the ruling system but wouldn't be a populist if they don't feel connected to "the people"; nor do they necessarily mistrust all elites. Thus, to measure populism as a single construct, we combine all three factor scores in a simple, additive *populism scale*.[23]

The importance of all three dimensions of populism is evident when we compare voters in the 2016 Democratic and Republican primaries.[24] As illustrated in figure 5.1, supporters of the top candidates vary in each of their populism scales.[25] The candidate with the least populist supporters was Bernie Sanders. Although Sanders was often given a populist label, this

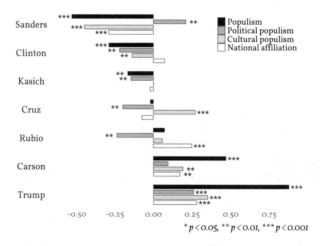

FIGURE 5.1. Average populism scores by candidate preference during 2016 presidential primaries.

description does not suit him well. Yes, Sanders's supporters score higher than average in political populism, but they score very low in both cultural populism and national affiliation. Unlike populists, Sanders's supporters don't feel mistrustful of science, nor are they strongly nationalistic. Indeed, Sanders, even by his own terms, was not a populist but a Democratic Socialist. Unlike other populists, he did not traffic in nativist claims, nor did he use a simplistic rhetoric. He actually has more in common with cosmopolitan leftist European parties than their right-wing populist counterparts.

The other two candidates associated with low populism scores were Hillary Clinton and Ohio governor John Kasich. On its face, this is not surprising. Both had long records of public service and ran more moderate campaigns emphasizing gradualist reforms rather than wholesale change. Senators Ted Cruz and Marco Rubio also had low aggregate populist scores, largely because their supporters score low in political populism. Cruz's supporters have high scores in cultural populism, a reflection of his strong link to Christian fundamentalists; Rubio's supporters score high in national affiliation. But cumulatively, neither candidate had an overall populist backing.

The two candidates whose supporters expressed the highest populism scores were the two true outsiders to the political system: Ben Carson and Donald Trump. Their supporters score high in all three populism dimensions. And of these, Trump's supporters are the most populist of all. According to our metrics, they have a total populism score nearly twice as high, on average, as Carson's supporters, who themselves score much higher than the average voter.

Looking at the population as a whole, roughly a quarter of the voting public scores high in total populism. This means a high score in all three dimensions: these voters feel alienated from political elites, are mistrustful of experts, and feel strongly nationalistic. It was they who disproportionately supported Trump and Carson. About half the nation scores high in one or two dimensions. This would mean that these voters aren't really populists as such but may be responsive to certain themes common in populism. Sanders's and Cruz's supporters tended to draw from this group. The remaining quarter of the population scores low in all three populist dimensions. These are people who don't feel that the system is working against them, have confidence in scientific experts, and don't have an especially strong nationalist orientation. In the 2016 primary election, these people tended to support Kasich and Clinton.

Beyond their populism, the supporters of the various candidates were also differentiated by their adherence to conspiracy theories. In our March 2016 survey, we measured belief in conspiracy theories by asking people whether they're in agreement with six conspiratorial statements:

1. The Food and Drug Administration is deliberately withholding approval for natural cures for cancer because of secret pressure of the pharmaceutical industry. (46 percent agree)
2. The financial crash of 2008 was secretly orchestrated by a handful of Wall Street bankers in order to extend the power of the Federal Reserve Board over the world economy. (26 percent agree)
3. Public health officials are hiding data which show that vaccines and many other medications contain toxins that can cause autism and other diseases. (23 percent agree)
4. Much of what happens in the world is determined by a small and secretive group of individuals. (38 percent agree)[26]
5. The US government secretly helped plan the attacks of 9/11 in order to justify going to war in the Middle East. (15 percent agree)
6. Barack Obama was not really born in the United States, and his "official" Hawaiian birth certificate is really a fake. (20 percent agree)

Although different people agree with some conspiracies and not others (for example, Birthers tend to be Republican, while Truthers tend to be liberal), they all load strongly on a single conspiracism scale.[27]

This conspiracism scale is highly correlated with the populism scale, especially its first two dimensions.[28] Americans who score high in political populism and cultural populism are far more likely to endorse conspiracy theories. The only dimension of populism not related to conspiracism is national affiliation. People who value being an American are no more conspiratorial than those who do not. These differences reflect some of the inherent tensions within populism. Populists think of themselves as patriots, and this usually entails some allegiance to governing institutions. Yet they also feel alienated from these same institutions. Conspiracy theories not only help differentiate populists from nationalists, they also provide a rationalization for the former. By implicating elites in a nefarious plot, the conspiracy theory rationalizes the alienation of the populist patriot. In this case, it is appropriate to rebel against the governing institutions, because these have been taken over by a small nefarious group. Conspiracy theories give credence to the populist not to engage in social revolution but to restore the governing order to its place as protector of the interests of "the people."

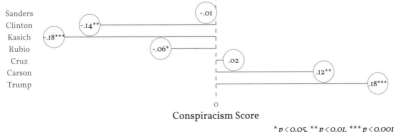

Sanders
Clinton
Kasich
Rubio
Cruz
Carson
Trump

Conspiracism Score

$* p < 0.05, ** p < 0.01, *** p < 0.001$

FIGURE 5.2. Average conspiracism scores by candidate preference during 2016 presidential primaries.

Not surprisingly, we see that conspiracism scores track very closely to populism scores in Americans' candidate preferences. As illustrated in figure 5.2, Clinton, Rubio, and Kasich, the most mainstream candidates, had the least conspiratorially minded supporters, all of whom tend to disagree with conspiracy theories more than not. Cruz's and Sanders's supporters tend to be agnostic or mixed in their opinions on conspiracy theories. Cruz supporters, for example, are more likely to be Birthers but less likely to be Truthers, while Sanders's supporters are the opposite. However, the two candidates with the most conspiratorially minded supporters were also the two most populist: Carson and Trump. And once again, Trump's supporters in particular stand out for their very high conspiracism scores.

Of course, our central claim here is not simply that populists like conspiracy theories or that Donald Trump's primary supporters are strong populists. These are fairly self-evident assertions. Rather, we want to establish the less obvious idea that populism and conspiracism are expressions of an intuitive approach to politics. Our supposition is that most Americans who believe in conspiracy theories or who endorsed Donald Trump or Ben Carson in the Republican primary do so from a visceral orientation: they comprehend politics through gut feelings more than reasoned deliberation. It is their innate intuitions and not some abstract ideology that guides their political views.

In our surveys, we find a great deal of evidence to support this claim. It starts with the Intuitionism scale. As we noted in chapter 2, that scale is highly predictive of a wide range of magical beliefs—as a person's score on the Intuitionism scale increases, he is more likely to believe in God, biblical inerrancy, ghosts, and many other magical phenomena. The Intuitionism scale is also highly predictive of people's populist and conspiracist attitudes. Figure 5.3 depicts the predicted differences along the populism and

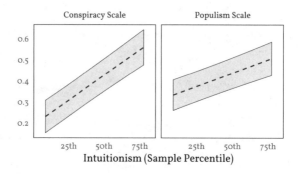

FIGURE 5.3. Conspiracism and populism scores as predicted by Intuitionism. Estimates include controls for gender, authoritarianism, church attendance, and religious conservatism. Ribbons indicate 95% confidence intervals.

conspiracism scales by the Intuitionism scale. These figures are derived from general linear models that also control for factors such as education, age, and ideology. The models also include controls for racial attitudes, nativist sentiments, and feelings of financial anxiety.

In our models, the Intuitionism scale is the single greatest predictor of both populism and conspiracism. The model predicts that Rationalists score twenty-three points lower on the populism scale and thirty-six points lower on the conspiracism scale than Intuitionists. While populists and conspiracists also are less educated, show higher nativist attitudes, and have feelings of financial anxiety, these effects are all smaller in magnitude than the differences along the Intuitionism scale. In short, if you want to predict whether someone is a populist or a believer in conspiracy theories, then the best way is to ask this person how she feels about stabbing family photos and shredding bills, and whether prospects for the future seem gloomy.

The intuitive character of populism is also evident when we compare supporters of the various presidential candidates. In fact, the Intuitionism scale almost directly tracks the populism and conspiracism scores. Figure 5.4 illustrates the difference between the Intuitionism scores of the various candidates and the sample average. Bernie Sanders's supporters, who are least inclined toward populism, also have the lowest average Intuitionism scores, four points below the national average. Hillary Clinton's supporters are also less Intuitionist than average. Ted Cruz's and Marco Rubio's supporters, meanwhile, have Intuitionism scores close to those for the overall population.

The candidates whose followers have the highest Intuitionism scores were the two true populists in the race: Ben Carson and Donald Trump. By far, their supporters have the highest Intuitionism scores. Carson's supporters scored four points higher than the sample average, while Trump's scored over five points higher.

The strong Intuitionism of Trump's supporters is the most telling. Beyond his espousal of conspiracy theories, Trump did not traffic in many common tropes associated with magical beliefs—he wasn't a paragon of Christian orthodoxy, nor was he especially New Age in orientation. He didn't claim that the Rapture was about to occur or that he had ESP. Instead, his resonance with Intuitionism seems to be more rooted in his populist rhetoric, gross stereotyping, and skepticism toward reasoned expertise. As embodied by Donald Trump, populism, conspiracism, and Intuitionism seem like dancers at a ball, distinct yet interconnected and always moving in sync.

We find further evidence of Intuitionism among populists and conspiracists in other measures. In earlier chapters, we identified a set of attitudes that reflect a more intuitive orientation toward the world. Intuitionists, as you'll recall, are much more likely to say they value their heart over their head. They are far more likely to believe in hidden Bible codes, end-time prophecy, and other fundamentalist beliefs. They are also likely to subscribe to bogus health claims, such as the claim that eliminating gluten will improve health. As illustrated in figure 5.5, all three of these attitudes also correlate with both populism and conspiracism.[29]

To be more specific, populists and conspiracists are more likely to say that the heart is a better guide than the head. They are also more likely to agree that many problems can be solved through prayer, or that the Bible is the inerrant word of God. People who believe in conspiracy theories and populist sentiments also think that eliminating gluten from their diet will

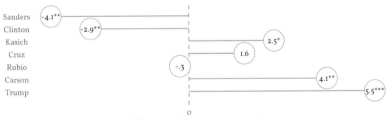

Difference from average intuition score

*$p < 0.05$, **$p < 0.01$, ***$p < 0.001$

FIGURE 5.4. Differences from average Intuitionism scores by candidate preference during the 2016 presidential primaries.

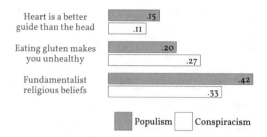

FIGURE 5.5. Correlates with populism and conspiracism scales. figures indicate partial correlation coefficients, with controls for education, age, gender, and ideology.

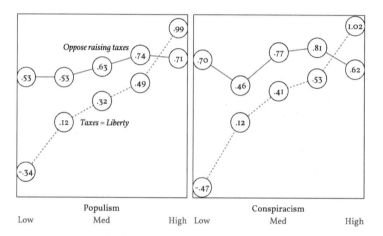

FIGURE 5.6. Opinions on fiscal policy as predicted by populism and conspiracism. Points indicate quintile divisions along populism and conspiracism scales.

make them healthier. In short, populists and conspiracists are strong magical thinkers.

A final example is also found in measures of policy opinion. As we noted in chapter 4, Intuitionists are more likely to be swayed when issues are framed in terms of emotional cues or relevant heuristics. We showed, for instance, that Intuitionists had slightly more liberal views than Rationalists about raising taxes, but changed their mind completely in response to the statement "Every time we raise taxes by 10 percent, we lose 10 percent of our liberty." We find the same pattern with both populists and conspiracists. Figure 5.6 lists the average response to the "tax equals liberty" statement and a more neutral statement of "Now that the economy is doing better, it is time to increase taxes on the very wealthy to pay down the deficit." Both questions are about taxes, albeit phrased very differently.[30] The former is phrased in a "hard"-issue way, the latter in an "easy"-issue way. We then compare the average responses by five quintiles of the populism and conspiracies scales.[31]

Here again, we see that populists and conspiracists, like all Intuitionists, are very sensitive to how issues get framed. When describing tax increases relative to economic circumstances and deficit reduction, we see few clear differences in political opinion. Populists are slightly more opposed than non-populists to raising taxes; conspiracy theorists show no differences compared with nonconspiracists. But when tax increases are framed as a trade-off with liberty, tremendous differences in populist opinion become apparent. Populists and conspiracists are far more likely to agree that raising taxes costs Americans their liberty. The 40 percent of Americans scoring lowest on the populism and conspiracism scales generally do not agree that taxes and liberty are equally comparable. But among people in the top fifth of the populist and conspiracist scales, these two issues are strongly equated. The vast majority of strong populists and conspiracists agree that raising taxes is equivalent to curtailing liberty. Like all Intuitionists, they are highly susceptible to metaphors, particularly those invoking a representativeness heuristic like the one above.

In sum, populism and conspiracism are borne by people's intuitions, especially those concerning issues of power and money. Populists do not have an overarching theory about the state's role in controlling the economy. Theirs is not a politics of ideology but a politics of feeling and symbol. Populists and conspiracists carry high levels of anxiety and apprehension, and are prone to taking metaphors literally. They strongly believe in the validity of their gut feelings, and are suspicious of any claims of expertise. In terms of public opinion, these sentiments often crystallize around issues of the state. Populists may want government to help the poor, but they are wary of any expansion of state power and are fearful of state military efforts. They are also highly nativistic in their orientation. Conspiracists in particular are very wary of any state intervention, be it in the fight against terrorism or in securing health insurance for the poor. The populist rant or the conspiracy theory may articulate a cogent analysis of a problem, but it's more a rationalization of another impulse than a reasoned deduction.

Conclusion

In modern American political history, few events have been more unexpected or improbable than the success of Donald Trump. Throughout both the primary and the general election campaign, a near-unanimous chorus of pundits and experts was predicting Trump's demise. "Trump has a better chance of playing in the NBA finals than winning the Republican nomination," wrote FiveThirtyEight's Harry Enten. Former Mitt Romney adviser Stuart Stevens predicted that Trump would be gone by the end of January, *New York Times* columnist Ross Douthat thought Marco Rubio would the inevitable nominee by the end of March, and *Slate's* Jacob Weisberg predicted that Trump's campaign would collapse in April.[32] During the general election, nearly every "prediction" site gave Hillary Clinton overwhelming odds of winning. In fairness to the pundits, Trump violated nearly every "rule" that predicts who wins a presidential nomination: he espoused inconsistent and sometimes liberal policy positions; he had no experience running a campaign or holding elected office; he had unprecedentedly high unfavorable ratings; and most important, until he secured the nomination, he had virtually no endorsements from any establishment Republican politicians. According to the dominant model in political science, these factors should have precluded Trump from securing the nomination.[33]

But secure the nomination he did. Although Trump's later victory in the general election came from a number of factors (the partisan adherence of Republicans, the anemic state of the economy in the first half of 2016, the problematic factors attached to Hillary Clinton), his success ultimately hinged on his ability to connect not only with a substantial portion of the Republican base but with a large number of rural voters in traditionally Democratic areas. And our data suggest that he did this by speaking to these voters' intuitions.

From his untiring promotion of the birther conspiracy theory to the nativist tinge permeating his campaign rhetoric, Donald Trump gave voice to the latent sentiments that animate Intuitionists' thinking. His was not a candidacy based on abstract theories about the role of the state or nuanced notions of American foreign affairs. There was virtually no policy content to his campaign beyond fantastical notions of building a wall along the Mexican border, canceling trade agreements, and reneging on military treaties with foreign allies. Instead, Trump's rhetoric was all aimed at visceral feelings among the less attentive elements of the electorate. He spoke in short sentences composed of simple words.[34] He bragged unceasingly about his own capabilities, and showed little regard for facts or truth. And he articulated the feelings of alienation and anxiety felt by millions of predominantly white Republicans. By railing against the political establishment, bombastically deriding intellectuals and experts, and spewing all types of nativist and ethnocentric invectives, Donald Trump spoke for a latent populism that was welling in much of America.

Consider, for example, an excerpt from Trump's final campaign commercial:

> Our movement is about replacing a failed and corrupt political establishment with a new government controlled by you, the American people. The establishment has trillions of dollars at stake in this election. For those who control the levers of power in Washington, and for the global special interests they partner with, these people that don't have your good in mind. The political establishment that is trying to stop us is the same group responsible for our disastrous trade deals, massive illegal immigration, and economic and foreign policies that have bled our country dry.[35]

This stridently populist rhetoric, when accompanied by ominous pictures of the Jewish financier George Soros and the Jewish heads of the Federal Reserve and Goldman Sachs, spoke to not just concerns about elite power but also long-standing conspiracy theories that targeted Jews.

Our findings here suggest that with messages like this, Trump tapped into the intuitions shaping how many people comprehend politics, especially issues of money and power. They start with strong feelings of apprehension. Like other magical thinkers, populists and conspiracists are both pessimistic about the future and anxious about their own financial circumstances. They report a lot of apprehensive behaviors: checking locks on doors, washing hands, and so on. In addition, populists and conspiracists are particularly drawn to the types of heuristics common in magical beliefs: they have exaggerated concerns about contagion and are overly sensitive to representative symbols. These Intuitionist tendencies, in turn, show up in other beliefs as well: populists and conspiracists overvalue common wisdom, hold erroneous beliefs about health and medicine, and are more likely to harbor strong supernatural beliefs.

The populists' and conspiracists' Intuitionism is exacerbated by the complexities of modern life. The proliferation of media sources, the globalization of trade, technological shifts, and high levels of migration are all changing American society. Each of these is a complex phenomenon that is not easily comprehended. Rather than follow the lead of experts in thinking about these issues, many Americans look to alternative accounts that come from populists and conspiracy theories. Such alternative claims validate many Americans' anxieties about the state of the world and address their suspicions that events are occurring because small groups of evil forces are willing them to happen. Much as with the monster in the child's closet, the wicked elites in Washington or on Wall Street are the lurking menace whose very existence is evidenced by our fears. This is a politics far different from the ideological battles between liberals and conservatives or the partisan wars in Congress. This is the politics of intuition. And in 2016, its loudest voice was Donald Trump's.

CHAPTER SIX

Feeling White and Hating Foreigners

Donald Trump's presidential campaign was not only notable for its strident populism, it was also distinctive in its overt hostility to immigrants, Muslims, and other non-Americans. Indeed, it was with these themes that Trump launched his presidential bid. In his first campaign speech, he proclaimed that America had become a "dumping ground for the world's problems." Mexico was "sending people that have lots of problems. They're bringing drugs. They're rapists." This bashing of Mexicans continued throughout Trump's campaign, punctuated by proposals to build a "beautiful" wall along the Mexican border, accusations against a federal judge of Mexican heritage, and talk of massive deportations of "bad hombres."

Trump's bigotry didn't stop with the putative failings of Mexican immigrants. It also extended to other groups, especially Muslims. Throughout his campaign, Trump characterized Islam as a "hateful" ideology, the historical successor to fascism and communism. After terrorist attacks in San Bernardino, California, and Orlando, Florida, Trump moved even further outside the American mainstream, promising an outright ban on Muslim immigration despite clamorous bipartisan criticism. Harking back to his earlier "birtherism," he even suggested that Barack Obama was complicit in the terrorist attacks, saying, "We're being led by a man who is either not tough, not smart, or else he's got something else in mind. [He] can't even mention the words 'radical Islamic terrorism.' There's something going on."[1]

For longtime political observers, Trump's attacks on Mexicans, Muslims, and most other non-Anglos were surprising, not simply in their naked bigotry but because they seemed to be causing him so little political harm. The conventional wisdom held that explicitly racist appeals, particularly those that denigrated minority groups, were not only anathema to modern US politics but counterproductive. Surveys showed that not only had most white Americans shed the blatantly racist sentiments of their grandparents, but they also would condemn racist practices.[2] Trump's nativist appeals would seem to be politically suicidal.[3] Yet his electoral support was largely impervious to the widespread elite's condemnation of his ethnic slurs. How, in a "post-racial" America, could such naked bigotry go so unpunished?

Part of the answer lies in the power of intuitions. Although overt racism is less common today, Americans still harbor many ethnocentric attitudes, especially when it comes to immigrants and foreigners. Much of this stems from their reliance on their intuitions in perceiving the world. Ethnocentrism is a "deep and perhaps irreversible human habit," as political scientists Donald Kinder and Cindy Kam describe, because it is rooted in how humans naturally make sense of others. As with their magical beliefs, they concoct ethnocentric beliefs based on their feelings. When we encounter people unlike us or hear troubling news involving groups different from ours, we often feel apprehensive. In response, we employ simple rules of thumb to make sense of our feelings. We assume that all members of other groups are similarly threatening, that they all share the same negative traits, and that they are best kept at arm's length lest they pollute "us" with their foreign ways. These ethnocentric tendencies are particularly strong for Intuitionists. Whereas Rationalists may seek to correct their negative stereotypes owing to their principled commitment to equality, Intuitionists are more likely to follow their negative "gut feelings" about other groups.

In this chapter, we examine the links between ethnocentrism and Intuitionism. Although strong links do exist, they depend a lot on the type of ethnocentric attitudes in question. With nativist attitudes, we find a strong connection between Intuitionism and ethnocentrism. Intuitionists are more likely to identify as American and to harbor negative views of immigrants. But with white racial resentment, the relationship between Intuitionism and ethnocentrism is less clear. White racial animosity is more pronounced among a particular subset of Intuitionists, namely conservatives and conspiracists, rather than Intuitionists as a whole. The differences between nativist and racial identities reveal the political complexities behind America's ethnocentric attitudes, and how these complexities get entangled with our inborn tendencies for making sense of the world. Intuitionism can often lead to ethnocentric attitudes, but which of these attitudes gets activated depends on a host of political circumstances.

Intuitions and Ethnocentrism

Throughout most of our history, we humans have lived in small tribes of hunter-gatherers. And like most of our primate ancestors, our forebears lived in fierce competition with their neighbors.[4] By most accounts, inter-tribal violence was common among early hominids and most premodern cultures.[5] This group competition was enabled by an inborn "tribal psychology." Early primates had to be able to not only differentiate friend from foe but marshal strongly aggressive and violent motivations to members of the same species whom they considered threats. They did this with a suite of psychological traits that recognized, sorted, and evaluated all other fellow species.

This psychological legacy of group competition continues with us today. Its most notable expression is what social scientists call ethnocentrism, the tendency to "put one's group in the center of everything."[6] As described by Kinder and Kam,

> Ethnocentrism is a mental habit. It is a predisposition to divide the human world into in-groups and out-groups. It is a readiness to reduce society to us and them. Or rather, it is a readiness to reduce society to us *versus* them. Members of in-groups are assumed to be virtuous: friendly, cooperative, trustworthy, safe, and more. Members of out-groups are assumed to be the opposite: unfriendly, unco-operative, unworthy of trust, dangerous, and more. Ethnocentrism . . . charts a safe path through a social world that may seem uncomfortable, difficult, and, at times, perilous.[7]

When social scientists first tried to explain ethnocentrism, they found its origins in material conflict. Just as primates and early hominids fought other tribes over food and mates, modern ethnocentrism was said to arise from competition over scarce resources. A large body of research over the past century seemed to validate this claim. From Muzafer Sherif's famous Robbers Cave experiments in the 1950s to quantitative analyses of contemporary racial attitudes, scores of studies suggest that when opposing groups are in competition, ethnocentric attitudes tend to arise.[8]

But by itself, "real conflict theory" doesn't entirely explain ethnocentrism. In fact, sometimes it hardly explains it at all. Partly this is because we often have ethnocentric attitudes toward groups that we aren't in direct competition with. Many Americans, for example, hold ethnocentric views about Muslims, even though they have virtually no contact with them. The real conflict theory gets even more complicated when we appreciate that in a complex society, it's often difficult to comprehend which groups "we" are actually competing with. For example, is an unemployed white coal miner in Kentucky competing with African Americans he hates, the wealthy mine owners he works for, or Chinese coal miners? Or is he actually not "in competition" with any of these groups? Perhaps his diminishing resources are a function of mechanization and technological advance, not conflict with other people. In many instances, one's feelings of competition may be completely misplaced.

A prime example of this misdirected ethnocentrism can be found in popular complaints against unauthorized immigrants to the United States. With their limited English language skills and low education, it is unlikely that most of these people are actually "stealing jobs" from American citizens; instead, they are working in demanding low-wage jobs, like farmwork or domestic service, that many Americans refuse to perform. Thus, Americans' hostility to these immigrants is rarely based on actual competition over jobs or government funds. Rather, it is more likely based on misattributing the decline in American low-skill, high-wage jobs, which is actually arising from factors like automation, globalization, and the shift to a service economy. But instead of appreciating these complex factors, unauthorized immigrants make a more compelling and convenient scapegoat.

The limitations with the real conflict theory of ethnocentrism are evident in a simple example. In the 2016 presidential election, Donald Trump gave voice to strong ethnocentric statements, particularly on immigration. His promise to build a wall along the Mexican border reflected this attitude. If real conflict was a source of Americans' ethnocentric hostility to Mexicans, then we would expect Trump's appeal to increase in places where voters felt themselves in greater competition with unauthorized immigrants. In other words, we'd expect Trump's support to be strongest in border states or in states with large populations of unauthorized immigrants. Instead, we find just the opposite. Figure 6.1 depicts the relationship between the change in the GOP presidential vote by state between 2012 and 2016 (the vertical axis) and the share of a state's unauthorized immigrant population (the horizontal axis). Any state above the dashed horizontal line in the figure indicates that Donald Trump improved on the vote share earned by Mitt Romney there four years prior.

Contrary to the expectations of realistic conflict theory, Trump did poorest, relative to Romney, in states with the largest shares of unauthorized

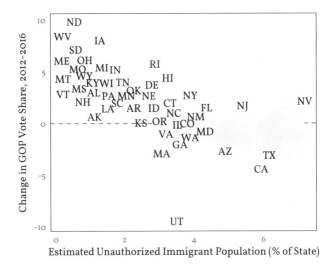

FIGURE 6.1. Unauthorized immigrant population and the 2016 presidential vote.

immigrants. In fact, the greater the size of this population in a state, the worse he did. For example, Trump received a smaller vote share than Romney in California, Texas, and Arizona. His biggest gains came from states with very few undocumented immigrants, including West Virginia, North Dakota, and Maine. Now obviously, such crude statistics don't immediately reveal people's perceptions of ethnocentric conflict. It may be that Trump's support was higher in these places for reasons that had nothing to do with his ethnocentrism. Nevertheless, if realistic conflict were true, we'd expect Trump to garner more appeal in the states with large populations of unauthorized immigrants. This, however, is not what we see.[9]

Given the weak explanatory power of real conflict theory, social scientists have concocted a trove of alternative *psychological* explanations for our ethnocentrism.[10] By these accounts, ethnocentrism is a function of both human cognition and emotional need. From the cognition side, ethnocentrism is thought to arise because humans are natural categorizers. Our minds habitually identify any object as part of a group: this car is a Ford, this tree is an oak, and so on.[11] We do the same with other people as well. We are quick to define people by their group identities, and to form judgments about them relative to our own groups. Are they in our group or not? Is their group a friend or a foe? These group identities can span an enormous range of criteria: we may judge people not just on their nationality but on what state or city they live in; we may sneer at people if they root for different teams or went to different schools; and of course, we may have strong aversions to others based on their race, religion, or creed. But the root elements of ethnocentrism are our innate tendencies to not only put people into distinct groups, but evaluate these groups relative to our own.[12]

This leads to the second important psychological aspect of ethnocentrism—emotional need. According to many social psychologists, ethnocentrism arises from our need to enhance our self-esteem. When we encounter other people, we don't simply categorize them as being in an "in-group" or an "out-group," we also categorize them as being in a "lesser group" or a "higher group."[13] By this reckoning, humans have a built-in reward system that comes with higher status—the higher our status, the better we feel about ourselves. One way we achieve this is by identifying with higher-status groups. A Cubs fan, for example, will wear a Cubs T-shirt after the team wins the World Series, because it makes him feel good to identify with a champion. Ethnocentrism may work in a similar way—we identify with in-groups and denigrate out-groups not only because of material competition, but because it enhances our feelings about ourselves.

But while the self-esteem explanation is often cited as a source of prejudice and ethnocentrism, it has not received much empirical support.[14] Some psychologists have offered instead a simpler motivational account: ethnocentrism is appealing because it helps us order our world. From this perspective, ethnocentrism, like all social identities, is a tool for comprehension. Given that we are natural categorizers, our stereotypes aren't only ways of bolstering our self-image, but ways of organizing reality. We see ourselves as superior to out-groups because it's an efficient way of rationalizing whatever future competition we may have with them. In other words, ethnocentrism arises as much from the anticipation of future conflict as by whatever existing conflicts might exist.

Either way, ethnocentrism seems a lot like an Intuitionist way of perceiving reality. Like other intuitions, it arises from strong emotional signals and quick cognitive shortcuts. And like most magical beliefs, it is also a way of making causal attributions—in this case, trying to explain the world in relationship to some "other people" who are typically seen as having a singular nefarious intentionality and often extraordinary traits. Ethnocentrism and magical beliefs both stem from feelings of apprehension and uncertainty. Just as magical beliefs are tools we use to quell our apprehensions, so too are ethnocentric beliefs. Our bigotry and prejudices are emotional palliatives, handy tools to make sense of the world and rationalize anxious feelings.

Ethnocentrism and magical thinking also share a similar "grammar." Consider one of the central expressions of ethnocentrism: the stereotype. As first described by Walter Lippmann, stereotypes are the simple portraits that we use to describe an entire group. They are, in Lippmann's words, "a distorted picture or image in a person's mind, not based on personal experience, but derived culturally."[15] But another way of describing stereotypes is as a representativeness heuristic, one of the central pillars of magical belief. When we use stereotypes, we assume that anyone who shares one trait of a group thus will automatically have all its other traits. The ethnocentric thinker applies stereotypes liberally: she assumes that all Jews are equally shrewd, that all Muslims are violent, or that all rich people are snobby. Just as the magical thinker believes that pictures of saints are endowed with a holy aura, so the ethnocentric thinker believes that all members of a group are endowed with the same common essence.

Ethnocentrism, like many magical beliefs, also employs the contagion heuristic. This is our innate tendency to think that contact with an emotionally potent object will "infect" or "transfer" the essence of the object itself. In magical beliefs, contagion heuristics take the form of holy relics or taboo spaces. The magical thinker believes that water blessed by the pope is holy or that a house previously owned by a serial killer is evil. For the ethnocentric thinker, contagion fallacies involve contact with other groups.[16] In this mindset, contact and commingling with out-groups is to be avoided, lest the other group somehow contaminates the purity of her own. Examples of these stigmas abound, ranging from the segregated bathrooms of the Jim Crow South to "untouchable" social castes in India. In nearly all cases, ethnocentrism typically expresses a very magical concern with proximity and social mixture.

Finally, like the magical thinker, the ethnocentric thinker will fiercely defend his stereotypical views. Just as religious zealots are loath to change their ideas about the world, so too are ethnocentric beliefs highly resistant to modification. Here again, this was well described by Lippmann nearly a century ago:

> The system of stereotypes may not be a complete picture of the world, but they are a picture of a possible world to which we are adapted. In that world people and things have their well-known places, and do certain expected things. We feel at home there. No wonder, then, that any disturbance of the stereotypes seems like an attack upon the Foundations of the universe. The stereotypes are, therefore, highly charged with the feelings that are attached to them. They

are the fortress of our tradition, and behind its defense we can continue to feel ourselves safe in positions we occupy.[17]

In other words, just as we use magical beliefs to help maintain our emotional equilibrium, so too our ethnocentric beliefs serve as emotional ballast, keeping our identities in a positive emotional space relative to other groups.

Given these psychological commonalities, we should expect ethnocentrism to be more prevalent among people who hold an Intuitionist worldview. As we have already seen, Intuitionists pay far more heed to their own emotional signals, taking their apprehensions and anxieties as important cues to the external world. Their feelings of fear are interpreted as something nefarious afoot, that is, the other group is up to no good. And just as Intuitionists are far more susceptible to the power of metaphors and symbols, they should also be more likely to view themselves in terms of their group memberships. In social situations, they will think of themselves more as "white" or "American" or "Christian" than as an individual. Similarly, Intuitionists will be more likely to embrace negative stereotypes about foreign groups. Most important, they will have a different relationship to their ethnocentrism. Whereas all people have ethnocentric tendencies, Intuitionists will give these social identities greater weight in comprehending the world. Rather than seek to correct or reconsider their stereotypes, Intuitionists will take their apprehensions as valid indicators that other groups are less trustworthy than their own, and rationalize their fears through a promiscuous application of stereotypes and other quick judgments.

But just because ethnocentrism and Intuitionism share a common psychological vernacular, it doesn't mean that all Intuitionists are uniformly ethnocentric or ethnocentric in the same way. Rather, the extent of the connection between Intuitionism and ethnocentrism will depend on a person's social context. And this is where things become complicated. At its core, ethnocentrism is a political sentiment. It's fueled by the *perception* of some type of zero-sum conflict with a different group, which is how it differs from mere prejudice. For example, a prejudiced American may dislike fat people without thinking of himself as skinny or even seeing himself in a group that competes with fat people. He may simply feel negatively toward people who are fat. Ethnocentrism, however, arises when people see their own group in conflict with other groups. Fat prejudice, in this case, is not a form of ethnocentrism because it doesn't involve group conflict. It would become ethnocentrism only if the fat hater suddenly started seeing fat people as a threat to his own group.

In a large and diverse country like the United States, however, it's difficult to know what might be triggering the ethnocentric feelings at any time. America is an incredibly diverse nation with a wide array of different groups. Not only do Americans identify themselves by gender, race, religion, sexuality, place, nationality, and a myriad of physical attributes, they also sort themselves by their politics, cultural tastes, consumer choices, and so forth. Drivers of pickups divide between Ford and Chevy, Houstonians sneer at Dallas, Cal fans hate Stanford . . . the list goes on. All these social identities, however, are culturally and socially contingent. In Chicago, White Sox fans may loathe Cubs fans in July, but feel deep unity with these previously hated North Siders during a November Bears game. Race may be a small concern for America's white majority, but is far more pressing for its different minority groups. Republicans were staunchly opposed to Russia when Reagan called that country the "evil empire," but softened their opposition when Donald Trump expressed admiration for Vladimir Putin.[18] Ethnocentric attitudes are thus ephemeral and transient, depending on which of our identities is being invoked under which particular circumstance.

Because our social identities are so fluid and pluralistic, we may not see a one-to-one correspondence between Intuitionism and ethnocentrism writ large. While Intuitionists may be more likely to embrace ethnocentric attitudes in general, their likelihood of embracing any one ethnocentric attitude will be highly contingent on their social position. An Intuitionist who is a Cubs fan may be more likely to embrace a negative view of White Sox fans only during baseball season; an Intuitionist Democrat will hold bad stereotypes of Republicans during a political campaign; a white Intuitionist may feel superior to blacks only if prompted to view conflict in racial terms. In other words, ethnocentrism may share many traits with magical thinking, and Intuitionists may be more susceptible to ethnocentric thinking. But the strength of this relationship will depend on the groups in question. Ethnocentric attitudes are not always triggered consistently. And we can see these differences when we compare two types of common ethnocentric attitudes in America today, race and nationalism.

Intuitions and Whites' Racial Attitudes

One of the most common sources of ethnocentric hostility is ethnicity, particularly in the United States. From its very beginnings, this nation has differentiated its citizens by race and ethnicity, with its white Anglo-Saxon Protestant majority regarding itself as distinct and superior to other groups.

From slavery and Jim Crow to restrictions against Jews, Irish, and Mexican immigrants, race and ethnicity have been central to the American political experience.[19] Thus, when it comes to politics and ethnocentrism, perceptions of racial and ethnic competition seem like a logical starting place for our empirical analysis.

But racial attitudes in the United States involve a complex mixture of political and social factors—whites' attitudes are subject to all types of ideological, cultural, and regional influences.[20] Given these complexities, how should we measure Americans' racial views? Our answer is to start with some of the most common measures of *white ethnocentrism*. We focus on white ethnocentrism in particular because of whites' predominant position in American society and long history of discrimination toward minority groups. Whites' ethnocentric attitudes are often measured with comparative stereotypes. Both the General Social Survey and the American National Elections Studies have long asked questions about how much Americans think qualities like "unintelligent," "lazy," or "violent" describe various racial groups. From these questions, Kinder and Kam crafted an ethnocentrism scale that measures the relative distance between the positive feelings toward one's own group and the negative feelings toward another. In other words, their scale measures how much a white person scores blacks or Latinos as lazier, less intelligent, or more violent than whites. They find that this scale predicts a host of political opinions, including opinions on social spending, moral issues, and foreign policy.[21]

Borrowing from their framework, we asked respondents in our December 2016 survey to rate whites, blacks, Latinos, and Muslims on these three traits.[22] We then employed a variant of the Kinder-Kam method for estimating the ethnocentrism scale, creating a measure of whether or not whites viewed out-groups more negatively than their in-group.[23] Next, we examined whether there were any differences in this white ethnocentrism scale using two methods: bivariate and multivariate models that control for both the Intuitionism scale and the measures of education, age, ideology, and a "conspiracism" scale, a single metric indicating how much respondents endorse a set of five conspiracy theories.[24]

If we don't take any other variables into account, it looks as though white Intuitionists are more likely to be ethnocentric. A simple bivariate model predicts that the percentage of whites who are ethnocentric will change by about four percentage points across the Intuitionism scale. Although this difference is statistically significant, it is not very large. How-

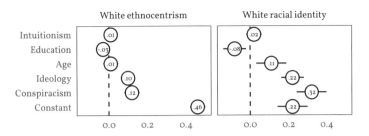

FIGURE 6.2. Predictors of white ethnocentrism and racial identity. Figures indicate ordinary least squares regression coefficients.

ever, the Intuitionism scale isn't the only way to gauge people's worldview. As we saw in earlier chapters, Intuitionists are also more likely to be conservative, to believe in conspiracy theories, and to be less educated. And these factors also predict differences in the ethnocentrism scale. According to our multivariate model (see fig. 6.2), once we account for other factors, the relationship between the Intuitionism scale and white ethnocentrism vanishes.[25] Instead, we find these other factors coming into play. We find that strong conservatives score ten points higher than strong liberals on the white ethnocentrism scale. An equally large difference occurs between people at either end of the conspiracism scale. People with advanced degrees score about four points lower than those with no college education.

It is important to keep in mind that we are using a very crude and noisy measure of white ethnocentrism. This measure is based simply on whether white respondents apply stereotypes in a more negative way toward other groups than their own. In addition, the Intuitionism scale in the December 2016 survey is truncated due to the political tremors following the recent election.[26] Nevertheless, the models do show that Intuitionism and white ethnocentrism are related, and that this relation is largely attributable to the fact that the other predictors of ethnocentrism (education, ideology, and conspiracism) are traits more common among Intuitionists.

These same patterns also are evident when we examine another key component of ethnocentrism: the centrality of white's own racial identity. Once again, we focus here on white racial identity because of the predominance of whites in American society. For America's racial minorities, living in a predominantly white country means that their racial identity tends to be continuously salient. To be black or Latino in America is, by many accounts, to be living in a society where one's race is always evident; but for whites, race may be something less prominent to their sense of self, particularly if they live in a predominantly white area.[27] We see this in our data. Only 22 percent of whites in our December 2016 survey report that their racial identity is "extremely important" for who they are; among African Americans, this number is 56 percent; among Latinos, it's 41 percent.

Given the lower salience of race to whites' identity, it's even more important to consider their race consciousness as a function of their ethnocentrism. After all, ethnocentrism is partly based on a strong notion of in-group identity. Obviously for minorities, this in-group identity is a by-product of living in a society where the majority is of a different race and has a long history of racial discrimination. For blacks and Latinos in America, their race is central to their identity because their living conditions make it largely unavoidable. But for America's segregated white majority, their racial identity may only be salient as a function of their feelings of ethnocentrism. In other words, a strong sense of racial identity among a majority group like whites is a more potent indicator of ethnocentrism than it is among blacks or Latinos. If Intuitionists are more likely to be ethnocentric, then they should have a stronger sense of white racial identity.

And indeed, this is what we find. In our December 2016 survey, we asked three questions that gauge the centrality of whites' racial identity.[28] They include the question of how important "being white is to who you are" mentioned above. They also include whether a white respondent agrees that "whites are unable to find jobs because employers are hiring minorities instead," and how important the respondent thinks it is that "whites work together to change laws that are unfair to whites." These three items are combined, via factor analysis, into a single *white identity* scale. Once again, we examine this scale using the same bivariate and multivariate models described above.

White Intuitionists are more likely to have a strong sense of white racial identity. In a simple bivariate model, the Intuitionism and white identity scales have a small but statistically significant relationship. If we score the white identity scale from 0 to 100, a Rationalist will score ten points lower than an Intuitionist. But as with the measure of ethnocentrism, the much greater effects of an intuitive worldview are more obliquely evident. As illustrated in figure 6.2, the greatest predictors of white racial identity are, once again, education, ideology, and conspiracism. According to our model, conspiracists score about twenty-eight points higher than nonconspiracists

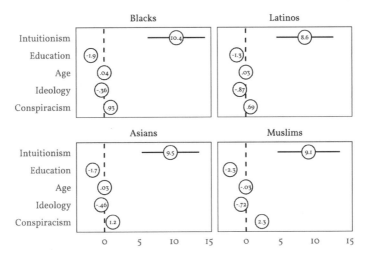

FIGURE 6.3. Predictors of whites' estimates of minority population size. Figures indicate ordinary least squares regression coefficients.

on the one-hundred-point racial identity scale. This is even higher than the twenty-two-point difference between strong liberals and strong conservatives. As with the ethnocentrism measure, the Intuitionism scale is not a great predictor of white racial identity; however, other parts of the white population with strong Intuitionist leanings (that is, conspiracists and conservatives) do have a stronger racial consciousness.

Where we do see a more direct effect of Intuitionism and white ethnocentrism is with the perceptions of minority group size (fig. 6.3). Ethnocentric thinkers will probably exaggerate an out-group's size to be more in line with their feelings of apprehension. An out-group may be a tiny portion of the population, but it will loom much larger to be proportional with their feelings of threat. Bearing this in mind, we asked respondents to estimate the size of four minority groups: African Americans, Hispanics, Asian Americans, and Muslim Americans. In general, whites tend to overestimate the size of these groups. On average, whites think that 27 percent of the population is black (it's really 13 percent), that 26 percent is Latino (it's really 15 percent), that 20 percent is Asian (it's really 4 percent), and that 18 percent is Muslim (it's less than 1 percent).

But while whites wildly overestimate the size of minority groups, the degree of this distortion varies a lot with their Intuitionism scores. Rationalists generate estimates of minority populations nine to twelve points lower, on average, than Intuitionists. For example, our models predict that a Rationalist will, on average, estimate that 20 percent of the population is black, while an Intuitionist will estimate that 32 percent of the population is black. Intuitionists do this no matter whether the target group is black, Latino, or Muslim. The less educated tend to overestimate the minority population sizes as well. And conspiracists overestimate the size of black and Muslim populations too.

In reviewing these findings together, we see a complex picture of Intuitionism and white ethnocentrism in the United States. Intuitionists are more likely to hold ethnocentric stereotypes. They have a stronger sense of white identity. And they are more likely to overestimate the size of minority groups. But many of these differences are attributable to certain types of Intuitionists—namely conservatives and those who subscribe to conspiracy theories. It is this subgroup that holds the strongest levels of white identity and white ethnocentrism. It is this group that has the most distorted view of Muslim populations.

These findings reflect the complexity of racial attitudes in America. Few whites today will endorse the overt bigotry of generations past. But perceptions of racial identity have also become more politicized. Conservatives have come to see themselves in opposition to the multiethnic identity politics embraced by the Left. As a result, whites' racial attitudes have become more aligned with their ideology. The fact that white conspiracists are more ethnocentric speaks to the complexity of race as well. In both these cases, feelings of racial threat and racial competition are consistent with how white conservatives' and conspiracists' intuitions inform their political beliefs, where the world is seen as a tribal struggle between positive in-groups and undeserving out-groups.

Intuitions and Nationalist Attitudes

Beyond race, another common way that Americans express their ethnocentrism is through their nationalism and their hostility to foreigners. Although Americans often pride themselves as being "a nation of immigrants," the United States has a long history of hostility to newcomers. From the Know-Nothing Party of the 1850s to the Chinese Exclusion Act of 1882 to Donald Trump's Muslim ban of 2017, the nation has periodically targeted certain nationalities and ethnic groups for exclusion. Such efforts originate in mass sentiments of nativist fervor, ginned up by political leaders looking for a way to court public favor.[29]

Much of this historic nativism arises from a particularly deep streak of nationalism in American culture. Although *nationalism* is a prosaic term, here we mean it in the psychological sense of strong identification with the "imagined community" of one's nation-state. Nationalists are those who view their own psychological well-being as intricately tied to that of their country. By many measures, Americans are much more nationalistic than citizens of other industrialized democracies. For example, the World Values Survey finds that 70 percent of Americans report being "very proud" of their nationality, compared with fewer than 50 percent of people in other democracies like France, Italy, Great Britain, or Denmark.[30] Being an American is far more central to Americans' sense of self than being British is to people in England or being Danish is to people in Denmark.

This strong nationalist sentiment often coincides with a mistrust of or condescension to foreigners that mainly originates in how Americans view other nations. Fifty percent see themselves as superior to other cultures— they agree that "the world would be a better place if other nations were more like America," a sentiment that's weaker in other nations.[31] Given this sense of cultural superiority, it's not surprising that immigrants, particularly those from nations regarded as more "foreign" to the American creed, are viewed with more suspicion. Such nativist condescension applies to economic policy as well. Trade deals and negotiations with other countries may seem more threatening than domestic matters, particularly if it seems like the deal is being made with an inferior partner.

Although we don't know exactly why Americans are so much more nativist than their peers, we do know that their nationalism is very complementary to their intuitive ways of perceiving the world. Nationalism is a tribal orientation, a sentiment based on commonalities derived from arbitrary political criteria. Much as with magical beliefs, nationalism is based on strong emotions and cognitive shortcuts—it derives from strong feelings of indignation and attachment, and lends itself to quick dichotomies of "us versus them." Given this, Intuitionists should be particularly susceptible to nationalist appeals. Whereas the Rationalist is more likely to see all people, regardless of nationality or ethnicity, as individuals with a common humanity, Intuitionists are more likely to view them in categorical terms. Because American ethnicity is based on political membership, American Intuitionists are more likely to see foreigners as threatening to some type of mythic "American" way. They are more likely to be responsive to nationalistic symbols and metaphors. They are also more likely to embrace a Manichaean "us versus them" approach to perceiving foreign affairs.

We can see these trends in our data, starting with national identity. In

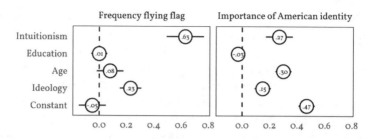

FIGURE 6.4. Predictors of American identity and flag flying. Figures indicate ordinary least squares regression coefficients.

our March 2016 survey, we asked respondents two questions about their sense of national identity: "How important is being an American to who you are?" and "How often do you fly the American flag?"[32] As with other surveys, we find a high level of nationalist sentiment. Nearly 70 percent of our respondents list being an American as extremely important to their sense of self; 30 percent say they fly the flag either "often" or "every day."

But these rates are also highly contingent on respondents' Intuitionism scores. Figure 6.4 depicts regression coefficients from a model that predicts American identity and flag flying by examining Intuitionism, education, age, and ideology. In both cases, Intuitionists are far more nationalistic than Rationalists. For instance, our models predict that the former score twenty-seven percentage points higher than the latter on the national identity scale. This is far greater than the fifteen-percentage-point difference between strong liberals and strong conservatives. Indeed, the only factor that has a greater difference in our models is between generations—older Americans have a far stronger attachment than younger ones to "being American." We see similar differences in flag flying as well. Here, we see that the biggest differences in our models are between Intuitionists and Rationalists; the former score sixty-three percentage points higher than the latter. This difference is twice as great as between strong liberals and strong conservatives. In short, if you want to predict what types of people fly the American flag, the Intuitionism scale is one of your most powerful tools.

Yet Intuitionism is not simply a strong predictor of national identity; it also predicts views on immigration and trade. In our same March 2016 survey, we asked respondents four questions about their perceptions of immigrants, US immigration policy, and whether free-trade agreements like NAFTA were harmful to ordinary Americans.[33] From these questions, we see that a large plurality of Americans is suspicious of immigrants and trade. Nearly 43 percent think that too many immigrants are cheats or criminals, 46 percent think that immigrants are more of a burden, and 27 percent think that free-trade agreements are harmful. Thirty-six percent of Americans think that the best way to deal with the problem of illegal immigration is through stricter border security and massive deportations.

But such nativist views also depend a lot on people's Intuitionism scores. Figure 6.5 illustrates the coefficients from multivariate models that predict differences of opinion on the four questions listed above. Once again, the models look at the impact of the Intuitionism scale in comparison with education, age, and ideology. With all four questions, Intuitionists are far more hostile than Rationalists to immigrants. The models predict that an Intuitionist will score, ceteris paribus, about thirty-four points higher on the question about immigrants being criminals and about fifty-one points higher on the question about whether immigrants are a burden. These differences are larger than those for education although not as great as the differences between liberals and conservatives.

Intuitionists also have different ideas from Rationalists about immigration policy and trade. They score about forty-four points higher, on average, in their support for massive deportations. This difference is roughly comparable to that between strong liberals and strong conservatives. Intuitionists are also more likely to think that free-trade agreements cause more harm than good. The model predicts that the average Intuitionist

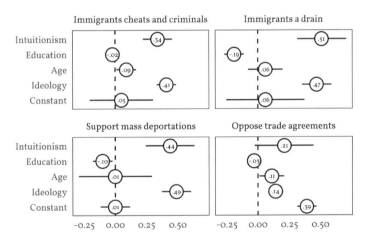

FIGURE 6.5. Predictors of immigration and trade attitudes. Figures indicate ordinary least squares regression coefficients.

will score about twenty-one points higher than the average Rationalist on the free-trade question. In this case, Intuitionism is the most potent predictor of trade opinions, greater in magnitude than either age or ideology.

In sum, nationalism and nativism are popular sentiments in the United States, and especially so among those with an Intuitionist worldview. Intuitionists are more likely to view "being American" as an important part of their identity and to fly the American flag. They also have a more negative view of immigrants and take a more strident view of immigration policy. Finally, they are more skeptical about the benefits of free-trade policies, believing that such policies are harmful to ordinary Americans. In this profile, they resemble political conservatives, who tend to share these sentiments. But once again, it's worth remembering here what the Intuitionism scale is measuring—pessimism, apprehension, and sensitivity to metaphors and symbols. None of its questions are ostensibly political, yet nevertheless are quite predictive of some strong political opinions. This suggests that once again, many political beliefs are rooted in an Intuitionist worldview, the same type of worldview that predicts magical beliefs, opinions on abortion and defense spending, and an adherence to conspiracy theories and populist rhetoric. Nativism aligns with these opinions because it too draws from our intuitive proclivities for understanding the world.

Conclusion

American ethnocentric attitudes arise from a rather self-evident fact: politics in the modern United States are quite complex. America's political institutions are vast and multilayered, and its political constituencies innumerable and convoluted. Its social divisions are intricate and ephemeral. And all this exists amid an increasingly interconnected global sphere in which dizzying technological advances and economic changes are constantly shifting the political order. These factors make politics a challenge for any American to comprehend. Given this, it's not surprising that people often revert to habitual and easy strategies for making sense of it all. Whether these strategies are perceiving events in terms of biblical prophecy or suspecting that hidden elites are weaving dastardly plots, our intuitions steer us toward explanations that comport with our innate ways of making judgments.

As with conspiracism and populism, nativism and ethnocentrism are yet other manifestations of this Intuitionist worldview. In searching for explanations to complex social and political problems, it's easy to fall back on a deeply ingrained mental habit to view the world as a dichotomous struggle between "us" and "them." Ethnocentrism not only justifies our apprehensions, it makes these feelings intelligible. By this reckoning, problems are occurring because some other group is making claims on what is rightfully "ours." Any kind of social problem can now be attributed to "their" illegitimate and reprehensible contrivances. For Intuitionists, an ethnocentric explanation is something that accords with their other magical and fantastical beliefs.

This doesn't necessarily mean that Intuitionists are uniformly more racist or bigoted. Our social identities are complicated and temporal. A person may identify strongly as Jewish in one time and place, as Republican in another, as white in still another, and as an American somewhere else. The power of the Intuitionism scale for predicting an ethnocentric attitude depends a great deal on the type of social identity being measured. This scale is a stable and powerful predictor of nationalism and nativist sentiments, because these sentiments are less controversial. Identifying as an "American" is not only easy, it's often celebrated as an indication of one's patriotism. Identifying as "white," on the other hand, is far more complicated. It involves a far greater range of complex factors that themselves are highly politicized. Not surprisingly, the Intuitionism scale is a less potent predictor of white ethnocentrism than other factors like ideology. In the United States, race politics and "whiteness" are issues far more polarizing than those concerning immigration reform and nationalism. Democrats are happy to wrap themselves in the flag, and many Republicans welcome some type of immigration reform; but such differences aren't evident when it comes to claims of racial grievance. Thus, even as Intuitionism has become more aligned with the political Right and the Right has become ever more racially conservative, the links between intuitive thinking and racial identity become even more confounded.

CHAPTER SEVEN

Scary Foods and Dangerous Medicine

In July of 2015, headlines around the country trumpeted alarming news: a woman in Washington State died of measles! Now, at almost any other point in history, this event probably wouldn't have been newsworthy. Until quite recently, deaths from measles were commonplace. But these days, Americans don't seem to be dying from measles anymore. Between 2005 and 2015, not a single measles-related death was confirmed in the United States.[1] In fact, in 2003 the Centers for Disease Control and Prevention declared that measles had been "eliminated" in America. Yet in the past few years, the disease has begun to reemerge. This is largely attributable to one of the most inexplicable and bizarre developments in the contemporary United States: people have stopped vaccinating their children.[2]

Of all the instances of magical thinking discussed in this book, perhaps none is more striking than opposition to vaccinations. Few things in modern times have made a more demonstrable improvement to our lives than vaccines. For centuries, smallpox, influenza, and polio ravaged human populations, killing and crippling hundreds of millions. Diphtheria, pertussis (whooping cough), measles, and rubella blighted childhood, killing millions more. Today, most of these diseases are either rare or contained.[3] And the primary reason is that vaccines not only protect individuals but prevent the spread of diseases by building "herd immunity" in the entire population. As one might expect, vaccines are often described as the single greatest achievement in public health.[4]

Despite these facts, millions of Americans remain suspicious. Over the past two decades, vaccine refusals have increased dramatically, with hundreds of thousands of parents now keeping their children from many inoculations. We also see this development in public opinion polls: roughly one in five Americans now believes that vaccines cause autism; one in ten thinks that vaccines are more dangerous than the diseases they combat.[5] Most remarkable of all is the fact that those holding such attitudes are often highly educated, liberal people who otherwise believe in scientific evidence about things like global warming or economic policy. From the wealthy enclaves of Los Angeles to the suburbs of Michigan, tens of thousands of affluent parents are delaying or avoiding vaccines for their children, despite any credible evidence of vaccines' harm and overwhelming evidence of their benefits.

Why has this backlash occurred? It's partly the result of our own success. As infectious diseases have become less common, the urgency of childhood inoculation has diminished. When people don't see the effects of infectious diseases, they don't appreciate the risks. But the backlash also comes from the political antics of antivaccine groups. Marshaling a trove of distorted statistics and erroneous claims, these groups have greatly exaggerated the threat of vaccines and mistakenly linked them to everything from allergies to autism spectrum disorder. But most important, the resistance to vaccines is growing because it violates our innate intuitions about what keeps us healthy. The idea of poking a sharp needle in our infants and injecting them with septic materials is unsettling to even the most rational among us. It's far too easy for apprehensive parents to worry about the consequences of injecting their children with a bunch of strange-sounding chemicals.

And this antiscientific backlash is not limited to vaccines. In policies ranging from foods containing genetically modified organisms (GMOs) to alternative medicine, millions of Americans are rejecting the evidence of well-established science in favor of ideas that have no empirical evidence. Many not only remain skeptical of modern medicine but entertain all kinds of fantastical notions about their health and diet. In 2016, Americans spent over $30 billion annually on "complementary health approaches," namely dietary supplements and herbal remedies.[6] Millions more engaged in alternative health practices ranging from acupuncture to homeopathy. And still millions more bought organic or gluten-free foods.[7] Governments across the nation, from small towns to Congress, are entertaining policy proposals that contravene evidence-based approaches to health and medicine.

Debates over these food and health issues are yet another example of how intuitions shape US politics. From GMOs to vaccines, many political arguments about nutrition, medicine, and health are based more on emotions and symbols than reason and fact. In this way, Americans' attitudes about alternative health practices are shaped by the same forces underlying other magical beliefs. Whether it's Donald Trump tweeting about vaccines or a fundamentalist Christian hawking dietary supplements, Americans who believe in supernatural myths or conspiracy theories are also drawn to alternative medicine or express apprehension over nonorganic food because these evoke the same patterns of judgment.

Everything Gives You Cancer

Few things cause us as much apprehension as threats to our health. Whenever we sense some toxin, disease, or sickness around us, our fear quickly rises. This emotional sensitivity has deep biological roots. Eons ago, our earliest vertebrate ancestors evolved flight responses precisely to keep themselves safe from danger.[8] As their descendants developed more complexity, they also became increasingly sensitive to all manner of environmental threats. Hominid species, in particular, developed highly acute fear responses.[9] Early humans were afraid not only of natural threats like predators, floods, and wildfires, but also of darkness, poisons, disease, and strangers.

In our evolutionary past, this penchant for fear was appropriate. Early humans saw only those threats that were close by. In a time of predators, natural disasters, and warring tribes, their apprehensions were highly adaptive to their surroundings. But today our fear responses are largely out of proportion to reality. This is the paradox of living in an information era. On the one hand, we are constantly assailed by alarms of looming catastrophe. The news is filled with threatening stories about adverse health correlates involving food, homes, cars, electronics, and seemingly every other aspect of modern life. These are typically combined with sensationalist stories of crime, mass shootings, child abductions, and other atrocities. Piling on are constant reports about global warming, terrorism, disease outbreaks, and geopolitical tension. Today's media bombards our mammalian brains with a very strong signal: *the world is a very dangerous place.*

Ironically, the world has never been safer. Across the globe, deaths from war, disease, famine, and natural disasters are at all-time lows. Americans are living longer and healthier lives than at any time in history. Rates of many chronic diseases are in fast decline: deaths from cancer, heart disease, and stroke are decreasing, and occurring much later in life.[10] Crime is at its lowest point in fifty years. The same improved outlooks are also happening with children. Since 1990, the mortality rate for children in the United States has declined by nearly half. Childhood abductions and pedestrian fatalities, two of parents' biggest fears, have also declined nearly as much (although these have always been rarer than people assume). If you are between five and fourteen years old in America today, you have only a seventeen in one hundred thousand chance of dying in any given year.[11]

Nearly all these gains are due to science. In medicine, vaccines and antibiotics have greatly reduced deaths from infectious diseases. In public health, malaria eradication, campaigns against smoking, and improvements in water and sanitation have saved millions more. In public policy, consumer and workplace regulations as well as better health, police, and food policies have also made a big impact. Americans have safer foods, safer cars, safer streets, and safer lives. These advances come from a Rationalist, empirical approach to solving problems. Yet Americans often fail to appreciate these facts. Millions not only live in a heightened state of apprehension but reject the very scientific approaches securing their well-being.

Why is this the case? Factors mentioned earlier in the book are partly to blame. Science is not the only worldview in our culture, and some of its competitors are quite fierce. Fundamentalist Christians, for example, often reject basic scientific claims about evolution as heretical anathema. The food and health industries have many competing industries that are eager to demonize their market competitors. Nor does science have a spotless history. Over the centuries, scientists have made erroneous or false claims, or have engaged in grossly unethical behaviors (for example, the Tuskegee syphilis experiment).[12] Many people view these past sins as a rationale for rejecting scientific methods entirely.

But the biggest reason people reject science lies with the counterintuitive nature of science itself. Science, the systematic building and testing of theories about the universe, is a relatively recent invention. Premodern cultures usually explained the functioning of the universe through myths, stories, and supernatural phenomena. Although some rudimentary scientific methods emerged during antiquity, a self-conscious method of systematically formulating and testing hypotheses took form only during the Enlightenment. And for all its dazzling achievements, our science is still primitive.

Take the science of medicine and health. Modern medicine as we know it is less than a hundred years old. We discovered the underlying mechanisms behind vaccines only in the 1910s, antibiotics in the 1930s, and the molecular structure of DNA in the 1950s. We still don't understand a great deal about chronic conditions like obesity, diabetes, cancer, and Alzheimer's disease, much less basic issues of nutrition. As a result, modern medicine is far from foolproof. Today's physicians often make incorrect diagnoses, and medicine often reverses itself on everything from medical treatments to cancer screenings. Even more confounding is how many medical reversals occur with treatments that make the most scientific sense. As Drs. Vinayak Prasad and Adam Cifu note, "The human body is so complicated, and our understanding of it so superficial, that what we believe should work often does not."[13]

The contingent nature of science and medicine leaves them ill-suited to serve our emotional needs, particularly in the terrifying specter of a health threat. As noted earlier, when we are afraid, we are highly motivated to make our uncomfortable feelings go away. Compressed in this apprehensive state, we don't necessarily want the right answer—we want the most comforting one. Science may provide many things, but it rarely offers the reassurance our anxiety craves. Most scientific models deal only in probabilities and not certitudes. Science can tell us about only the chances of diseases, death, or other catastrophes, not when and where they will occur. Medicine can give us only an approximate diagnosis and not always the correct one. Science also cannot validate our egocentric longings for immortality or our constant need for reassurance. From its cold, analytic perspective, science views human existence as simply another incarnation of a self-generating chemical reaction. All the grandiose importance we convey to our lives is a delusion. Disease and death can happen randomly and at any time.

Given the emotional potency of illness and the limitations of medicine, it's not surprising that people have long fallen for magical claims regarding sickness and health. From witch doctors to snake oil salesmen, from elixirs to medicine dances, humans have invented innumerable types of magic to combat illness and restore health. These magical remedies tend to follow the "grammar" of magical thinking outlined in chapter 1: they are informed by fear and apprehension, they invoke contagion and representativeness heuristics, they focus on recent events rather than long-term trends, and they tend to anthropomorphize the forces of nature. And it's these same intuitive tendencies that underlie much of the antiscientific movements related to food and health in America today. Nearly all the resistance to science, medicine, and food production is centered not in rational concerns but in gut feelings. To get a better sense of this, let us take a closer look at a few examples.

Vaccines

Ever since Europeans and Americans began inoculating themselves against smallpox in the early eighteenth century, vaccines have had their opponents. At a commonsense level, this is quite understandable. The very idea of exposing oneself to a disease (especially via the septic pus of an infected cow) is completely contrary to our intuitive response, which is to get away as quickly as possible. Even with the great success of Edward Jenner's smallpox vaccine in the early 1800s, critics and opponents remained. Their early fears weren't completely unfounded. Compared with the products of today's pristine laboratories, the first vaccines sometimes were contaminated with other diseases. Nor were early vaccines always completely effective. Even today, vaccines can only reduce one's risk of infection, not eliminate it entirely. This is why "herd immunity" is so important—the greater the percentage of vaccinated people in a population, the less likely someone is to get the disease, even if that individual has been vaccinated as well.[14]

But the biggest historical complaint about vaccines was simply that they *seemed* like a repulsive, unnatural intrusion into our bodies. People disliked vaccines because *the very idea* of the vaccine just didn't feel right. A poignant example of this last sentiment can be found in a 1907 speech published by John Pitcairn, a Pittsburgh industrialist and antivaccine crusader:

> The vaccinists [*sic*] tell us that the injection of the matter from the putrid sore of a diseased calf will set up a chemical action that will increase the white blood corpuscles and thus the resisting power of the blood itself. The sacred blood of a healthy person, as God made it, is not good enough for them. They seek to interfere with Nature's laboratory which the Creator gives to a healthy child! With their man-made science, they would improve upon God's handiwork. The mere statement of this presumptuous claim is enough to lead the man of common sense to bring vaccination into question. . . . Can it be right to pollute the human blood? Does it agree with the dictates of good, plain common sense?[15]

This same type of rationale underlies today's antivaccine movement. Although vaccine opponents offer an array of "evidence" to show that vaccines are either ineffective or harmful, such claims are without merit. For example, one common trope among antivaccinators is that vaccines hold "dangerous" chemicals like thimerosal. Twenty years ago, vaccines contained thimerosal as a preservative until, ironically, health officials removed it out of concern that it would deter people from getting inoculations. Although thimerosal contains trace amounts of mercury, there was never any evidence that thimerosal had any negative health impacts. Despite many lawsuits and extensive research, no one has conclusively established a causal link between thimerosal or any chemical preservative in vaccines and autism. Nevertheless, antivaccine activists continue to insist that one exists, and that chemicals in vaccines are causing unhealthy effects.[16]

Why do antivaccine campaigners continue to resist the scientific evidence? The answer is largely psychological. Vaccines represent a perfect storm of elements that entice magical thinking: contemporary parents' intense fear for their children's health and future; the inexplicable origins of autism spectrum disorder and many other childhood maladies; growing suspicion over the financial and political machinations of the pharmaceutical industry; and the powerful symbolism of the vaccines (that is, painfully injecting a foreign compound into a new baby). Absent a clear measles or polio threat, many parents feel little urgency to get their child vaccinated, particularly in comparison with the highly negative symbolic power of the vaccine itself. They comprehend vaccines not through their reason but through their intuitions.

We can see the intuitive power of the antivaccine movement in any of its proponents. Consider, for example, an excerpt from an e-mail that was widely distributed by a mother in California. In the fall of 2014, she was lobbying against a bill that would eliminate vaccine exemptions. While she claimed that this bill would intrude on her right not to vaccinate her children, her opposition to vaccines ultimately boiled down to her own personal experience:

On December 10, 2012, less than 6 weeks after he was born, Sebastian was given the Hepatitis B vaccine. He screamed during and after the shot but seemed to calm down after a nursing session. For the next 24 hours he was not our happy smiling baby. He was cranky and very lethargic. Within days he had developed a cough and one night he started coughing so hard he was having trouble catching his breath. We called CPMC emergency and they said to bring him in immediately. He was diagnosed with a respiratory illness. We were new parents and scared to death. They explained the treatment and thankfully he recovered within a week *but we didn't*. We had no idea at the time that respiratory illnesses were a side effect of vaccines.[17]

This brief testimony encapsulates the real power of the antivaccine campaign: the anxieties of new parents, the trauma of seeing one's infant get a shot, and the association between the vaccine and any subsequent adverse behaviors. This parent never mentions all the other times that Sebastian might have been cranky and lethargic. Nor is there any notion that respiratory illnesses typically come from viruses, which can be picked up anywhere. Rather, this parent evaluates all negative behaviors of her child relative to the vaccine. Given the fact that dozens of health problems are listed as possible side effects of the hepatitis B vaccine, it's easy for a parent to attribute anything from a cold to a rash as a postvaccine reaction. And even though her child is fine, this parent continues to hold on to the idea that the vaccine was a poison.

Our innate tendency to link proximate events (that is, the availability heuristic) is nowhere more pronounced than in the putative link between autism and vaccines. At one level, it's easy to sympathize with the parents who think that vaccines caused their child's disorder. Autism spectrum disorder (ASD) is an extremely challenging condition. Although much scientific progress is being made, we still know relatively little about what specifically causes ASD or how it can be prevented. For parents who suddenly find their child withdrawing or engaging in odd or antisocial behaviors, feelings of bewilderment and anguish are understandable. In trying to comprehend why their seemingly normal infant has changed, their intuitions direct them to proximate causes. Since ASD often becomes manifest around the age of two years, roughly the same age that the MMR vaccine gets administered to children, it's understandable that parents could connect the two.[18] And when a seeming expert like Andrew Wakefield not only publishes fraudulent claims about the links between vaccines and autism but actively promotes this idea to parents, it's easy to see how parents would try to rationalize their anguish.[19]

The tenacity of the antivaccine movement, despite all the scientific evidence of vaccine safety and the discrediting of Wakefield's claims, also speaks to the power of intuition and the stickiness of magical beliefs. As noted in chapter 1, because magical beliefs ultimately serve emotional needs, they often become integral to a person's emotional stability. People will persevere in their delusions, because these ensure a homeostatic set point. They become like weights at either end of a seesaw, helping to keep it in balance. Few people may be willing to endure the emotional costs of abandoning their prejudices, particularly when such prejudices are what provide a coherent and intuitively compelling picture of the world. Our magical beliefs are sticky precisely because they keep us steady.

Genetically Modified Foods

A similar type of impulse informs opposition to genetically modified foods. Genetically modified organisms (GMOs) are agricultural products whose genetic code has been deliberately manipulated in a laboratory by splicing genes from other species. Over the past two decades, GMOs have become increasingly prevalent in agriculture (mostly in maize, soy, cotton, and rapeseed). These new strains are typically more resistant to pests, are more tolerant of adverse environmental conditions, and produce greater yields. Proponents of GMOs see them as a way of improving nutrition, tackling hunger, and reducing pesticide use around the world. But GMOs also elicit a lot of concern and political activity. According to opinion polls, only 37 percent of Americans think GMOs are safe (unlike 88 percent of scientists).[20] Opponents of GMOs are lobbying for everything from food labeling disclosing GMO content to outright bans. Grocery stores like Whole Foods and Trader Joe's are replacing or eliminating foods with GMOs from their shelves. In July 2016, the federal government passed legislation requiring GMO labeling, partly to preempt strident labeling requirements already passed in states like Vermont.[21]

Although there are some legitimate concerns about the impact of GMOs on local agricultural economies, these are not typically the arguments marshaled by opponents. The American public doesn't really consider questions of monoculture or the economic vulnerabilities of South Asian farmers. Rather, American opposition to GMOs comes from intuitive fears of contamination and fears of corporate power. Consider the following excerpt from "What's Wrong with Genetic Engineering?" on the website of the environmental organization Greenpeace:

> Genetic engineering enables scientists to create plants, animals and micro-organisms by manipulating genes in a way *that does not occur naturally*.

> These genetically modified organisms (GMOs) *can spread* through *nature* and interbreed with *natural organisms*, thereby *contaminating* non "GE" environments and future generations in an unforeseeable and uncontrollable way.

> Their release is "genetic pollution" and is a major threat because GMOs cannot be recalled once released into the environment.

> Because of commercial interests, the public is being denied the right to know

about GE ingredients in the food chain, and therefore losing the right to avoid them despite the presence of labelling laws in certain countries.[22]

Ironically, Greenpeace, an organization that uses science in its campaigns against global warming, offers no scientific rationale against GMOs. This is because the scientific consensus is that GMOs are safe for consumption. It's just as likely that GMOs could offer more environmental benefits than costs. Instead, Greenpeace's campaign is based largely on irrational apprehensions and intuitions. GMOs are depicted as being like pollutants, ready to spread and contaminate pristine environments—a common trope in other magical beliefs. In evoking the populism we saw in chapter 5, Greenpeace says that GMOs come from "commercial interests" that it characterizes as infringing on the public's right. But most notably, Greenpeace repeatedly uses the term *natural* without specifying what it means. This makes a rather arbitrary distinction that organisms coming from either crossbreeding or selective breeding (which is true of nearly all the food we grow and eat) are somehow "more natural" than organisms whose genes are specifically altered in a lab.

There is, however, no scientific basis for this distinction. Genes are merely collections of nucleic acids composed of the same four nucleobases, regardless of the species they are in. Most plant and animal families share enormous percentages of the same genes. Indeed, there is little difference in the 70 percent of genes that humans share with tapeworms.[23] Genetic differences between species are usually just ones of elaboration. The notion that the genomes of different species are somehow sacrosanct and immutable is one without any clear scientific rationale.

Greenpeace's preoccupation with "naturalness" is based not on science but on our intuitive concerns. One of these goes back to the representativeness heuristic and how we understand categories of objects. Philosopher Stefaan Blancke argues that we intuitively equate an organism's DNA with its essence, "an unobservable and immutable core that causes the organism's behavior and development and determines its identity."[24] This psychological essentialism, our tendency to conflate mental categories with underlying realities, is a trait that appears early in life. When children think that fathers can't be ballet dancers or mothers can't be firefighters, it's because they are relying on this intuitive tendency to think that categories of things are sacrosanct.[25]

GMOs violate this intuitive tendency toward essentialism. Mixing the genes of species violates our essentialist norms and gives rise to images of

"Frankenfoods," natural abominations that seem repulsive and disgusting. Moreover, the Frankenfood image conjures not just a monstrosity but something that rampages out of control. The fear behind GMOs is that they will "escape" the areas where they are planted, displacing indigenous plants and ruining entire ecosystems.[26] To the extent that a person anthropomorphizes nature, this intrusion seems like introducing a disease. To the Intuitionist, a GMO is not simply an ecological atrocity but a defilement of some type of imaginary Eden. GMOs trigger not only our representativeness heuristics but our contagion fears as well. Like vaccines, they seem alien and threatening, something that violates our basic notions of what is natural and thus good.

Natural Foods

The preoccupation with naturalness and purity in the food supply does not stop with GMOs. In fact, it predates it. Since the beginning of recorded history, humans have invoked all types of taboos and magical beliefs about what they eat, often stemming from concerns of purity and cleanliness, but also notions of power and virility.[27] Examples range from food restrictions listed in the Bible to the appetite for tiger penises and rhino horns in China.[28] Although these notions sometimes have practical concerns (for example, Hindu prohibitions on beef originate in the importance of cow dung as a source of fuel and fertilization), often they serve largely spiritual or magical functions.[29] Regardless of their sources, however, humans' food-related taboos and fetishes are rarely based on any scientific understanding of health and nutrition. Instead, our ideas about food are largely informed by the same magical, intuitive processes that arise whenever we face uncertainty.

In contemporary America, one of the most common instances of magical thinking about food is the preoccupation with the "naturalness" of food products and a phobia of anything "chemical." This development started in the 1960s, after the publication of Rachel Carson's *Silent Spring*. Carson's exposé of the harmful environmental effects of the insecticide DDT made Americans increasingly wary of the effects of chemicals in their foods.[30] This fear was compounded by the expansion of laboratory testing for carcinogens. As the public heard about a slew of unfamiliar-sounding chemicals that were giving lab rats cancer, fears of chemicals in the food supply began to increase.[31]

One of the earliest examples of this chemophobia involved monosodium glutamate (MSG). The public concern about MSG arose not from any scientific tests or major laboratory findings but rather from a single letter to the *New England Journal of Medicine* from a physician speculating on his own adverse reaction to eating in a Chinese restaurant.[32] This prompted a wave of other letters reporting similarly adverse effects. "Chinese Restaurant Syndrome" suddenly became perceived as a real medical phenomenon, and the likely culprit was a chemical pervasive in Asian seasoning: MSG. The fight against this additive was soon taken up by consumer advocate Ralph Nader, who lobbied to have it removed from all types of food products.[33] Upon hearing that MSG was bad, millions of other Americans began claiming all types of adverse reactions to it. Since then, MSG has become a chemical pariah, the target of all types of invectives from natural food groups.

The problem, however, is that the scientific evidence against MSG is negligible. For starters, it's naturally present in many foods. Despite its foreign-sounding name, it's a natural ingredient in everything from tomatoes to cheese. The MSG commonly used in the food additive is extracted from seaweed. Moreover, MSG has not been shown to be harmful. Following a review of the clinical evidence, the Food and Drug Administration has recognized it as safe.[34] Most of the adverse reactions to MSG appear to be psychological rather than physiological in origin.[35] Nevertheless, large percentages of Americans continue to think that it is dangerous. As writer Alan Levinovitz points out, "When it comes to food sensitivities, people are incredibly unwilling to question self-diagnoses."[36]

Indeed, since the 1960s, America's anxiety about chemical additives and contaminants has only grown. Our culture is filled with books, news items, magazines, websites, and companies dedicated to the advancement of "natural" foods and the demonization of chemicals. Although sometimes these concerns are grounded in scientific evidence—some contaminants, like mercury, lead, and arsenic, are truly harmful—more often they simply reflect intuitive processes common to most magical beliefs: they deal with a subject of great uncertainty (nutrition); they amplify feelings of apprehension by highlighting indeterminate threats (cancer, aging, and disease); and they rely on intuitive heuristics to frame how the topic is understood.

One of the most common heuristics is found in the common refrain that "we are what we eat." This cliché does more than simply equate healthy eating with healthy living; it actually reflects a long-held magical belief that by ingesting a substance, we incorporate its metaphysical essence into

ourselves. When cannibalistic cultures (or Roman Catholics for that matter) think that by ingesting the body of another they will be imbued with
its powers or holiness, a representativeness heuristic is at work. The same
holds today. When people look to eat "natural" foods, their intuition is that
such foods will transfer their core goodness, making those who eat them
feel better, live longer, seem younger, and so on. People think that organic
foods taste better or that raw milk is healthier precisely because they understand the world by links of association.

The converse of this is the contagion heuristic: things with negative connotations, especially chemicals, will impart harmful effects. This heuristic
is commonly associated with not only fad diets and health cleanses but
many public health crusades. A glaring example can be found in the popular blog of activist Vani Hari, the self-proclaimed "Food Babe."[37] Hari has
gained a wide following by trumpeting the dangers of chemicals in various
food products. Her website boldly announces that she's "hot on the trail
to investigate what's really in your food." One of her common strategies is
to identify an ominous-sounding chemical in a packaged food, show how
that same chemical is also found in a very unpalatable substance (a rubber
shoe or coal tar), and then conclude that this link demonstrates how the
food is harmful.

One of Hari's most famous efforts was a massive petition drive aimed at the
Subway sandwich chain to remove azodicarbonamide from its bread.[38] Why
did she target this chemical? Beyond its daunting name, azodicarbonamide
does hold a danger: if, in its raw form, it's inhaled in large amounts, it can
cause respiratory problems, which is why it is banned in Europe as a blow-
ing agent in manufacturing plastics. But it wasn't the health of bread makers
that motivated the "Food Babe." Nor was it because azodicarbonamide has
had any negative health effects among Subway's sandwich eaters—the Food
and Drug Administration hasn't found any harmful effects from consuming
the trace amounts found in bread (it breaks down upon baking).[39] Rather,
Hari was able to mobilize support by noting that azodicarbonamide is also
used in other foam products such as yoga mats. And this was the big selling point. After all, who wants "the yoga mat chemical" in their bread? By
Hari's logic, if a chemical is found in something unpalatable or could have
some noxious alternative functions, it should never be in a food—even if
that same chemical is a natural substance. When it comes to elements in
food, guilt by association is all the proof that she requires.

A similar type of magical thinking occurs with many contemporary
diet plans. In the past several decades, Americans have witnessed the rise
and fall of a wide range of health fads. Although these may take aim at a

wide array of problematic targets (fat, saturated fat, wheat, sugar, meat, and so on), they typically share the same formula. First, the author of the plan offers his own story of salvation—a time of struggle typically followed by a moment of enlightenment in which the truth to healthy eating is discovered. Then, he follows a stock formula: identify the problematic food group, speculate on a long list of health woes and problems that come from its consumption, invoke some scientific-sounding terms to bolster his claim, and offer a diet plan that avoids this type of food, usually accompanied by the idea of a "detox" period.[40]

This pattern is similar to the one associated with superstitious and supernatural beliefs. The implicit notion is that our heavy weight or ill health reflects some "sinful" behavior, in this case the consumption of an impure contaminant (be it sugar, salt, butter, or bread). Henceforth, consumption of this food item becomes taboo. By avoiding the taboo food, the body begins to "cleanse." In turn, the dieter offers a type of nutritional atonement and will find redemption through the sacrifice of the diet. As writer Malcolm Gladwell observes, "In conception and execution, diet books are self-consciously theological. It is the appropriation of this religious narrative that permits the suspension of disbelief."[41]

A poignant example of this monological thinking is the current popularity of gluten-free diets. In our surveys, roughly a third of Americans agree with the notion that eliminating gluten from their diet will make them healthy. But less than one percent of the population suffers from celiac disease, so this widespread aversion to gluten is not based on medical evidence.[42] Rather, the antigluten sentiment stems from the popularity of best-selling diet books like Dr. William Davis's *Wheat Belly* or Dr. David Perlmutter's *Grain Brain*. By the reckoning of their authors, grains containing gluten cause an extensive list of health ailments ranging from autism to cancer to heart disease. Echoing populist and conspiratorial sentiments, these diet books implicate the food industry, mainstream medicine, and the government in cover-ups to hide the truth about the dangers of carbohydrates. They also invoke a nostalgic romanticization of a long-ago time when one's grandparents were thin, healthy, and happy.[43] Building on these messages are the entrepreneurial food makers who produce all types of gluten-free products, thereby helping to reinforce the notion that gluten must be avoided.

Ultimately, this magical thinking about food arises from the fact that the science of health and nutrition is still very indeterminate. For all the clinical trials comparing low-carb with low-fat diets, for all the hundreds of millions of dollars spent tracking the eating patterns of nurses in

Framingham, Massachusetts, and other locales, and for all the billions of dollars invested by the National Institutes of Health on nutritional studies, our scientific knowledge regarding the health impact of diets remains fuzzy. Beyond the age-old adage of "eat more vegetables," little scientific consensus exists concerning what makes a healthy diet, largely because there's probably no such thing as a single healthy diet. Consuming nothing but ice cream, cheesesteaks, Doritos, and soda is clearly not a pathway to health, but it's unlikely that eliminating just salt or sugar or wheat or fat is by itself a miracle cure. Nevertheless, for someone in the grips of apprehension or self-doubt, the powerful lure of the fix-all diet plan remains, largely because the snake oil sales pitch resonates so deeply with our instinctive ways of understanding the world. And if this is the case with diets, it's triply so when it comes to medicine.

Snake Oil and Alternative Medicine

If humans have a long history of following fad diets, they have an even longer history of following unscientific health remedies. Every culture has some type of "folk" or superstitious practice said to cure illness or disease.[44] The overwhelming majority of these practices are based not in any type of medical science (which simply didn't exist for most cultures) but rather in some magical notions of spirits, elixirs, or charms. These types of practices continue today. Even in the United States, with its very advanced science, "alternative" medicine continues to be quite popular and pervasive. Americans spend tens of billions of dollars on nonscientific medical cures ranging from acupuncture to vitalism.[45]

But even though alternative medicine continues to be widely popular, it's highly contentious. Traditional practitioners of medicine criticize the wide array of treatments that fall under the alternative medicine umbrella, because these haven't been subject to scientific scrutiny.[46] Support for alternative medicine is typically anecdotal and not published in peer-reviewed scientific journals. Without such testing, the claims of alternative medicine are unverifiable. Proponents of alternative medicine counter that traditional medicine itself is often untested, anecdotal, or subject to reversal.[47] They argue that Western medicine doesn't embrace the "holistic" approach to health taken by non-Western cultures. They claim that even if there is no scientific backing for some alternative medicines, merely their placebo effect is sufficient to justify their usage.[48]

In truth, the real function of alternative medicines, like other magical beliefs, is as an emotional palliative. They function to make patients *feel* better, even if they have no direct effects on the ailments they are claimed to target. Perhaps this alone will produce some benefits—it seems likely that a rested, emotionally balanced patient will recover faster than an agitated, apprehensive one. But this is also like saying that a baseball player who wears a lucky necklace will hit better than he would without it. The real power of alternative medicines lies in how they resonate with our intuitions. And they do so largely by tapping into the same heuristics undergirding all our magical beliefs.

Consider homeopathy. At its core, homeopathy is literally a representativeness heuristic. Founded in 1796 by Samuel Hahneman, it is based on the idea that "like cures like." In other words, any substance causing the symptoms of a disease in a healthy person can, if given in very small doses, cure that same disease in a sick one. Drawing from the self-described "law of infinitesimal doses," homeopaths dilute plant, animal, and mineral substances in water or alcohol in tiny doses and then administer these doses at regular intervals (typically in small pellets). In other words, if I have a rash, homeopathy suggests that I can cure this rash by ingesting infinitesimally small doses of poison ivy.[49]

In reality, this homeopathic approach violates many established theories of science: its medicines typically contain no molecules of the original substance in diluted form, it lacks any biologically plausible mechanism, and it does not accord with basic laws of chemistry. At their core, homeopathic remedies are nothing more than sugar pills. Nevertheless, Americans spend over $2.5 billion annually on homeopathic remedies. Part of the popularity may be due to the attention patients receive from the homeopathic doctor—homeopathic consultations are typically quite lengthy and involve a great deal of discussion between patient and practitioner. But most important, homeopathic medicine appeals to our intuitions. We believe in it because we deeply believe that like equals like. This same tendency is evident in modern magical beliefs. When Wiccans use the ideas that the color gold can impart financial success or that sage can promote wisdom, they are invoking the very same psychological predilections that make homeopathic cures seem effective.[50]

The biggest appeal of alternative medicines is that they are somehow more "natural" than synthesized ones. As with vaccines and GMOs, this presumption is based on the power of the contagion heuristic. Because they are manufactured in a laboratory, traditional medicines seem somehow less "natural" than medicines made from harvested plants. This apprehension of manufacturing often gets infused with populist prejudice: pharmaceutical companies are typically viewed with conspiratorial disdain, as they produce synthetic compounds that violate the body's natural functioning, all in the name of corporate profits. So instead of choosing medicines that have undergone many clinical trials, many people will choose the various herbal or mineral remedies because they are free from human investment. The vast array of natural remedies (what some people jokingly call "the Middle of Whole Foods") exists largely because of this prejudice. From a biological standpoint, the cells in our bodies don't "know" and can't distinguish whether a palliative chemical comes from a hand-tended, organic sage plant or a compound synthesized in a lab. When it comes to medicine, natural is a category that is subjectively and capriciously applied.

Nevertheless, our biases toward "natural" are strong, and adherents of natural medicine are often vulnerable to swindle. Much of the rhetoric surrounding natural medicines echoes the type of carnival barking common in traveling medicine shows of the nineteenth century. Consider the promotion of dandelions from the website naturalremedies.org:

> Dandelion herb has been associated with improving liver function and liver diseases such as hepatitis and jaundice. It has been shown to improve both constipation and diarrhea. It purifies the blood, cleanses the digestive system, removes heavy metals from body tissues, and can help dissolve kidney stones. It has been shown to help weight loss, cure acne, lower high blood pressure, cure anemia, lower serum cholesterol levels, reduce acid indigestion and gas, improve some cancers, and help control diabetes all with no negative side effects. The dandelion herb is full of so many vitamins, minerals and micronutrients that alone might be the reason it is so beneficial in so many different areas.[51]

Given these many benefits, it's hard to believe that we're not all grazing voraciously on our front yards. But what's really going on in this promotion is its symbolizing the product. As with the advocacy for so many other natural medicines, the emphasis here is on the removal of taboo or foreign substances: the "purification" of blood, the "cleansing" of the digestive tract, and the "detoxification" of heavy metals.

Scientific trials of alternative medicines like dandelion roots have revealed few tangible benefits that cannot be attributed to either placebo effects or spontaneous recovery. After twenty years and over $2 billion in grants, the National Center for Complementary and Integrative Health, an agency founded to extol the benefits of alternative medicines, has yet to find any demonstrable benefits from herbal remedies. Much of this research is based on highly questionable assumptions to begin with.[52] The real reason the US government spends so much money funding such questionable research is because members of Congress who partake in magical thinking, like former Iowa senator Tom Harkin, are convinced of its efficacy.[53] They want the NCCIH to validate their firmly held convictions that alternative medicines are effective, regardless of whether science is actually behind them.

This leads us to the third way that natural medicines seem to have a powerful hold on the American public: the availability heuristic. Most testimonies about the benefits of alternative medicine come from people who have experienced relief from some ailment after an alternative treatment. Often, advocates claim that after finding no help from traditional medicine, the alternative treatment offered real benefits. What they fail to appreciate is that perhaps the treatment was either entirely psychological or simply coincidental to any inevitable healing. As with vaccines, the adherence to natural medicine comes mostly from its emotional functions rather than its physiological benefits.

The Intuitive Sources of American Health Attitudes

In reviewing the antiscientific movements concerning health and diet, similar themes are apparent: the preoccupation with "naturalness"; the populist and conspiratorial suspicions about agribusiness, pharmaceutical companies, and government health agencies; and the heavy reliance on heuristics for making judgments about the world. These tendencies, however, aren't only in the anecdotes given above but also in the attitudes of the population at large. We can see this in our survey data. In two nationally representative survey samples in 2013 and 2015, we started with some questions about Americans' attitudes toward alternative medicine.[54] These questions covered the efficacy of alternative medicines as well as opinions on issues like gluten, GMOs, and vaccines. The results are listed in figure 7.1.

Americans are enthusiastic supporters of alternative medicine and natural foods. For example, over half the public think that herbal remedies and positive thinking can heal illness, and over 40 percent think that acupuncture and homeopathy are effective healing techniques. Roughly

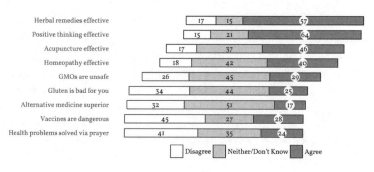

FIGURE 7.1. Attitudes toward alternative medicine and health.

25 percent think that vaccines are dangerous, that eliminating gluten will make you healthier, or that many health problems can be solved by prayer. Roughly three in ten Americans think that GMOs should be banned, and 17 percent think that alternative medicine is actually superior to Western medicine. Even more telling are the high percentages of Americans who have no opinion on these same issues. Roughly half the public don't know whether GMOs should be banned, whether gluten is bad for you, or whether alternative medicine is better. In fact, the only two issues where anything close to a majority of Americans holds scientifically validated views are vaccines and prayer, but these numbers are still small: only 45 percent of Americans disagree with the idea that vaccines are dangerous, and only 41 percent think that prayer cannot cure disease.

Given this uncertainty and suspicion about health and medicine in contemporary America, it's not surprising that these transgressive ideas are correlated with our other measures of both Intuitionism and other magical beliefs. Figure 7.2 depicts standardized regression coefficients from multivariate regression equations between the Intuitionism scale and health and food attitudes. The standardized coefficients are a way of comparing the size of differences in health attitudes across not just the Intuitionism scale but also the variables controlling for education, age, gender, ideology, and the conspiracism and antiscience scales.

Transgressive attitudes about alternative medicine, vaccines, gluten, and GMOs are all positively related to the Intuitionism scale. As we reported in chapter 4, Americans who think that eliminating gluten will make them healthier or who want to ban GMOs are more likely to be Intuitionists. Intuitionists are also more likely to endorse alternative medicine and reject vaccines. Even more striking are the high correlations between these health attitudes and the conspiracism scale. To put it more bluntly, people who believe that the 2008 recession was part of a secret plot or that a secret cabal controls important events (see chapter 5) are more likely to endorse alternative medicine, reject gluten and GMOs, or think that vaccines are dangerous. Indeed, the differences in health attitudes between people scoring low on the conspiracism scale and those scoring high are greater than for any other predictors in our models.[55]

There are many reasons why Intuitionists are drawn to transgressive health messages. First, as mentioned above, most of the transgressive health beliefs we focus on here invoke the same types of heuristics that are common in magical thinking (that is, vaccines seem dangerous, GMOs are called contagions, natural medicines seem, well, more "natural"). But these intuitive tendencies also get reinforced in other ways. For example, people who hold conspiracist beliefs are far more likely to rely on alternative sources of health information. In the 2013 survey, we asked people where they get their health information. People with lots of conspiracist beliefs are more likely to say that they get information from "alternative health sites" or media stars like Dr. Mehmet Oz or Dr. Andrew Weil. They are less likely to say that they get their information from a physician or a nurse-practitioner.

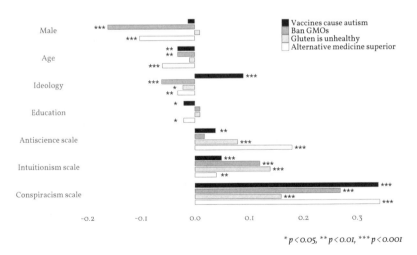

$^*p < 0.05,\ ^{**}p < 0.01,\ ^{***}p < 0.001$

FIGURE 7.2. Predictors of nonscientific beliefs about health and wellness. Bars indicate ordinary least squares regression coefficients.

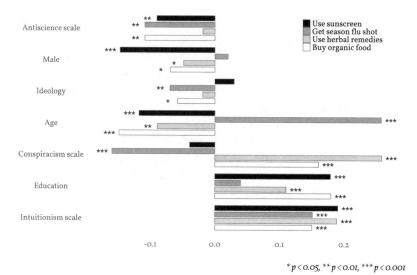

FIGURE 7.3. Predictors of health behaviors. Bars indicate ordinary least squares regression coefficients.

We see a somewhat more complex picture when it comes to predictors of health behaviors (fig. 7.3). In the January 2015 survey, we asked people how often they engage in different health practices. Two of these, using sunscreen and getting an annual flu shot, are well within the parameters of traditional medicine; it would be difficult to find a traditional physician or medical organization that doesn't advocate for both. Two other behaviors, prioritizing organic food and using herbal remedies, are not.

Intuitionists are far more likely to engage in all types of preventative health behaviors, regardless of whether they are traditional or not. As one moves up the Intuitionism scale, respondents are more likely to report buying organic foods and using herbal remedies; but they are also more likely to get flu vaccines or regularly use sunscreen. This relationship may partly be a function of how we measure Intuitionism, especially the apprehension measures. It's not surprising that people who report that they check their locks and wash their hands more frequently are also more likely to report using medicines and sunscreen.

More surprising are the differences among people who hold magical beliefs. As we reported in chapters 3 and 5, Intuitionists are strong believers in conspiracy theories and hold a lot of beliefs that contradict scientific explanations. Yet rather than behaving as Intuitionists, they tend to behave in very different ways. Conspiracists are more likely to embrace nontraditional health behaviors (herbal remedies and organic foods) but less likely to embrace traditional medicines (flu shots and sunscreens). They are highly suspicious of traditional medicine, just as they are more likely to hold nontraditional health beliefs. Meanwhile, people who reject science also report less frequent health practices across the board. In other words, people who reject Darwin's theory of evolution or who think that humans and dinosaurs coexisted are less likely to use sunscreen, get flu shots, buy organic food, or take herbal remedies. Intuitions thus relate to people's health behaviors in multiple and complex ways that vary with other factors and beliefs.

Conclusion

Berkeley, California, isn't the type of place where one finds a lot of support for Donald Trump. This Bay Area enclave of liberalism is the cradle of American hippie culture. In 2016, it gave Trump less than 10 percent of the vote. Nevertheless, there is one thing that many Berkeley residents have in common with the populist president—a suspicion of vaccines. Berkeley schools have some of the lowest vaccination rates in California, and it is not uncommon to find vaccine resisters in its many coffee shops and organic food stores. This sentiment is shared by Donald Trump. In 2014, he tweeted, "Healthy young child goes to doctor, gets pumped with massive shot of many vaccines, doesn't feel good and changes—AUTISM. Many such cases." Later, he clarified: "No more massive injections. Tiny children are not horses—one vaccine at a time, over time." Still later, he tweeted, "Spread them out over a period of time & autism will drop!"

Intuitions can sometimes create very strange political bedfellows. Up until this chapter, we've seen that Intuitionists tend to congregate more on the political Right. The Christian fundamentalism and populism that embody Intuitionist politics are more common among conservatives and Republicans than among liberals and Democrats. But as we move away from questions of policy, populism, and ethnocentrism, we see Intuitionism cutting more broadly across the ideological spectrum. Indeed, most of the activists we mention earlier in this chapter (for example, Greenpeace, Vani Hari) are politically quite liberal. Nevertheless, when it comes to food and medicine, they too engage in the same types of Intuitionism underlying fundamentalists' concerns with abortion or populist conspiracy theories. Much of the antiscience rhetoric about GMOs, vaccines, and alternative medicine not only is quite magical in its ideas of what is "natural" and good for us, but also tends to be quite populist in its suspicion of food manufacturers, doctors, drug companies, and public health agencies.

The interesting question is why issues of health and food are able to transcend ideological boundaries, but issues of sex and death or money and power do not. Partly, this relates to scientific uncertainty. Nutrition and medicine are still nascent fields in which much of the science is unclear. In areas without a clear consensus, there may be less of a scientific elite for Intuitionists to rally against.

But mostly, this relates to America's recent political history. As we'll describe in the conclusion, the confluence of racial and religious politics in the 1960s and 1970s led a lot of Christian conservatives to not only identify themselves as conservative but identify as Republican as well. Similarly, many of the populists that were so enthusiastic for Donald Trump in 2016 might have been drawn to a Democratic candidate if he or she had been able to combine the suspicion of power with a nationalist and anti-elite message. The Republican Party, traditionally the party of big business, has been able to cast itself as a "people's party" by articulating suspicions about cultural elites and embracing a fervent white nationalism. But what neither party has done is to differentiate itself on issues of alternative medicine and organic foods. These intuitive concerns with health and diet are as common among fundamentalist Christians as they are among Berkeley hippies. Without a clear ideological fault line, food and medicine continue to be issues where Intuitionism flowers across the political spectrum.

CHAPTER EIGHT

A Nation Divided by Magic

with Calvin TerBeek

Throughout the long presidential campaign of 2016, America's political elites were desperately trying to comprehend the improbable success of Donald Trump. During the Republican primaries, the greatest confusion was on the Right. As Trump recorded one victory after another, traditional conservatives scrambled for an explanation. Their general conclusion was that the Republican leadership was failing to hear its base. *National Review* columnist Dan McLaughlin offered a common assessment: there was "an overdose of mistrust of Republicans, fed both by the fecklessness of a Beltway GOP and by a talk-radio-led environment in which no charge against Republican leaders was too extreme or hyperbolic."[1] By this reckoning, Trump's success reflected the concerns of "ordinary Americans," who were highly agitated by a steady diet of extremist media and put off by the arrogance of their own leaders. To reclaim control of the party, conservative leaders were told that they needed to better understand the passions of their rank and file.

After Donald Trump's surprising victory in the general election, the soul searching moved to the Left. Now it was the liberals' turn for gross confusion. Interestingly, they too found blame with their own elites. According to columnist Thomas Frank, it was the liberal media who drove working-class voters to Trump, because it "chose insulting the other side over trying to understand what motivated them."[2] Sociologist Arlie Hochschild claimed that liberals bore "the bigger responsibility" for failing to empathize with white working-class America and their feelings of victimhood.[3] Michael Lerner, editor of *Tikkun* magazine, argued that it was wrong for liberals to "shame" Trump voters for the racism and sexism of their candidate. Instead,

> Democrats . . . need to reach out to Trump voters in a spirit of empathy and
> contrition. Only then can we help working people understand that they do not
> live in a meritocracy, that their intuition that the system is rigged is correct (but
> it is not by those whom they had been taught to blame) and that their pain and
> rage is legitimate.[4]

Lerner didn't specify whether his suggestions also held for "NeverTrump"
conservatives, or what sins, exactly, Democrats were supposed to be con-
trite for. Nor did he seem to appreciate his own condescension in assuming that Trump voters needed to be corrected about the real source
of their "pain and rage." Trump had won, and the onus was squarely
on liberals to first understand the other side and then dutifully correct its
misconceptions.

It's easy to appreciate why pundits across the political spectrum were
expressing these sentiments. Trump's victory was as perplexing as it was
surprising. Not only did Trump lack many qualifications assumedly necessary for a president (for example, experience, temperament, honesty),
he espoused policies that would directly harm many of the very working-
class voters that so enthusiastically supported him. Given all this, it was
reasonable that they would try to comprehend why so many Americans
were behaving so "inexplicably."

And how was Trump able to persuade millions of voters to look beyond
his obvious flaws? As we've suggested in the previous chapters, he found
success by giving voice to how many ordinary Americans understand issues of race, money, and power.[5] Trump's conspiracy theories, his bigotry,
and his populism all reflect how many Americans intuitively comprehend
politics and the world at large. In his demonization of immigrants, trade
deals, and Washington elites, he tapped into a deeper "folk politics," a
way of perceiving issues based on personal feelings and common sense.
Trump's rhetoric echoed a perspective common among many conservatives and fundamentalist Christians: mistrust of the American neoliberal
order and nostalgia for a "simpler" time in America's past.

But "folk politics" is nothing new; indeed, it's always been with us.
Donald Trump was not the first candidate to appeal to voters' intuitions,
and he certainly won't be the last. So what, then, made 2016 so different?
Although the election was determined by a host of particular circumstances, it was also a culmination of some long-developing changes within
modern US politics. Trump was the apotheosis of modern American conservatism. His conspiracy theories, ethnic hatreds, and profound distrust

of science, the media, and the professional classes in general are not limited to the fringes of talk radio and blogs; they have become *the* principal orientation of the conservative movement. Donald Trump won the election largely because he was the Republican nominee; but he won the nomination because the Republican Party has become dominated by Intuitionists. With his presidency, Intuitionism became a force in US politics largely because it is the defining feature of modern conservatism.

And this has created a significant political problem. As conservatism and Intuitionism have become more closely aligned, America has become even more polarized. It's one thing for liberals and conservatives to disagree over tax cuts, government programs, or even prayer in public schools; it's another thing when they disagree about the veracity of facts, the usefulness of science, or the very nature of reality. When Americans are divided by both ideology and ontology, it makes it extremely difficult to solve problems of common concern. With its absolutism and intolerance for ambiguity, Intuitionism is not amenable to the compromise and consensus that a reasoned democracy requires. Its ascendancy over the conservative movement makes it a genuine threat to the values of the Republic. But before we discuss how to address this situation, we first need to appreciate why Intuitionism thrives and how it came to dominate conservative politics.

Why Intuitionism Thrives in Contemporary America

Perhaps the most curious thing about Enchanted America is that it's not supposed to exist. A century ago, many eminent thinkers were predicting that the era of Intuitionism was at an end. "The fate of our times," sociologist and philosopher Max Weber famously observed, "is characterized by rationalization and intellectualization and, above all, the disenchantment of the world."[6] With its breathtaking advances in medicine, industry, politics, and science, the post-Enlightenment world was eradicating the maladies that brought about so many common myths and superstitions. Louis Pasteur showed that plagues and diseases were not the wraths of angry gods but the by-products of microbes. Thomas Edison's electric bulb banished the evil spirits that lurked in the night's inky darkness. Chemical fertilizers, pesticides, and mechanical reapers ended the biblical famines. The Wright brothers conquered the very skies from which Icarus plummeted. And across the world, the autocratic prerogatives claimed by kings and popes were succumbing to rational principles of human rights and democratic governance. No wonder the end of magic seemed upon us. A highly advanced and educated society like the United States was going to become ordered by the cool rationality of the modern age.

And as late as 1960, it looked as though Weber's prediction was coming true. The United States, spurred on by Soviet advances in rocketry and weaponry, was enthusiastically embracing science. Billions of dollars were pumped into public universities and the National Science Foundation. Science and technocratic skill defined public policy, law, and medicine. And while nearly all Americans still believed in God, most of the country embraced a placid, generalist spirituality that was embodied in mainline Protestantism.[7] As was fitting the largely consensual culture of the time, most Americans clustered around a rather centrist and pragmatic type of spirituality that sat easily with its growing Rationalism.[8] It was an era when Americans believed in both science and God.

But magic did not disappear. Instead, Americans began to polarize in their ontologies. On one side, a growing minority of Americans were becoming explicitly Rationalistic, repudiating their parents' traditional beliefs. For the first time in US history, large swaths of the American population began disavowing organized religion. Rationalism was ascendant among the intellectual elite, and much of the lay populace as well. On the other side, an even larger proportion of Americans were embracing a more charismatic and fundamentalist Christianity that not only espoused wildly supernatural beliefs but also was actively hostile to science. For these Christians, the advances of modernity were not a cause for celebration but a source of spiritual destabilization. What's more, this split became increasingly politicized, with Rationalists congregated more on the political Left while Intuitionists affiliated with the Right.

How did this happen? Although this question has no single answer, the most likely explanation is to be found at the confluence of human psychology and recent historical circumstance. The simple fact is that as a species, humans remain hypersensitive to the chronic uncertainty that constitutes their existence. Scientific and technological wonders may have dispelled most of the famines, diseases, darkness, and violence that fostered so many of our ancestor's magical beliefs, but they have not removed uncertainty from the human condition, even in an economically advanced nation like the United States. But this uncertainty has not been felt in equal degrees. Instead, it has become polarized, reflecting seismic technological, economic, and political shifts in the American landscape. The unifying consensus of the 1950s has given way to a society highly stratified by social class, culture, and politics. Many of the same factors that have polarized Americans in the areas of wealth, religion, and politics are also dividing them by worldview. Let us briefly consider a few.

The information age. One source of America's ontological polarization is the changing way we get information about the world. A century ago, most Americans relied on local print media as their primary source of information, and most newspapers were largely preoccupied with local issues. A small handful of magazines like the *New Republic*, *Harper's Weekly*, and the *Saturday Evening Post* added a more national or international perspective, but American media was still a parochial concern. But with the advent of radio, televised news, and the Internet, ordinary Americans gained access not only to more information sources but to a media that is both more global and visceral in orientation. Radio and television made the broader world more vivid and immediate: Edward Murrow's radio broadcast of the London Blitz made World War II seem close to the home front, much as CBS's televised coverage of the Vietnam War would do in the 1960s. Today, news about a terrorist attack in Istanbul or an Ebola outbreak in Liberia not only comes nearly instantaneous to the event, but is usually accompanied by video footage that is stored online, making its impact all the more compelling and long-lasting.

The explosion of media has also created a paradox for ordinary Americans. On the one hand, the torrent of information should diminish our reliance on our intuitions. Over the past two hundred years, the spread of scientific knowledge demolished the fantasies and superstitions of the medieval mind.[9] On the other hand, the modern news environment does not always promote more rational inquiry. This is partly a matter of time and energy. Most people simply don't have the time or the inclination to sift through all the information coming at them. They usually don't go to the trouble of generating a scientifically accurate picture of the world. Rather, many Americans consume information that actually promotes magical thinking. In the modern news environment, this comes from at least three sources.

First, most information about the world is presented in a way that appeals to our emotions. Humans have an appetite for hearing about other people's catastrophes and misfortunes or simply negative events.[10] We are riveted by news of murders, natural disasters, or scandal. Most news sources recognize this and seek to meet this demand. Consider the ways the news is typically covered. Few newspapers will report if a coal mine goes twenty years without an accident, but if it collapses, the headlines take note. The same trend generally holds with crime, fires, diseases, or kidnappings. News reporting is typically about highlighting the salacious. For example, in health reporting, a headline trumpets a "link" between a particular chemical and some disease, but the fine print actually reports a minuscule statistical probability of actually getting sick. This inundation of negative information is likely to distort our image of the world— hearing so much about terrorist attacks, kidnappings, or infectious diseases, we're likely to get a highly exaggerated picture of threats to our well-being.[11] In short, the wealth of information available to us creates not an accurate picture but an overly threatening one.

Second, most people will seek news that aligns with their prior beliefs. Before the 1980s, most Americans were exposed to relatively consensual news coverage. Television news came mostly from the three major news networks. Although they also produced editorials, the major newspapers and news networks were bound by professional norms of objectivity and nonpartisanship.[12] But today, Americans increasingly gravitate to sources that program their news coverage to reaffirm a prior ideology. Conservatives watch Fox News or listen to Rush Limbaugh; fundamentalist Christians watch Pat Robertson or read James Dobson; liberals watch MSNBC or read the *Nation*; and so on. This "silo" effect is exacerbated by the Internet and social media. Highly partisan websites disseminate news to like-minded users, while on social media platforms like Facebook, people who make egregious posts are ostracized and "unfriended," thus furthering the cycle of social conformity. Consequently, the fragmented nature of today's media environment allows a great deal of misinformation, gossip, and rumor to be spread as truth. People with prior magical beliefs aren't likely to see much correction to those beliefs, but instead find news sources that are in line with their prior expectations.[13]

Third, today's media environment allows for the spread of transgressive viewpoints, magical views, and untruths. This is not any more evident than in the blossoming of conspiracy theories. Twenty years ago, conspiracy theorists were largely limited to disseminating their own ideas by self-publishing books and handing out leaflets in public venues. But with the growth of talk radio and the Internet, they have found a platform for disseminating their narratives that can launch these ideas virally through other social media. Take the example of Alex Jones and infowars.com. This talk show provocateur weaves fantastical stories that typically involve common conspiracy tropes (the CIA, George Soros, the Black Lives Matter movement, and so on) with little regard for fact. In an earlier time, Jones would have found few national venues for his deeply paranoid musings; but between his syndicated talk radio show and his ability to rebroadcast his musings online, he has amassed a large following.

In short, the information age is not disenchanting us; in fact, in some ways it may be exacerbating our Intuitionist proclivities. The shocking imagery and righteous indignation of much talk radio, social media, and news analysis trigger our viscera. Under the sway of our emotions, we are far more susceptible to the expedient explanations and distorting symbols that come with magical beliefs, conspiracy theories, and ethnocentric screeds. With all our science and information, we may be less enchanted than our ancestors, but our news environment doesn't necessarily foster a more Rationalist perspective.

Education and religion. Another reason Americans are polarizing in their worldview is due to the evolution of two important cultural institutions—education and religion. On one side, the continued expansion of higher education has greatly contributed to the "rationalizing" of the American public. Since the end of World War II and the implementation of the GI Bill, the percentage of Americans with a college degree has doubled. At the same time, millions have abandoned the religious beliefs and practices of their parents. These two facts are related. As we noted in chapter 3, college-educated Americans are much less Intuitionist than those with only a high school diploma. And since the early 1960s, the percentage of Americans who believe in God or regularly attend church has steadily declined.

But a college degree remains elusive to most. Although more Americans are earning high school diplomas than at any time in history, two-thirds still do not have a college degree. The absence of a college education not only undermines the Rationalism of many Americans, it also increases their economic vulnerability. In the US postindustrial economy, those with only a high school diploma are five times more likely to live in poverty, are three times more likely to be unemployed, and earn nearly half as much, on average, as their counterparts with a college degree.[14]

These educational statistics mask a growing fragmentation in the American educational environment. In the 1950s and 1960s, the overwhelming majority of students attended public schools. Since then, more have begun attending religious schools and universities. Even more noticeable is the tremendous growth in homeschooling, which included less than 5,000 children in 1970 and today encompasses over 1.7 million.[15] Homeschoolers are drawn largely from religious fundamentalists who want to shield their children from secular influences. Meanwhile, the scientific orientation of the public education curriculum continues to be challenged by conservative religious groups.

A growing bifurcation is also occurring in America's religious landscape. Sixty years ago, the nation was much more homogeneous in its religious beliefs. As late as 1960, 99 percent of Americans professed a belief in God, and most belonged to the Roman Catholic Church or one of the seven mainline Protestant faiths.[16] Today, less than 80 percent believe in God. This decline in belief has been accompanied by a decline in membership in mainline Protestant denominations and among European Catholics.[17] Religious beliefs have changed as well. For example, the General Social Survey has long asked Americans whether they believe that the Bible is the literal word of God, the inspired word of God, or a collection of historical fables. Although the percentage believing that the Bible is the literal word of God has remained at about 32 percent of the population over the past twenty-five years, the percentage believing that the Bible is a collection of myths has increased from 15 to 22 percent.[18] America has thus shifted from a nation largely unified around a mostly diffuse theology to two increasingly polarized camps—one largely devoid of religion and one highly fervent in its beliefs.

In looking at education in conjunction with religiosity, we can see an important source of America's growing divide. The nation's less educated majority is much more likely to believe in God, affiliate themselves with fundamentalist or conservative churches, and profess the importance of religion in their daily life.[19] But among the minority of Americans with college degrees, and especially among the even smaller minority with advanced degrees, there is far less belief in God or the importance of religion in life.[20] The mainline Protestantism and Catholicism that softened the differences between America's educated elites and its fervent masses have eroded with time. The nation's technocratic classes are increasingly secular and rational, while its less educated majority is increasingly fundamentalist or conservative in its religious orientation.

Declining trust in civic society. Another source of division is the massive decline of Americans' trust in their public institutions. In the 1950s and 1960s, they expressed high levels of confidence in government, industry,

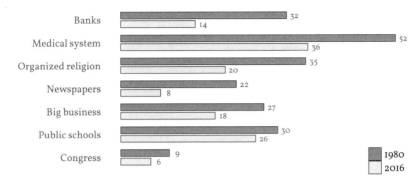

FIGURE 8.1. Percentage of Americans with a "great deal of confidence" in public institutions, 1980 and 2016. *Source*: Gallup, 2017.

scientists, teachers, the news media, and organized religion. For example, in 1964 over 70 percent of Americans said they trusted the federal government to "do what's right most of the time." Such confidence was extended to most other public institutions as well. When the General Social Survey began asking Americans about their levels of trust in the 1970s, large majorities reported high levels of confidence in the police, public education, banks, network news, and the medical system.

But today, these types of trust have plummeted. The biggest change has been with the federal government. In the past forty years, trust in government has declined to just 20 percent of the population.[21] And lest we think that this is just a reflection of unhappiness with party politics, similar declines have occurred with other institutions as well: the number of Americans who say they have considerable trust in banks, public education, newspapers and televised news, big business, and the medical system has dropped by at least 50 percent since the mid-1970s.[22] Indeed, today fewer than one in three express much confidence in any of these core social institutions (fig. 8.1).

Such declines only exacerbate the schism between Rationalists and Intuitionists. When confidence in public institutions withers, the public is left without authoritative guides to help it navigate the complexities of the modern world. And in a secular, democratic state, this is a serious problem. Contemporary democracies are products of the Enlightenment. Just as seventeenth-century Europeans were employing new scientific ways of thinking, so too they started using reasoned deduction in addressing the question of human governance. Philosophers like Locke, Montesquieu, Hume, and Voltaire were champions of civil liberties. In their revolutionary view, human liberty came not from the condescension of royal prerogatives but from the very social contract on which the state was formed; and nothing was more central to the liberalism project than the freedom of speech. There could be no room for open scientific inquiry as long as Christian dogma about the natural world was enshrined in state power.

But the importance of free inquiry also posed a political challenge to Enlightenment liberalism—who or what should adjudicate reality? In sixteenth-century Europe, all claims to truth were drawn from sectarian interpretations of biblical scripture. But once the church was displaced as the ultimate arbiter of truth, an ocean of indeterminacy was left in its wake. Science could answer a few questions authoritatively, but mostly it was confined to theory, hypothesis, and conjecture. In public affairs, this presented a crisis: if the church was no longer the unquestioned authority on how we should eat, act, and otherwise govern ourselves, what should be?

For many in the emerging democracies of the eighteenth century, the answer was found in civil society.[23] In western Europe and the United States, a bounty of scientific and professional organizations, book and newspaper publishers, public schools and universities, hospitals, and businesses emerged as alternatives to church authority. These groups not only argued about new discoveries and disseminated new technologies, they offered their collective imprimatur on claims to truth. For example, nineteenth-century scientists legitimized their theories by gaining acceptance from scientific groups and publishing their research. Then as now, the news media buttressed these claims through its own reporting. And professional associations came together to offer authoritative interpretations and judgments on issues of health, medicine, food, and science. In a liberal society, the network of independent associations buoys public discourse and provides grounding social knowledge.

When the public loses confidence in its civic organizations, this creates a vacuum of authority. In recent times, this vacuum is being filled by alternative narratives and news sources. A very good example of this has been occurring in science and medicine. Between the 1930s and the 1950s, health claims by organizations like the American Medical Association went largely unchallenged. And little wonder why. In the first half of the twentieth century, American medicine had made sweeping advances in public health—for example, the average female life expectancy in the United States had increased from fifty-four years in 1920 to over seventy-three years by 1960. American medicine was in "a golden age."[24] But starting in the late 1960s, it, like many other public institutions, started coming under fire. In the wake of various health scandals, it came to seem less of a benevolent source of good and more of a politicized entity.[25] Alternative medicine became a means of resistance to the overly chemical and corporate nature of traditional medicine.

This type of contestation is one of the central paradoxes of liberalism: free societies are based on principles that undermine their own sources of authority. After all, in a liberal society any organization or entity that makes truth claims is bound to be challenged, because the very nature of a scientific worldview is based in skepticism. While such questioning is a powerful vehicle for the advancement of knowledge, it creates a conundrum for ordinary citizens who are trying to make sense of a complicated world. How can people figure out the highly complex and global forces in their life when scientific authorities can't be trusted? When public institutions lose their legitimacy, it opens the possibility for nonscientific institutions to take preeminence. And as we've argued above, magical beliefs often seem more compelling precisely because of their ability to seem more intuitively plausible. But the questioning of secular authority didn't simply happen on its own. In America, it came from the politicization of reason and the rise of modern conservatism.

The Rationalism of the American Left

Of all the sources of American polarization, none are as profound as the evolution of both modern liberalism and conservatism. Over the past century, the political Left and the Right not only formalized their ideological differences, they came to be separate in worldview as well. The Left came to identify itself as largely Rationalist, while the Right became increasingly Intuitionist. To appreciate how this happened, let us first go back a little in time. In the 1950s, American society was not only centralized in its magical beliefs, it was also centralized in its politics. This was most evident in the major political parties. Instead of being the fiercely polarized entities of today, the two parties operated as broad, overlapping coalitions. The Democratic Party included staunch Southern white conservatives, civil rights activists, trade unionists, and urban intellectuals. The

Republican Party was centered on its traditional probusiness, Chamber of Commerce supporters but also included Midwestern farmers, pragmatic suburbanites, a sizable portion of African Americans, and a wide array of liberals. There was no single "conservative" movement, and a wide consensus in support of New Deal policies held sway.

Many observers of the day believed that this broad consensus was the inevitable culmination of American political culture. A pragmatic and technocratic liberalism reflected the "common wisdom" informing so much of the the nation's political tradition. Candidate-centered elections, heterogeneous parties, and ideological concurrence were the very hallmarks of American democracy. The "end of ideology" was at hand, and "the Vital Center" reigned as dominant.[26] Pluralism, the comforting notion that political power was widely dispersed, was the preeminent theory of governance, while the equally sanguine "median voter theorem" proposed that moderate voters would always draw parties toward the center.[27] In both popular and academic discourse, moderation, pragmatism, and technocratic expertise were the baseline against which political decisions would and should be made. The landslide election of president Lyndon Johnson over conservative senator Barry Goldwater in 1964 only appeared to cement these notions.

But the liberal consensus of the 1950s was not inevitable. It was the culmination of a long pattern of political activism going back to the Progressive movement and, in hindsight, the consequence of historical circumstances. It started in the late 1800s, when new "progressive" ideas of governance were taking root among intellectuals and political reformers. Seeking to address the social and economic dysfunctions of a rapidly industrializing America, Progressives advocated for more vigorous state action. Central to their political agenda was the notion that government decisions and policy should be based on scientific principles.[28] Just as scientific discoveries were revolutionizing the economy, industry, and medicine, so Progressives believed that science could also pave the way for engineering a more harmonious and just society.

Although Progressives had some moralistic agendas, it was largely a Rationalist movement. And crucial to the Progressive cause were two interrelated institutions—the research university and the independent bureaucracy. During the late 1800s, America's major universities, especially its new public land-grant institutions, were evolving into research centers featuring laboratories, graduate schools, and policy missions. Part of this new mission involved training the professionals who would construct and staff the expanding governmental bureaucracy that would address America's burgeoning social problems.[29] The Rationalism of the Progressive movement was also evident in its many policy successes. The national income tax, the direct election of senators, women's suffrage, the Interstate Commerce Act, the Federal Reserve banking system, the Federal Trade Commission, and the Department of Labor all arose from a reason-based understanding of government and justice.[30] This scientific approach to solving social problems was furthered with a host of other Progressive institutions, like the Social Science Research Council, the Spelman Fund, the National Bureau of Economic Research, and the Institute for Government Research.[31] The tight links between the academy and the rational bureaucracy, the bête noire of the modern conservative movement, were forged in conjunction with the Progressive Era.

Although the Progressive movement eventually faded in the 1920s, it laid the groundwork for a modern, "Rationalist" liberal movement. During the Great Depression, the political Left in America not only became dominant in the nation's politics, it also realized the technocratic spirit of its Progressive forebears.[32] This can be seen in three pillars of the liberal agenda. First, liberalism advocated for scientific responses to the social problems of industrial capitalism. Many New Deal policies aimed to "rationalize" the free market by developing a "purely neutral technocracy" based on scientific principles.[33] This was accomplished through a fusillade of laws that created a massive bureaucracy to both regulate the economy and protect farmers, senior citizens, and other groups from "want."[34] However, his mushrooming bureaucracy did not come into being by itself. It needed a phalanx of experts to formulate and implement policy. Here again, public subsidies to universities allowed for the creation of schools for public administration, public health, education, and social welfare.[35] During the New Deal, higher education, expertise, and a liberal social agenda became inexorably linked.

Second, liberalism adopted civil rights as a central part of its movement. This was done partly in response to world events. Seeing themselves as a bulwark against Italian and German fascism, New Deal liberals sought a political order based on not simply scientific principles of rational governance but Enlightenment principles of individual equality and freedom.[36] But this also meant tackling issues of racial and ethnic discrimination at home. Liberals came to view both racism and chronic black poverty as social pathologies, things that could be "treated" like clinical aberrations.[37] Despite the opposition of Southern Democrats, many New Deal reformers placed their concerns with race and civil rights at the center of liberal politics.[38] Liberals also came to embrace a nascent multiculturalism. As anthropologist Margaret Mead's work reached new audiences, liberals embraced religious pluralism and encouraged tolerance among Protestants, Catholics, and Jews (the term "Judeo-Christian" was coined during this period).[39]

Third, as World War II ended and the Cold War began, liberal Rationalism embraced a robust internationalism. While conservatives like Robert Taft were calling for a return to America's prewar isolationism, liberals made America's global role central to their political agenda. They championed organizations like the United Nations, the World Bank, and the International Monetary Fund. In their view, these groups would address global problems through reasoned deliberation and technocratic expertise. As American competition with the Soviet Union escalated, liberals also became enthusiastic supporters of the military. Here again, Rationalist institutions like universities and think tanks played a central role in developing technology, strategy, and policy formulation.[40]

In sum, by the early 1960s, the American Left had defined itself in strongly Rationalist terms. Scientists, policy experts, government workers, and academics were not only the primary architects of the liberal agenda—they infused the Left with an indelibly Rationalist character. A technocratic state with a strong emphasis on redressing social inequalities and promoting civil liberties and cultural tolerance was at the center of the liberal movement. And up until the 1960s, this liberal, Rationalist vision was preeminent in US politics.

The Rise of the New Right

But amid this liberal ascendance, the seeds of ideological rancor were taking root. While most traditional conservatives had acceded to the New Deal, a handful of intellectuals and activists was defining a new, stridently oppositional political movement—modern conservatism. Coalescing first around publications like William F. Buckley's *National Review*, modern conservatism wove together the various political strands that would eventually propel Ronald Reagan into the White House, dominate Republican politics, and define much of today's political agenda.[41]

Given the intellectual pretensions of its founders, modern conservatism may seem to be a Rationalist enterprise. Many of its promoters certainly like to characterize it that way, often citing highly Rationalist thinkers like John Locke, Edmund Burke, Friedrich Hayek, or Milton Friedman as principal sources of inspiration. But from its early beginnings, modern conservatism was largely infused with an Intuitionist worldview. Consider two of its "founders," William F. Buckley Jr. and Russell Kirk. Both rose to fame writing books bemoaning secularism. For them, conservatism was less about laissez-faire economics and more about the Christian tradition-alism that was "necessary" for Western civilization. This spiritual orienta-tion was particularly evident in the mission statement of *National Review*. Buckley and Kirk saw a "profound crisis" in the conflict between "the Social Engineers, who seek to adjust mankind to conform with scientific utopias, and the disciples of Truth, who defend the *organic moral order*." They declared a holy war on communism, which was a "blatant force of *satanic* utopianism." At home, the principal battle lines would be drawn against the New Deal liberalism, where a "team of Fabian operators is bent on controlling both our major political parties."[42] Modern conser-vatism, as seen in its founding publication, was founded as a polarizing, antisecular movement casting itself in spiritual terms.

But while conservatism always revered the supernatural, such tenden-cies were often hemmed in by the intellectualism of its founders. Mod-ern conservatism arose from a clique of highly educated elites, not as a groundswell from the masses. William F. Buckley Jr. went to great lengths to marginalize the John Birchers and other reactionaries. But his efforts to relegate the strongly Intuitionist elements of the Right to the periphery of the movement eventually gave way. As modern conservatism expanded in the 1960s, it became fiercely populist in its orientation, hostile to the established political order, and enthusiastic in its embrace of conspiracy theories and strong magical beliefs.

One of the earliest exemplars of this "New Right" was Phyllis Schlafly. Before her fame as an opponent of the Equal Rights Amendment, Schlafly was best known as a crusading opponent of communism.[43] She was no Ra-tionalist, however. Communism was not simply an ideological adversary to capitalism, but an "international criminal conspiracy founded on athe-ism, materialism, and economic determinism . . . a life-and-death struggle with the criminal underground."[44] Schlafly applied this conspiratorial, Manichaean thinking to domestic issues as well. The New Deal was cre-ated by "a small group of secret kingmakers, using hidden persuaders and psychological warfare techniques." These "eastern [*sic*] elites" created "Manchurian candidates who were quite willing to have their candidate talk like a real Republican when seeking the nomination. But once he is nominated, switches from a fiery fighter to a milktoast [*sic*] 'me too' candidate." Behind it all were the *New York Times* and the federal government, who sustained a "hidden policy of perpetuating the Red empire in order to perpetuate the high level of Federal spending" that was revealed in "secret studies made by the Kennedy Administration."[45]

Schlafly's cultural populism and penchant for conspiracy theory had a long historical pedigree. At the time she rose to fame, historian Richard Hofstadter was famously labeling her way of thinking as emblematic of a long tradition of the "paranoid style" in US politics. Even as early as the 1930s, many conservatives began expressing deep suspicions of not just big government but academics, scientists, newspapers, and all professional classes.[46] Father Charles Coughlin, a prototype of today's conservative media provocateurs, exemplified this mistrust: "Too many of us do not realize that the Marxists' greatest victory, to date, has been won not in Europe nor in Asia but at the city of Washington, D.C."[47] This type of rhetoric later set the stage for Wisconsin senator Joseph McCarthy, who combined conspiratorial thinking and cultural populism into a seamless whole.[48] For McCarthy, like many opponents of New Deal programs, a communist conspiracy had thoroughly infiltrated Franklin Roosevelt's Ivy League–educated "brain trust."[49]

By the late 1960s, many conservatives were making the attack on scientific and technical expertise central to their mobilizing strategy. None accomplished this more explicitly than the segregationist presidential candidate George Wallace. Wallace characterized his voters as "all the little people who feared big government in the hands of phony intellectuals and social engineers with unworkable theories."[50] He wielded this populist rhetoric like a cudgel. "Workin' folk," he told the press, are "fed up with bureaucrats in Washington, pointy-headed intellectuals, *swaydo-*intellectual morons tellin' 'em how to live their lives."[51] Not to be outdone, Richard Nixon appropriated this cultural populism, hoping to woo white Southern Democrats disillusioned with both the civil rights movement and the youth counterculture. In Nixon's famous formulation, the "silent majority" of Americans were being undermined, not just by "hippies" and "agitators" but by arrogant intellectuals and other experts. His 1972 presidential campaign explicitly sought to portray his opponent, Democrat George McGovern, "as the pet of Eastern Liberalism, the darling of the *New York Times*, the hero of the Berkley Hill Jet Set: Mr. Radical Chic."[52]

Even after Nixon's resignation, right-wing populism continued to grow as a mainstay of the New Right. For many conservatives, all proponents of rational liberalism, be they government workers, scientists, or experts of any kind, were "acting upon a hidden agenda" to destroy capitalism.[53] As conservative journalist Matthew Continetti describes, "The enemies of the New Right were compromise, gradualism, and acquiescence in the corrupt system. Conservatives and Republicans with Ivy League degrees were sellouts, weak, epiphenomena of the social disease."[54] Modern conservatism was not simply appropriating a cultural populism but attacking the Rationalist order.[55]

And among all these public institutions, none garnered more scorn than the mainstream press, especially the *New York Times*. From the beginning, conservatives made attacking the media a central part of their movement. Barry Goldwater's 1964 presidential campaign warned supporters, "Do not trust the newspapers, radio, TV, and newsmagazines for your information. These are the main weapons the enemy has to use against us."[56] The Nixon administration took criticizing the elite media to a new level both in volume and in rhetoric, and many best-selling books emerged that decried the media bias.[57] Twenty years later, media bashing had become part of the conservative mainstream. Republican presidential candidate Bob Dole urged his supporters to "stop the liberal bias in this country. Don't read the stuff. Don't watch television. You make up your own mind. . . . This country belongs to the people, not the *New York Times*."[58] Media "bias" also became the central preoccupation of newly emerging conservative venues, including talk radio and "outrage-based political blog[s]" and websites such as Townhall, Breitbart News Network, and Drudge Report.[59] As with talk radio, a staple of political blogs and websites is criticism of the mainstream media and a "deeply emotion- and symbol-laden view of American politics."[60]

The rise of nationally syndicated talk radio, Fox News, and websites has given conservatives not just alternative sources of information but venues that attack much of the secular public sector (that is, news services, science, government, and educators). The effects of decades of attacks on these public institutions are now clear. Not only has trust in such organizations plummeted, but conservatives have been made *more* extreme, indelibly convinced of the correctness of their views and intolerant of alternatives.[61] This was recently described by conservative talk radio host John Ziegler:

> Talk radio, in the era of Trump, isn't remotely conservative. It's also no longer about the truth. It's about telling people what they want to hear. It's very much like a cult now, where the purpose is to substantiate what the religion is telling you and anything that runs counter to the religion is inherently false and blasphemous, even evil. So anyone who breaks from orthodoxy is a traitor.[62]

Such zealotry within the New Right has been bolstered by the proclivities of its largest constituency—fundamentalist Christians. Until the
1970s, political conservatism and fundamentalism weren't strongly connected. The conservative thinkers who first trumpeted the importance of
Judeo-Christian values weren't doing so from fundamentalist pulpits—
William F. Buckley Jr., Irving Kristol, and Russell Kirk, for example, did
not espouse biblical inerrancy or the coming of the end of time. And until
the 1970s, most fundamentalist leaders tended to sequester themselves
from partisan politics. Fundamentalism usually had its own concerns that
were separate from the mundane world of politics.

But in the 1970s, political entrepreneurs recognized that the fundamentalists' general outlook aligned well with modern conservatives' central
preoccupations. This general outlook started with a strong Manichaean
view of the world, "a view of history as a struggle between the forces of
good versus evil, light versus darkness, Christianity versus paganism."[63]
For most fundamentalists, evil did not come in the form of poverty, racial
injustice, or other liberal concerns. Rather, it was manifest in Darwin-
ism, the United Nations, Hollywood, and communism.[64] But more than
anything else, modern conservatism and Christian fundamentalism found
a common cause fighting the rational secularization and liberalization of
American public life. Supreme Court decisions banning prayer in public
schools and legalizing abortion, coupled with the civil rights movements
for minorities, women, and homosexuals, not only mobilized the newly
formed "Religious Right" but made them staunch allies of modern conservatism.[65] Fundamentalist thought leaders began to draw the rank and
file into the political process to fight for their eschatological worldview.[66]

The fusion of fundamentalism and modern conservatism culminated
with the political ascendance of Ronald Reagan. Although he was not a
particularly observant Christian, Reagan adeptly employed fundamentalist rhetoric to draw the religious faithful into the Republican fold. For example, in his nomination battle with President Ford in 1976, Reagan told
a radio interviewer, "There has been a wave of humanism and hedonism
in the land. However, I am optimistic because I sense a great revolution
against that. . . . The people of this country are not beyond redemption."
After his election in 1980, Reagan told a sympathetic crowd of religious
conservatives that evolution was a "theory only and it has in recent years
been challenged in the world of science. . . . If it is going to be taught in the
schools, then I would think that also the biblical theory of creation, which
is not a theory but the biblical story of creation, should also be taught."

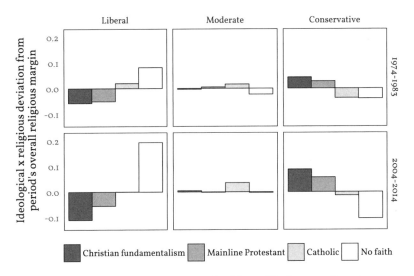

FIGURE 8.2. Association between ideology and religious affiliation, 1974–83 and 2004–14. *Source*: Smith et al., 2015.

He told the National Association of Evangelicals in 1983, "There is sin and evil in the world and we're enjoined by Scripture and the Lord Jesus to oppose it with all our might." Tapping into the Manichaean sensibility so common to fundamentalists, he characterized the Soviet Union as an "evil empire," and declared that "the struggle between right and wrong and good and evil" was the stakes of the battle.[67] With such outreach, Reagan unified traditional conservatives, the New Right, and Christian fundamentalists into a powerful coalition.

Looking back, we can now see evidence of Reagan's efforts to bring fundamentalists into the conservative fold. Figure 8.2 depicts the differences in religious affiliations across ideological groups in two ten-year periods (1974–83 and 2004–14).[68] In the 1970s, American conservatives were not all that more likely than the rest of the population to be fundamentalist. Liberals had slightly more nonreligious folks (roughly 10 percent more than the nation as a whole) and slightly fewer fundamentalists and mainline Protestants. Conservatives were a mirror image, with slightly more Protestants and slightly fewer Catholics and others. But by the 2000s, this pattern had dramatically changed. Americans with no religious affiliation were dramatically overrepresented on the liberal side of the spectrum. Meanwhile, the percentage of Protestants, especially fundamentalist ones, identifying as liberal plummeted. At the same time, conservatives became disproportionately fundamentalist and less secular compared with the general population. Over the past few decades, ideology and religion have grown increasingly aligned.

But the ascendance of fundamentalism within the New Right also divided its more Rationalist and Intuitionist elements. This was clearly evident during the 2016 presidential campaign, when many Rationalist conservatives, such as Ross Douthat, David Brooks, George Will, David French, and Kevin Williamson, fiercely opposed the nomination of Donald Trump. For such traditional conservatives, Trump's moral failures and lack of conservative principles disqualified him from even being considered a "real conservative." But rather than finding sympathetic audiences, such traditionalists were ostracized. Like many in the "Never Trump" movement, they were subjected to all types of harassment and threats by Trump's supporters on the Right.[69]

Much of this reaction relates to the propensity toward Intuitionism that had long been simmering in conservative discourse. This is well described by Charlie Sykes, a prominent conservative talk radio host in Wisconsin:

> One staple of every radio talk show was, of course, the bias of the mainstream media. Over time, we'd succeeded in delegitimizing the media altogether— all the normal guideposts were down, the referees discredited. That left a void that we conservatives failed to fill. For years, we ignored the birthers, the racists, the truthers and other conspiracy theorists who indulged fantasies of Mr. Obama's secret Muslim plot to subvert Christendom, or who peddled baseless tales of Mrs. Clinton's murder victims. Rather than confront the purveyors of such disinformation, we changed the channel because, after all, they were our allies, whose quirks could be allowed or at least ignored. We destroyed our own immunity to fake news, while empowering the worst and most reckless voices on the right. This was not mere naïveté. It was also a moral failure, one that now lies at the heart of the conservative movement even in its moment of apparent electoral triumph.[70]

As Sykes's comments suggest, the intuitive and apocalyptic thinking of many Intuitionists has become pervasive among lay conservatives. This was no better seen than in Donald Trump's success with Christian voters. More than anything, it revealed that the connection between fundamentalism and the New Right has less to do with religious doctrine and more to do with the power of intuitions. Trump, a lying, venal, serial womanizer, violated more traditional Christian values than any candidate in recent history. Yet his support among fundamentalists was largely unaffected.[71] This was because he tapped into the deeper feelings of mistrust, alienation, and animosity that have come to define modern conservatism. The same intuitions underlying fundamentalist beliefs (and also present in populism, conspiracy theories, ethnocentrism, and hostility to science) are now at the center of conservative thought.

The ascendance of the New Right has also left Rationalist conservatives on the margins. Conservative intellectuals who make reasoned deductions, respect facts, or express a regard for science are now pilloried by talk radio hosts and bloggers as sellouts, RINOs (Republican in Name Only), or cuckolded conservatives. As a movement, conservatism is divided between its intellectual, establishment roots and, as Matthew Continetti describes, "the blue-collar radio and television hosts with million-dollar contracts, the billionaire-supported populist website that attacks renegade Jews, the bloggers and commenters and trolls estranged from power, fueled by resentment, lured by the specter of conspiracy, extrapolating terrifying and chiliastic scenarios from negative but solvable trends."[72] The ascendance of Intuitionism as the organizing principle within modern conservatism is fundamentally changing the nature of American political discourse and the role of rationality in American democracy.

The Political Challenge of Intuitionism

In the West, the first death of Reason came in 475 ACE. This was the year that the Greek philosopher Proculus recorded the last astronomical observation in the ancient world. For the next thousand years, western Europeans abandoned the scientific study of the stars, and nearly everything else. The deductive proofs, empirical research, and reasoned philosophy of classical Greece, along with its democratic values, were displaced by the unquestionable authority of tyrants, kings, and popes. The Western mind slipped back into the totalizing grip of myth and superstition. Christian theologians besmirched the "wisdom of the wise" and "the empty logic of philosophers" as distractions from the truth that could only be had through divine revelation; reason was often viewed as anathema to Christianity.[73] Civilization in western Europe deteriorated. It wasn't until the Renaissance and the Enlightenment that Europeans rediscovered the science of their classical forebears and with it the means to challenge arbitrary autocracy.

In the three hundred years since the Enlightenment, the West has enjoyed an unprecedented rise in the human condition. By any measure, Americans are living better, longer, and freer lives than at any time in recorded history. Such gains are largely attributable to the scientific and philosophical advances that came with the resurgence of reason. It was science, not superstition, that eliminated plagues, famines, squalor, and misery; it was experimentation, not doctrine, that gave us electricity, mass transportation, and the agricultural revolution; it was reason, not blind faith, that yielded democracy, civil liberties, and freedom.

Yet despite all these gains, science and reason remain under assault. Most Americans still harbor all manner of irrational and fantastical beliefs, and magical thinking remains pervasive in American life. And this is a problem for the Republic. The Intuitionist/Rationalist split is not like other political divisions in the United States. Intuitionism poses an existential threat to democracy. It is neither benign nor temperate. It bristles against open inquiry, is intolerant of opposition, and chafes at the pluralism and compromise modern democracy requires. It is prone to conspiracy theory, drawn to simple generalizations, and quick to vilify the other.

The political intolerance of Intuitionists can be seen with a simple example. In the December 2016 survey, we asked respondents how much they agree with the statement "Americans who burn the flag should lose their citizenship." This statement was accompanied by a provocative illustration of a flag burner. Americans' responses varied highly by their Intuitionism score: 60 percent of Intuitionists want to strip the flag burner of his citizenship, compared with less than 10 percent of Rationalists. In short, Intuitionists are far more intolerant of dissent.

Now, when Intuitionism is diffused across a population or unaligned with any particular party, its authoritarian tendencies are less of a threat. But as Intuitionism congeals into political forms, it becomes dangerous to democratic values. When modern democracies fail, it's often because citizens start believing in the "magical" powers of charismatic leaders to solve all their problems. In Weimar Germany, Fascist Italy, or Chavez's Venezuela, populist demagogues rode to power on waves of Intuitionist enthusiasm. Once in charge, they quickly began to dismantle democratic institutions. And Donald Trump is the embodiment of this. The bullying, hatred, and harassment directed toward anyone, liberal or conservative, who criticizes Trump or the government is emblematic of such authoritarian impulse.

And as Intuitionism has come to dominate modern conservatism and the Republican Party, it becomes more of a threat to America's democratic norms.

What does this mean for the future of American democracy? In a book such as this, it's tempting to offer some type of specific solution or, more commonly, to make some bold prognostication. We offer neither. Partly, this is a function of our knowledge. Our research is more of a first than a final step. Our Intuitionism scale, for all its predictive punch, is still a crude instrument. There is much left to learn about how our intuitions function and how they shape our political beliefs. We hope that this work will inspire further research into the ways that intuitions structure our political beliefs. Nevertheless, we are only at the beginning of this effort.

But part of the problem comes from knowing exactly where Intuitionism resides in our democracy. Intuitionism is both a structural and a psychological challenge. Structurally, it is manifest within the American conservative movement and, increasingly, within the Republican Party. And there are several ways this structural challenge will play out. It's possible that Intuitionism will ebb as a political threat. The United States benefits from the fact that power is dispersed and shared across so much of the government. The framers of the Constitution were keenly sensitive to the power of "passions" and the discord these could wreak on democratic governance. And the system of divided and shared powers has generally worked—apart from the Civil War, America has enjoyed a long stretch of stable and increasingly democratic governance. In American history, populist movements tend to wax and wane with the tides of partisanship and the vicissitudes of the economy. The creedal passions of the Jacksonian era, the populist movement, and the 1960s eventually resettled.[74] Intuitionism periodically ascends in US politics, but it also regularly abates. As we write this, Donald Trump's presidency continues to fumble, and further missteps may discredit an Intuitionist approach.

That noted, we should not simply assume that Intuitionism will soon wither as a political force. Intuitionism not only pervades American life, it has become thoroughly entrenched within the political Right. It is also sustained by a fractured media environment in which political raconteurs make millions playing to people's innate prejudices and passions. In an era of talk radio, cable news, and social media, dozens of programs regularly stoke indignation and fear. Add to this a robust fundamentalist movement and a growing economic dislocation among America's white working classes. Taken together, these create fertile conditions for Intuitionism to thrive.

What can a Rationalist do? One common idea, especially among liberal commentators, is to "empathize" with Intuitionists: by understanding
their feelings, one could then communicate with them. It's easy to see
where this notion comes from. Ask any parent, and she'll probably tell you
she has much better success at calming an anxious child by empathizing
with his fears than by trying to reason them away. Perhaps this approach
would also work for Enchanted America, but it seems unlikely that simply
empathizing with some Trump supporter, conspiracy theorist, or "anti-
vaxxer" will bear much fruit. As psychologist Leon Festinger noted a half
century ago, "A man with a conviction is a hard man to change. Tell him
you disagree and he turns away. Show him facts or figures and he questions your sources. Appeal to logic and he fails to see your point."[75] In
other words, Intuitionists may feel alienated from a Rationalist, liberal society, but it's not clear how to mollify them. Nor is it clear that Intuitionists
even want to be "understood" by those elites who they already see as un-
trustworthy and evil. Empathy may placate scared children because they
trust the authority of the parent, but it's probably insufficient for wrathful
populists bewildered by changes that seem beyond their control.[76]

A more fruitful approach may be to start by recognizing that many ordinary Americans have a much different way of viewing the world than most
intellectuals, pundits, and political elites. While Rationalists may hold sway
over newsrooms, bureaucratic agencies, universities, and Washington's halls
of power, ordinary Americans have a more Intuitionist perspective. We see
this in our data. By any number of measures, Intuitionists outnumber Rationalists in America by at least two to one. Yet despite this fact, America's
governing classes often try to communicate with the public as if it shared a
Rationalist perspective.

Take the example of Hillary Clinton, whose knowledge of policy and
government function were probably unmatched among recent presidential candidates. For all her considerable expertise, Clinton's long position
papers and multipoint plans did little to motivate many Intuitionists. A
similar problem existed for Mitt Romney, another highly competent Rationalist. His reasoned approach to politics did little to rally his base. Such
highly Rationalist candidates often struggle in "connecting" with ordinary
voters.

Much of this difficulty is based in a style of communication. To reach
beyond their small minority, Rationalists need to speak in terms Intuitionists comprehend. This does not mean embracing the populist, ethnocentric
bombast of a demagogue like Donald Trump. As Mitt Romney and Hillary

Clinton both show, when a dyed-in-the-wool Rationalist tries to mimic an Intuitionist politician, he or she usually comes across as cloying and inauthentic. Rather, Rationalists need to first appreciate how Intuitionists perceive the world. Nelson Mandela famously said, "If you talk to a man in a language he understands, that goes to his head. If you talk to him in his language, that goes to his heart."[77] Rationalists need to learn how to talk to Intuitionists in their language.

And what language do Intuitionists speak? We hope that we have identified some of its key elements. Intuitionists "speak" a language that's familiar to all of us. It's the language we spoke as children. It acknowledges the emotional power of uncertainty, fears, and apprehensions. It is structured around the primordial heuristics that underlie our naive judgments. It recognizes the appeal of gut impulses and common sense. Yet when Rationalists "speak" the language of Intuitionists, it doesn't mean abandoning the principles of science, reason, and fact. Rather, it means translating Rationalist values into terms that resonate with an Intuitionist worldview. It means recasting elaborate ideas into terms that are emotionally compelling. It means countering the bigotry, fantasy, and terror of Intuitionist rhetoric with competing ideas of equality, pragmatism, and hope. It means translating abstract notions like individual rights, due process, and civil liberties into compelling narratives that are easy to comprehend. In short, it means appreciating the dynamics of intuitions, which we have described throughout this book.

A useful example of this strategy can be taken from scientists who have been working to change attitudes about climate change. Edward Maibach of George Mason University suggests that "simple clear messages, repeated often, from a variety of trusted sources" are the best way to change public attitudes.[78] And what types of simple clear messages? Research by Stephen Ansolabehere and David Konisky indicates that the general public is much more attuned to the immediate threats of local toxic pollution than to general concerns about global temperature increases.[79] Thus, by recasting the debate on carbon emissions as one of mercury and lead poisoning (thereby activating contagion heuristics) and carbon dioxide levels, one can increase support for a more scientific position.

A similar strategy could be used by Rationalists to communicate across a wider variety of political issues. Whether these issues concern civil liberties or immigration policy or criminal justice, there are many areas where illiberal intuitions can be counteracted by simple messages that resonate with ordinary Americans' apprehensions and commonsense ways of understanding the world. And this is a project that liberals and conservatives can join in to-gether. Upholding the rational values that underlie the American Constitu-tion can be a unifying cause for those who otherwise see little in common. For all the discussion of ideological polarization that dominates American political discourse, true liberals and true conservatives can unite in protect-ing and sustaining the basic values and principles that define the American Republic.

Acknowledgments

This book had its beginnings in 1996, when I (Oliver) was a disheveled graduate student in Berkeley, California. As I was walking down Telegraph Avenue, I was approached by an equally disheveled guy who anxiously pressed a flyer into my hand: "Read this; it'll show you what's really going on." Covered in his small, frantic handwriting, the flyer was a rambling and mostly incoherent conspiracy theory involving space aliens, the Trilateral Commission, and Queen Elizabeth. Rather than dismiss this guy as yet another Berkeley eccentric, I was instead struck by the thought that something interesting was going on here. Perhaps this conspiracy theory could shed some light on how people think about politics? At the time, I was finishing other projects, so I made a mental note and tucked it away.

Fast-forward ten years to 2006. I had some extra space on a national survey, and, remembering the Berkeley guy, I decided to see how much Americans agreed with some common conspiracy theories. When the results came back, I was stunned: about half the public believed in conspiracy theories! Clearly, the guy in Berkeley wasn't as odd as I had thought. By then, Tom had joined Chicago's PhD program, and we decided to run some more surveys to double-check these results and see what explained them.

It turned out that the best predictor of whether someone believed in conspiracy theories was if that person also believed in end-time prophecy. This begged the question, what do conspiracy theories and apocalyptic visions have in common? Plenty of things, but mostly they're both examples of magical thinking—ways of explaining the world that contradict empirical explanations. And Americans, it turned out, are really enthusiastic magical thinkers. Large percentages of the country embrace everything from horoscopes to ghosts to Satan. In fact, magical thinkers outnumber nonmagical thinkers by at least two to one.

This gave us a bigger idea: perhaps the key to understanding irrational voters was to look at their magical beliefs. We started designing survey questions that gauged people's susceptibility to magical thinking. Not only did we find ways of predicting whether or not people believed in angels, ESP, or the "birther" conspiracy theories, the same measures predicted a lot of political attitudes as well, including support for a certain Republican presidential candidate from New York. *Enchanted America* is the result of this research.

This book wouldn't have happened without the contributions of many generous colleagues and institutions. The surveys were funded by grants from the Pioneer Fund of the Robert Wood Johnson Foundation as well as research support from both the University of Chicago and the Democracy Studies Center at Ohio State University. Early help from colleagues in the Cooperative Congressional Election Study and attendees at the 2012 conference greatly helped this project along. Oliver enjoyed support from the Institute of Governmental Studies at UC Berkeley during a sabbatical in the 2014–15 academic year. Much of chapter 5 came from separate collaborations with Wendy Rahn. Much of chapter 8 came from research assistance from Calvin TerBeek. Many of the scales were crafted with invaluable help from Jack Citrin. Paul Sniderman and William Howell gave great advice on shaping the argument. Ethan Porter helped in our early efforts to develop the survey experiments. Jamie Druckman and Larry Bartels provided incredibly detailed and useful comments and joined Diana Mutz, Hans Noel, Brendan Nyhan, John Hibbing, James Stimson, and Marc Hetherington at a miniconference on the book in April of 2016. Their terrific suggestions greatly improved the manuscript. We are also grateful to comments from Chris Achen, John Brehm, Cathy Cohen, Martin Gilens, Kirk Hawkins, William Howell, Gabriel Lenz, Tali Mendelberg, Michael Neblo, John Patty, Maggie Penn, Eric Schickler, Laura Stoker, and our many students. Benjamin Westerbrink also provided great research assistance. Lorna and Ed Goodman gave us helpful comments on early drafts. Chuck Myers remains the most outstanding editor in academic publishing, and his feedback pervades this work. Sandra Hazel provided outstanding copyediting. And of course, we are greatly indebted to the conspiracy theorist in Berkeley who triggered this project twenty years ago.

Most important, *Enchanted America* was sustained by our families. Tom would like to thank his gorgeous wife, Megan, who moved to Canberra, Chicago, and then Columbus so that he might pursue his ambition of making plots. He would also like to thank his two daughters, Eleanor and Margaret, for being constant reminders of what's important in life. Eric's wife, Thea (who's also gorgeous), offered a zillion smart insights along with unending patience in listening to him constantly ask people whether they would rather stab family photos or stick their hands in a bowl of cockroaches. Esme and Ethan, Eric's kids, truly instructed him on how intuitions work. It goes without saying, but we'll say it: none of this book would exist without their love and support.

Notes

Preface

1. Lippman, Samuelsohn, and Arnsdorf, "Trump's Week of Errors, Exaggerations and Flat-Out Falsehoods."
2. Marks and Miller, "Ten Years of Research on the False-Consensus Effect," 72.
3. Once Trump became the Republican Party's nominee, many "reasonable" Republicans supported him because they presumed he would better represent the general interests of their party's coalition.
4. Lieberman, "Intuition."

Introduction

1. Achen and Bartels, *Democracy for Realists*, call this the "folk theory" of democracy: the common assumption that citizens meet the high demands of citizenship.
2. "Large numbers of American citizens are woefully under-informed . . . and overall levels of knowledge are modest at best": Delli Carpini and Keeter, *What Americans Know about Politics and Why It Matters*, 270. Perhaps even more troubling is that "voters' perceptions of a politician's performance do not always reflect reality, such as Republicans believing that the deficit worsened under President Bill Clinton or Democrats believing that unemployment rose under President Ronald Reagan": Lenz, *Follow the Leader?*, 224.
3. Phillip Converse's seminal essay is the starting point: "The Nature of Belief Systems in Mass Publics."
4. Chong and Druckman. "Dynamic Public Opinion."
5. Oliver and Wood, "Conspiracy Theories and the Paranoid Style(s) of Mass Opinions."
6. Achen and Bartels, *Democracy for Realists*.

7. Carmines and Stimson, "The Two Faces of Issue Voting."

8. Chong and Druckman, "Framing Theory"; Kinder and Sanders, *Divided by Color*, 272; and Gilens, *Why Americans Hate Welfare*, 29.

9. Zaller, *The Nature and Origins of Mass Opinion*; Jacobs and Shapiro, *Politicians Don't Pander*; Lenz, *Follow the Leader?* For an important comparison on this point, see Lee, *Mobilizing Public Opinion*.

10. Oliver and Wood, "Conspiracy Theories and the Paranoid Style(s) of Mass Opinions"; Shermer, *Why People Believe Weird Things*; Vyse, *Believing in Magic*; Kahneman, *Thinking, Fast and Slow*; Whitehouse, "Cognitive Foundations of Religiosity." For an example in a Gallup poll, see Newport, "In U.S., 42% Believe Creationist Views of Human Origins."

11. This, of course, doesn't always mean that they are thoughtful and contemplative; indeed, they are often just the opposite, as is evident in the rigid certainty of the ideologue or the brash predictions of the pundit. In fact, it is precisely experts' reliance on these preexisting beliefs that often makes most of them bad at making accurate political predictions. For a good description of the biological sources of belief, see Hibbing, Smith, and Alford, *Predisposed*, 8–15. See also Tetlock, *Expert Political Judgment*.

12. This has been apparent since Walter Lippmann was writing in the 1920s and Columbia sociologist Bernard Bereleson and colleagues pioneered empirical research on public opinion in the 1950s. Berelson, Lazarsfeld, and McPhee, *Voting*. For more recent examples, see Achen and Bartels, *Democracy for Realists*, 9–12; Lenz, *Follow the Leader?*; Delli Carpini and Keeter, *What Americans Know about Politics and Why It Matters*. Indeed, even scholars who argue (problematically) that the "magic of aggregation" can result in collectively rational decisions, start from the premise that individual preferences are ill-informed and unstable. Page and Shapiro, *The Rational Public*, 14.

13. Sniderman, Brody, and Tetlock, *Reasoning and Choice*; Lodge and Taber, *The Rationalizing Voter*; Marcus, Neuman, and MacKuen, *Affective Intelligence and Political Judgment*; Neuman et al., *The Affect Effect*; Brader, "Striking a Responsive Chord"; Albertson and Kushner Gadarian, *Anxious Politics*.

14. Orwell, "In Front of Your Nose," 124.

15. Hume, *A Treatise on Human Nature*, 415.

16. For excellent summaries of studies looking at the innate origins of political thinking, see Hibbing, Smith, and Alford, *Predisposed*; Hatemi and McDermott, *Man Is by Nature a Political Animal*.

17. Shellnutt and Anderson, "The Divine Rise of Multilevel Marketing."

18. Oliver and Wood, "Conspiracy Theories and the Paranoid Style(s) of Mass Opinions."

19. For a good overview, see Vyse, *Believing in Magic*. See also Rozin and Nemeroff, "Sympathetic Magical Thinking"; Berenbaum, Boden, and Baker, "Emotional Salience, Emotional Awareness, Peculiar Beliefs, and Magical Thinking."

20. A well-established literature demonstrates that partisans are susceptible to engaging in motivated reasoning vis-à-vis political issues and politicians. For recent examples, see Bartels, "Beyond the Running Tally"; Gaines et al., "Same Facts, Different Interpretations"; Gerber and Huber, "Partisanship, Political Control, and Economic Assessments." Indeed, there is some evidence that even those with higher levels of political knowledge suffer from this same bias: "Party identification colors the perceptions of even the most politically informed citizens far more than the relatively less informed citizens." Shani, "Knowing Your Colors" (paper), 31.

21. This is the same type of "motivated reasoning" that permeates contemporary political thought. When conservatives think that climate change is a hoax or when liberals believe that raw milk is healthier, they are driven by the same impulses of people who believe in astrology or faith healing—the need to restore emotional balance in the midst of threatening circumstances.

22. Two seminal texts on this are Frazer, *The Golden Bough*, 1990 ed., 701–11; and Jung and Von Franz, *Man and His Symbols*.

23. Amos Tversky and Daniel Kahneman pioneered psychological research in this field. Tversky and Kahneman, "Belief in the Law of Small Numbers"; "Judgment under Uncertainty"; and "Extensional versus Intuitive Reasoning." See also Kuran and Sunstein, "Availability Cascades and Risk Regulation"; Bar-Hillel, "The Base-Rate Fallacy in Probability Judgments"; Kahneman and Lovallo, "Delusions of Success." For a comprehensive overview of this literature, see Kahneman, *Thinking, Fast and Slow*.

24. Kahneman, Knetsch, and Thaler, "Anomalies."

25. Jean Piaget is the towering figure in this area for his pathbreaking work exploring magical thinking in children. For example, see his classic works, *The Child's Conception of Space*; *The Child's Conception of the World*; and *The Moral Judgment of the Child*. More recent work on this topic includes Vyse, *Believing in Magic*, 177–94; Zusne and Jones, *Anomalistic Psychology*, 26–32; and Berzonsky, "The Role of Familiarity in Children's Explanations of Physical Causality." A thorough overview of the literature on children and magical thinking can be found in Subbotsky, *Magic and the Mind*, chaps. 2, 4.

26. Shtulman, *Scienceblind*.

27. See Hartz, *The Liberal Tradition in America*.

Chapter One

1. Like the ancient Greek astronomer Eratosthenes of Cyrene. He noticed that the same vertical sticks would cast shadows of different lengths, depending on how far north or south they were. He deduced that this was because the earth is curved. Even more impressively, by comparing the length of the shadows,

Eratosthenes was able to calculate a remarkably accurate estimate of the earth's actual circumference.

2. In fact, most of the world's cultures have started with the idea that the world is a flat disk or plane. See Ascher and Ascher, "Ethnomathematics."

3. Gmelch, "Superstition and Ritual in American Baseball."

4. In reality, there is absolutely no scientific evidence that Phiten necklaces are altering anyone's energy levels. Yes, there is electricity in our bodies, and yes, Phiten necklaces hold trace amounts of titanium. But there is no possible way these tiny flecks could make any difference in our bodies' electrical flow. From a scientific perspective, the energy benefits of Phiten necklaces are an illusion. Boyles, "Phiten Necklaces."

5. Chase, "10 of Baseball's Greatest Fan Superstitions, Ranked by Effectiveness."

6. Malinkowski, *Magic, Science, and Religion and Other Essays*. Related to this, see Styers, *Making Magic*.

7. Malinkowski, *Magic, Science, and Religion*.

8. Malinowski concluded, "Magic is to be expected whenever man comes to an unbridgeable gap, a hiatus in his knowledge or in his powers of practical control, and yet has to continue in his pursuit. Forsaken by his knowledge, baffled by the results of his experience, unable to apply any effective technical skill, he realizes his impotence. Yet his desire grips him only the more strongly. His fears and hopes, his general anxiety, produce a state of unstable equilibrium, by which he is driven to some sort of vicarious activity. . . . Fear moves every human being to aimless but compulsory acts." Ibid., 108.

9. Indeed, psychological experiments show that magical thinking often can do this. Take, for instance, recent psychological experiments with putting a golf ball. In one experiment, half the research subjects were told they were putting a "lucky" ball; the other half were not. Those who were told they were putting a lucky ball subsequently had much better putting scores than those who did not. Damisch, Stoberock, and Mussweiler, "Keep Your Fingers Crossed!" But note that Robert Calin-Jageman and Tracy L. Caldwell could not replicate these findings in a subsequent study: "Replication of the Superstition and Performance Study by Damisch, Stoberock, and Mussweiler (2010)."

10. Visions of a watching and judgmental God may have been essential for human development in larger societies away from small foraging tribes. See Norenzayan, *Big Gods*.

11. Kahneman, *Thinking, Fast and Slow*, pt. 1 and chap. 4; Cacioppo and Petty, "The Elaboration Likelihood Model of Persuasion."

12. "System 2 allocates attention to the effortful mental activities that demand it, including complex computations": Kahneman, *Thinking, Fast and Slow*, 21.

13. "Anxiety is the output of the surveillance system, identifying the unexpected appearance of unfamiliar and or threatening circumstances": Marcus, "The Psychology of Emotion and Politics," 203. See also Salovey and Mayer, "Emo-

tional Intelligence"; Mayer and Geher, "Emotional Intelligence and the Identification of Emotion."

14. Kahneman, *Thinking, Fast and Slow*, 39–49.

15. This is Herbert Simon's famous notion of "satisficing": Simon, "Rationality as Process and Product of Thought." This is also where we part ways with George Marcus, W. Russell Neuman, and Michael MacKuen's *Affective Intelligence and Political Judgment*. In their model, uncertainty in the political environment forces us to become more deliberative and rational in our thinking. When we detect an anomaly or some uncertainty in the political environment, we become anxious and our brains shift from System 1 to System 2 types of thinking. As Marcus, Neuman, and MacKuen assert, "When we find ourselves in the political geography of uncertainty, we cannot safely rely on past lessons, especially lessons that are embedded in automatic judgments. The theory of affective intelligence holds that in such circumstances we turn to the less often used mode of explicit consideration. Rationality is critical to managing uncertain circumstances": *Affective Intelligence and Political Judgment*, 127. For political scientists, this was a pathbreaking effort to integrate emotions into the psychology of political decision making. It also was crucial for getting researchers to consider how System 1 and System 2 thinking shape public opinion. But Marcus, Neuman, and MacKuen's theory has not had great empirical support. Ladd and Lenz, "Reassessing the Role of Anxiety in Vote Choice."

16. For an exceptional and accessible overview of Kahneman and Tversky's and others' work on this influential concept, see Kahneman, *Thinking, Fast and Slow*, 109–95.

17. Even Gerd Gigerenzer, a critic of Kahneman vis-à-vis heuristics, accepts that many heuristics are unconscious in nature. Gigerenzer and Gaissmaier, "Heuristic Decision Making." On the physiological process of human eyesight, see Sernagor et al., *Retinal Development*.

18. See, for example, Tversky and Kahneman, "Extensional versus Intuitive Reasoning."

19. This question was asked in a pilot survey for this book conducted in July of 2014 with 1,294 respondents.

20. When we gave this question to a nationally representative sample, 65 percent thought Steven was a mathematical technician, 16 percent said a stockbroker, 11 percent a fast-food worker, and 9 percent a retail salesperson—proportions that are directly opposite of the frequency of these occupations in the labor market. For a detailed breakdown of labor statistics by occupation, see the U.S. Department of Labor's "Labor Force Statistics from the Current Population Study."

21. Converse's seminal essay is the obvious starting point here: "The Nature of Belief Systems in Mass Publics." See also Zaller, *The Nature and Origins of Mass Opinion*, 101; McCarty, Poole, and Rosenthal, *Polarized America*; Lewis-Beck et al., *The American Voter Revisited*, 287–89. As partisan polarization has increased, a

veritable cottage industry of political science literature has sprouted, debating the extent to which voters are truly ideological. Fiorina, Abrams, and Pope, *Culture War?*, 2nd ed.; Levundusky, *The Partisan Sort*; Abramowitz, *The Disappearing Center*; Abramowitz and Webster, "The Rise of Negative Partisanship and the Nationalization of U.S. Elections in the 21st Century."

22. Damasio, *Descartes' Error*; Evans and Cruse, *Emotion, Evolution, and Rationality*; Bechara, "The Role of Emotion in Decision-Making"; Ratner and Herbst, "When Good Decisions Have Bad Outcomes." For a dissenting view, see Pham, "Emotion and Rationality."

23. Lodge and Taber, *The Rationalizing Voter*.

24. Ibid., 58.

25. Sears, "Symbolic Politics," 138; Druckman, "Priming the Vote"; Valentino, Brader, and Jardina, "Immigration Opposition among U.S. Whites"; Druckman and Jacobs, *Who Governs?*, 73–81.

26. Mendelberg, *The Race Card*, 116–19.

27. Cunningham-Parmeter, "Alien Language."

28. Lodge and Taber, *The Rationalizing Voter*, 23.

29. Sniderman, Brody, and Tetlock, *Reasoning and Choice*; Lenz, *Follow the Leader?* On the obverse of this—negative partisanship—see Abramowitz and Webster, "The Rise of Negative Partisanship and the Nationalization of U.S. Elections in the 21st Century."

30. Frazer, *The Golden Bough*.

31. Schwarz et al., "Base Rates, Representativeness, and the Logic of Conversation."

32. This also why water buffaloes and hippos are some of Africa's deadliest animals; because they possess few of the hallmark traits of dangerous animals (sharp teeth, fur, etc.), people tend to underestimate their danger.

33. Rozin, Millman, and Nemeroff, "Operation of the Laws of Sympathetic Magic in Disgust and Other Domains."

34. The data for this book come primarily from on-line public opinion surveys collected by the authors. To collect our data, we constructed surveys on Qualtrics, an online survey platform. We then subcontracted with a research company, Survey Sampling International, to send a nationally representative sample of respondents to the site, where we gathered their responses. The respondents were subject to several quality screening questions to ensure they were paying attention to the content of the questions. The data were then weighted to be representative of national trends. In all, we conducted six national surveys between August 2014 and December 2016.

35. Interestingly, about two-thirds of our sample says that the least-dangerous shape was object E. Something about this abstract shape failed to elicit any negative feelings, although what this is, exactly, is not especially clear. The only conclusion we can draw is that if you really want to trick someone, hide a trap under something that looks like a fried egg.

36. Lakoff and Johnson, *Metaphors We Live By*.

37. This question was first asked in our July 2014 pilot study, where 60 percent said they would rub the ticket on a dollar bill, compared with only 40 percent who said they would use a napkin. When we followed up with our August 2014 study, we included a slight variant. In addition to randomly assigning people to groups in which the talisman was either a paper napkin or a dollar bill, we added a third category of a hundred-dollar bill. Interestingly, only 45 percent of the participants said they would rub the ticket on the hundred-dollar bill, compared with 53 percent who said they'd use the dollar bill, although this response was still higher than the 40 percent who said they'd use the paper napkin. We suspect this result was due to the fact that fewer people have hundred-dollar bills. In any event, representativeness heuristics don't always seem to grow in a linear fashion.

38. Gilovich, Griffin, and Kahneman, *Heuristics and Biases*.

39. "Disgust has humble origins. At root, it is a biological adaptation, warding us away from ingesting certain substances that could make us sick. This is why feces, vomit, urine and rotten meat are universally disgusting; they contain harmful toxins. We react strongly to the idea of touching such substances and find the notion of eating them worse. This Darwinian perspective also explains why we see disgusting substances as contaminants—if some food makes even the slightest contact with rotting meat, for instance, it is no longer fit to eat. After all, the microorganisms that can harm us spread by contact, and so you not only should avoid disgusting things, you should avoid anything that the disgusting things make contact with": Bloom, "To Urgh Is Human."

40. Rozin, Millman, and Nemeroff, "Operation of the Laws of Sympathetic Magic in Disgust and Other Domains."

41. Klaczynski, "There's Something about Obesity."

42. Douglas, *Purity and Danger*.

43. Eskridge, "Body Politics."

44. Faulkner et al., "Evolved Disease-Avoidance Mechanisms and Contemporary Xenophobic Attitudes."

45. Biss, *On Immunity*.

46. Ansolabehere and Konisky, *Cheap and Clean*.

47. Nussbaum, *Upheavals of Thought*; Morone, *Hellfire Nation*; Sehat, *The Myth of American Religious Freedom*.

48. Guthrie, *Faces in the Clouds*.

49. On the Heider and Simmel experiment, see Kahneman, *Thinking, Fast and Slow*, 76–77.

50. In their classic article, David Premack and Guy Woodruff noted, "An individual has a theory of mind if he imputes mental states to himself and others. A system of inferences of this kind is properly viewed as a theory because such states are not directly observable, and the system can be used to make predictions about the behavior of others": Premack and Woodruff, "Does the Chimpanzee Have a

Theory of Mind?," 516. See also Simon Baron-Cohen, "Theory of Mind in Normal Development and Autism."

51. "Any appearance of guilt or contrition in dogs is the result of the animals having adapted to live with humans over thousands of years—basically, they've learned to act in a submissive way when their masters express anger or glower downwards at them": Dockrill, "Dogs May Look Ashamed, but They Don't Feel Guilt."

52. Epley, Waytz, and Cacioppo, "On Seeing Human."

53. Fenster, *Conspiracy Theories*. For a good example of how millennialist Christians view the world, see Robertson, *The New World Order*.

54. "We defined the availability heuristic as the process of judging frequency by 'the ease with which instances come to mind.'" Kahneman, *Thinking, Fast and Slow*, 128.

55. Mueller and Stewart, *Terror, Security, and Money*, 19.

56. Schultz, Dayan, and Montague, "A Neural Substrate of Prediction and Reward."

57. Baddeley, *Human Memory*.

58. See Achen and Bartels, *Democracy for Realists*; Egan and Mullin, "Local Weather and Climate Concern."

59. Nickerson, "Confirmation Bias."

60. Festinger, *A Theory of Cognitive Dissonance*, vol. 1.

61. Brugger and Graves, "Testing vs. Believing Hypotheses."

62. On Pentecostal and charismatic Christians in the United States and around the world, see "Spirit and Power" (survey).

63. Bettelheim, *The Uses of Enchantment*.

64. See, for example, the following by Nyhan and Reifler: "Displacing Misinformation about Events"; "Does Correcting Myths about the Flu Vaccine Work?"; and "When Corrections Fail."

65. Smith and Tau, "Birtherism."

66. Oliver and Wood, "Conspiracy Theories and the Paranoid Style(s) of Mass Opinions."

Chapter Two

1. Depending on the wording of the survey question, between 79 and 89 percent of Americans profess a belief in God. Newport, "Most Americans Still Believe in God" (survey). The *New York Times* summarized recent research on an active God: "Most Americans believe God is directly involved in their personal affairs, and that the good or bad things that happen 'part of God's plan.'" Parker-Pope, "Most Believe God Gets Involved."

2. Seventy-two and seventy-one percent of Americans believe in angels and heaven, respectively. Newport, "Most Americans Still Believe in God" (survey). Ac-

cording to Rasmussen Reports, 64 percent of Americans believe in Jesus Christ's resurrection. "64% Believe Jesus Christ Rose from the Dead" (survey).

3. Oliver and Wood, "Conspiracy Theories and the Paranoid Style(s) of Mass Opinions," 956.

4. On belief in ghosts, see Wen, "Why Do People Believe in Ghosts?"; Moore, "Three in Four Americans Believe in Paranormal" (survey).

5. In 2013, perhaps in light of the reelection of President Obama, the number of Americans who told the Barna Group, a Christian polling firm, that humans are living in end-time shot up to 41 percent. Chumley, "4 in 10 American Adults."

6. Of Americans, "31 percent are theistic evolutionists, and 19 percent are atheistic evolutionists": Green, "You Can't Educate People into Believing in Evolution." On humans and dinosaurs roaming the earth together, see Moore, "Over 40% of Americans Believe Humans and Dinosaurs Shared the Planet" (survey). Indeed, the most prominent creation science museum, located in Petersburg, Kentucky, prominently features humans and dinosaurs cohabitating. Goldberg, "Were There Dinosaurs on Noah's Ark?"

7. For many Americans, religious beliefs may exist more as empty ideas rather than expressions of ontology. They may believe in God, for example, not because they've had a supernatural experience or that they rely on their innate intuitions but because God is an idea they were brought up with. In this case, their belief in God is no different from the belief that the earth revolves around the sun, that George Washington was the first president, or any other notion that they haven't perceived firsthand. For such people, their magical beliefs are less of a worldview and more of a cultural affectation.

8. See our online appendix for a full description of the surveys. Unless otherwise indicated, the results in this chapter come from combining our January and September 2015 surveys.

9. The scale is generated from a factor score, which comes from a single solution to a principal component analysis. The factor score has a mean value of 0 and a standard deviation of 1.

10. Butler and Mathews, "Cognitive Processes in Anxiety."

11. Our survey questions were inspired by some very innovative experiments by psychologists Paul Rozin and colleagues. Drawing from the work of Malinowski and Fraser, Rozin, Linda Millman, and Carol Nemeroff wanted to gauge the sensitivity of ordinary people to cues of homeopathic and contagious magic. In their experiments, they did things like comparing how well subjects rated juices associated with a sterilized roach, how highly they rated sugar taken from a bottle marked Cyanide (even though they are explicitly told the powder is sugar), how they rated fudge in the shape of dog feces, or how well they can throw darts at pictures of someone they dislike (e.g., Hitler) versus someone they like (e.g., John F. Kennedy). Rozin, Millman, and Nemeroff found that simple associations with unpleasant factors had a big impact on their subjects' evaluations. Subjects, for

example, rated fudge as less tasty if it came in the shape of dog feces than not, or drinks less flavorful if sweetened with sugar from a bottle that said Cyanide than from one that said Sugar. See Rozin, Millman, and Nemeroff, "Operation of the Laws of Sympathetic Magic in Disgust and Other Domains."

12. Unlike with the pessimism and apprehension scales, the symbolic thinking scale is simply an additive scale of the six (or sometimes first five) items.

13. This scale comes from combining the apprehension, pessimism, and symbolic thinking scales via a single factor analysis, where all three of our subscales load strongly on this single dimension. Their strong loading is not surprising, as all three subscales are highly correlated with one another: symbolic thinkers tend to be more apprehensive (and vice versa), and both symbolic and apprehensive thinkers are more pessimistic. Given that we were adjusting survey items through the course of our research, our Intuitionism measures were not always identical across all surveys. For example, in our January and September 2015 surveys, we had questions only on the first five items for the symbolic thinking scale and not the ticket-buying question. In the October 2014 survey, we had a question about economic recession only for the pessimism scale. In the August 2014 survey, we did not have any questions for the apprehension scale. And in the December 2016 survey, we found sharp differences in the pessimism responses following Donald Trump's election. This changed the predictive power of the Intuitionism scale regarding many magical beliefs, so we excluded the pessimism items from this survey. Doing so left us with a noisier Intuitionism scale, but one that still predicted magical beliefs in a manner similar to the other surveys.

14. The principal component analysis generates a factor score with a mean of 0 and a standard deviation of 1. To compute our Intuitionism scale, we rescaled the variable so that the minimum value was 0 and the maximum value was 1. Because of the relatively high level of magical thinking in the public, this gave us a measure with a mean score of .54 (not .5) and a standard deviation of −14 in our combined 2015 data set.

15. "Specifically, young children promiscuously assert that entities of all types, including non-living natural objects, are 'made for something'": Keleman, "Function, Goals, and Intention," 177.

16. Piaget, *The Origins of Intelligence in Children.*

17. Keleman, "The Scope of Teleological Thinking in Preschool Children"; Keleman, "Are Children 'Intuitive Theists'?"

18. For recent comprehensive efforts by political scientists to "explain" such matters, see Scholzman, Verba, and Brady, *The Unheavenly Chorus*; Lewis-Beck et al., *The American Voter Revisited.*

19. Another version of the question asks the respondents which statement about "their existence" they most agree with: (1) it is "an accidental and arbitrary by-product of animal evolution"; or (2) it is "something with a particular purpose." About 70 percent choose the latter.

20. This figure describes the predicted probabilities derived from a logistic regression of the Intuitionism scale on four questions about supernatural beliefs while controlling for education, age, gender, and whether respondents identify as "fundamentalist, conservative, or orthodox in their religious beliefs." Once again, these figures come from the January and September 2015 surveys.

21. Similar results also occur when we use a differently worded question. If we ask respondents how much they agree with the statement "The things that happen in their life do so for a particular reason," we find only 40 percent of non-Intuitionists agreeing, compared with over 70 percent of Intuitionists.

22. Piaget, *The Moral Judgment of the Child*.

23. We asked our respondents how much they agree with the statement "Even if you don't get caught, eventually you'll pay for your bad deeds."

24. When we asked respondents why they believe that they will eventually pay, we find that Intuitionists are much more likely to think that God would punish them for bad deeds or that they would be haunted by feelings of guilt. Rationalists are far less likely to invoke God or guilt as a source of retribution.

25. Interestingly, across the Intuitionism scale, there are no major differences in the percentage of Americans seeing God as an indifferent cosmic force: roughly a quarter of them subscribe to this view, no matter their Intuitionist tendencies.

26. For an authoritative history, see Marsden, *Fundamentalism and American Culture*.

27. Steensland et al., "The Measure of American Religion."

28. Marsden, *Understanding Fundamentalism and Evangelicalism*.

29. Torrey et al., *The Fundamentals*. Specifically, see chap. 34, "The Atonement," by Franklin Johnson; and chap. 37, "Salvation by Grace," by Thomas Spurgeon. Additionally, see the journal article "Chicago Statement on Biblical Inerrancy," and chap. 3, "John Nelson Darby and Dispensationalism," in Sandeen, *The Roots of Fundamentalism*.

30. Luo, "On Abortion, It's the Bible of Ambiguity." Polkinghorne, *Testing Scripture*, 33: "What is true of life in general is true also of the bible in particular. An honest reading of scripture will acknowledge the presence in its pages of various kinds of ambiguity."

31. Respondents could answer these statements with a five-point scale ranging from Strongly Disagree to Strongly Agree. These percentages are those who answered Strongly Agree/Agree.

32. See Marty and Appleby, *Fundamentalisms Observed*.

33. These estimates were calculated by dividing the sample into quintiles along the Intuitionism scale.

34. For positive thinking, respondents were asked if they agree with the statement "We can help people in need by sending them positive thoughts." Paranormal beliefs bear a strong substantive resemblance to Christians' beliefs in prayer, intervention by an active God, heaven, hell, and angels.

35. Once again, we calculated this simply by dividing the Intuitionism scale into quintiles. Among Rationalists (the lowest quintile), 18 percent say they've seen a ghost, and 7 percent say they've generated luck; among Intuitionists (the highest quintile), 32 percent say they've seen a ghost, and 17 percent they've generated luck.

36. Masci, "For Darwin Day, 6 Facts about the Evolution Debate" (survey).

37. "Our predilection for causal thinking exposes us to serious mistakes in evaluating the randomness of truly random events. . . . We are pattern seekers, believers in a coherent world, in which regularities appear not by accident but as a result of mechanical causality or of someone's intention": Kahneman, *Thinking, Fast and Slow*, 115.

38. In our August 2014 survey, we see big differences along the Intuitionism scale. Among Rationalists (the lowest quintile on the Intuitionism scale), 29 percent would rub the lottery ticket on a dollar bill and 31 percent on a napkin; among Intuitionists (the highest quintile), 60 percent would rub the ticket on a dollar bill and 40 percent on a napkin.

39. Although not listed here, we also found some other differences in judgment along the Intuitionism scale. In our October 2014 data, for example, we found that Intuitionists were less likely than Rationalists to take the optimal choice when facing the "Monty Hall" problem (see https://en.wikipedia.org/wiki/Monty_Hall _problem). They were also more likely to think that a general horoscope-type description was more likely to apply to them after they were arbitrarily labeled as an "under-estimator."

40. The exceptions are believers in an observant God, biblical inerrancy, prayer, and Bible codes, where the differences between self-described fundamentalists and nonfundamentalists are slightly greater than between Rationalists and Intuitionists.

Chapter Three

1. Unless otherwise noted, the findings in this chapter were generated using a data set from the combined January and September 2015 surveys.

2. The bootstrap method we employ is from a class of methods called nonparametric resampling. We take the survey data that we collected and construct a new data set comprising a random subset of the rows of the original data set. Some of the original cases might be included multiple times in the new data, or they might be omitted. A linear model is estimated on the new data, and predicted values are computed and stored, before discarding the new data set. This process is repeated one thousand times so that we can observe the variance in the predicted values. The fitted values are predictions of a latent variable, whose values are on an arbitrary scale. To aid in the interpretation of these figures, we compute the sample

percentiles for each variable. The figures report distribution of these expected percentiles. The distributions thus don't reflect the distribution of the underlying cases—they instead represent the difference in the statistical predictions (controlling for the indicated variables).

3. Keleman, Rottman, and Seston, "Professional Physical Scientists Display Tenacious Teleological Tendencies."

4. The literature on this point is vast, and, it should be noted, social causation theory demonstrates that poverty precedes psychological problems. For recent studies on this and related points, see Lipman and Boyle, *Linking Poverty and Mental Health* (report); Breslau, "Mental Disorders and Subsequent Educational Attainment in a US National Sample"; Hudson, "Socioeconomic Status and Mental Illness." Nor is the issue limited to adults: McLeod and Shanahan, "Trajectories of Poverty and Children's Mental Health." These issues can carry into adulthood. See Evans and Cassells, "Childhood Poverty, Cumulative Risk Exposure, and Mental Health in Emerging Adults"; Wadsworth et al., "An Indirect Effects Model of the Association between Poverty and Child Functioning."

5. For each of these questions, respondents could choose an answer on a five-point scale. For those feeling "anxious about having enough money" and or that "things are spiraling out of control," their answer could range from Never to Every Day. For the state of their finances in the coming year, they could choose an answer ranging from Get Much Worse to Get Much Better.

6. This was done with a confirmatory factor analysis.

7. The financial anxiety scale was recoded from 0 to 1. The lowest income group (those making less than $20,000 a year) had a score of .65; the highest income group (those making over $150,000 a year) had a score of .45. There is a steady linear drop in scores between these two poles as one moves up the income ladder.

8. When we regress the nine-point income scale on Intuitionism, we find a statistically significant coefficient of −.036. But when the financial insecurity item is added to the model, the income coefficient drops to −.001 and loses statistical significance.

9. See the online appendix for a full description of the relationship between income and the measures of social alienation.

10. Tobacyk and Milford, "Belief in Paranormal Phenomena"; Vyse, *Believing in Magic*; Dag, "The Relationship among Paranormal Beliefs, Locus of Control and Psychopathology in a Turkish College Sample"; Wolfradt, "Dissociative Experience, Train Anxiety and Paranormal Beliefs."

11. Davis, "Measuring Individual Differences in Empathy." "Women have more intimate relationships, are more concerned about them, and feel more empathy toward their friends, though not toward strangers": Pinker, *The Blank Slate*, 345.

12. Adorno et al., *The Authoritarian Personality*.

13. For example, using the Feldman and Stenner measure of authoritarian child rearing (see below), we find significant correlations between the authoritarianism

scale and the immanent justice, Manichaean, and gender roles measure (typically between .22 and .26) as well as the intuition measure.

14. Feldman and Stenner, "Perceived Threat and Authoritarianism."

15. See Altemeyer, *Right-Wing Authoritarianism.*

16. See Duckitt, "Authoritarianism and Group Identification."

17. Feldman and Stenner, "Perceived Threat and Authoritarianism"; Hetherington and Weiler, *Authoritarianism and Polarization in American Politics.*

18. Meaning they score in the top third of our fundamentalism scale.

19. In the online appendix, we specify this in more detail. But to briefly summarize, regression equations predicting the authoritarianism scale reveal very large coefficients with fundamentalism, supernaturalism, and folk science beliefs. They show negative coefficients with the paranormal scale.

20. See, for example, Dobson, *Dare to Discipline*; Tripp and Powlison, *Shepherding a Child's Heart.*

21. We also ran tests for viewing the effects of the "big five" personality measures. Although we found some correlates with these measures, we didn't have much confidence in the construct itself, so we aren't including it here. Our discussion can be found in the online appendix.

22. Rozin et al., "The CAD Triad Hypothesis," 574. See also Rozin, Haidt, and McCauley, "Disgust."

23. Schnall et al., "Disgust as Embodied Moral Judgment."

24. Rozin, Millman, and Nemeroff, "Operation of the Laws of Sympathetic Magic in Disgust and Other Domains," 703.

25. Rozin, Haidt, and McCauley originally devised thirty-two measures. Drawing from this work, we chose eight questions in two different formats. We slightly changed the wording in some of them to better fit our survey format. In four of the questions, respondents were asked to evaluate how well the following statements describe them (Very Unlike, Unlike, Neither, Like, Very Like): "I feel very sick if I see a cockroach at someone else's house"; "It would bother me a great deal to touch a dead body"; "It would make me uncomfortable to hear another couple having sex"; and "I try to avoid letting any part of my body touch a toilet seat in a public restroom, even if it is very clean." The other four questions asked people to rate how disgusting they found the following (Not Disgusting at All, Slightly Disgusting, Moderately Disgusting, Extremely Disgusting): "realizing you accidentally took a sip from a soda can that a stranger was drinking from"; "hearing a story of a thirty-year-old man having sex with an eighty-year old woman"; "smelling urine while waiting at a public bus stop"; and "accidentally touching the ashes of someone who was cremated." This scale has a Cronbach's alpha of .77.

26. When we regress the disgust sensitivity scale on the big five personality measures and indicators for age, income, and gender, we find that gender and age are the strongest predictors (with women and younger people registering higher on disgust sensitivity) as well as strong effects for neuroticism, agreeableness, and

conscientiousness. More educated people also have less disgust sensitivity, although this difference is not great.

27. The August 2014 data had large batteries on various personality measures. It did not have, however, the standard apprehension scales, so we used measures of hand washing, using lucky items, and using herbal remedies as a stand-in to calculate the Intuitionism scale. Our models controlled for education, income, gender, and authoritarian child rearing, and featured two scales for disgust sensitivity and need for cognition. The table is listed in the online appendix on p. A2.

28. Cacioppo and Petty, "The Need for Cognition," 116.

29. Cacioppo et al., "Dispositional Differences in Cognitive Motivation," 197.

30. In response to the following six questions, survey respondents were asked to put themselves on a forty-point sliding scale, with −20 indicating Not at All like Me; 0 indicating Somewhat like Me; and 20 indicating Very Much like Me. The other statements included "I only think as hard as I need to"; "I like reading about scientific discoveries and theories"; and "The more complex the idea, the more likely I am to think about something else." A factor analysis showed two loadings of these items. One was on items relating to how difficult people found thinking to be. The other related more to intellectual curiosity, such as solving problems or learning about new things or scientific theories.

31. Newport, "In U.S., 77% Identify as Christian" (survey).

32. Among nonconservative Protestants, only 22 percent believe in end-time prophecy, 48 percent believe in an intentional God, and 32 percent believe in the power of prayer.

33. Percentage believing in the power of prayer (60 percent of conservative Catholics, 31 percent of Catholics); an observant God (77 percent of conservative Catholics versus 61 percent of Catholics); end-time prophecy (31 percent of conservative Catholics versus 19 percent of Catholics).

34. In our surveys, we asked respondents to locate themselves along a five-point ideological scale, from very liberal to very conservative. Similar to other surveys, we find that about a quarter of Americans identify as liberal or very liberal, 34 percent identify as conservative or very conservative, and the rest place themselves in the middle of the ideological spectrum, either from true moderation or because they simply have no ideological predilections.

35. These measures are a three-point ideological scale (liberal, other, conservative) and a three-point party identification scale (Democrat, Republican, other) which also includes people who first identify as independent but say they lean toward one party or another as a partisan. We also divided the Intuitionism scale into thirds.

36. For example, among those identifying as strong conservative 88 percent believe in an intentional God, 85 percent believe in angels, and 73 percent believe in the power of prayer.

Chapter Four

1. The literature on polarization is both vast and contentious. Abramowitz, *The Disappearing Center*; Fiorina, Abrams, and Pope, *Culture War?*, 3rd ed.; Levundusky, *The Partisan Sort*. On the lack of "floating voters" who cross party lines, see Smidt, "Polarization and the Decline of the American Floating Voter." On partisan media, see Levundusky, *How Partisan Media Polarize America*. For a good overview of the literature on partisan media, see Dilliplane, "Activation, Confirmation, or Reinforcement?" On polarization and geography, see Sussell and Thomson, "Are Changing Constituencies Driving Rising Polarization in the U.S. House of Representatives?" (paper). On romantic partners, see Cohn, "Polarization Is Dividing American Society, Not Just Politics." On children's names, see Oliver, Wood, and Bass, "*Liberellas versus Konservateeves.*"

2. Haidt and Abrams, "The Top 10 Reasons American Politics Are So Broken."

3. Noel, *Political Ideologies and Political Parties in America*; Layman, "Party Polarization in American Politics."

4. As Christopher Achen and Larry Bartels recently put it, "The evidence demonstrates that the great majority of citizens pay little attention to politics. At election time, they are swayed by how they feel about the 'nature of the times,' especially the current state of the economy and political loyalties typically acquired in childhood." Achen and Bartels, *Democracy for Realists*, 1. See also Delli Carpini and Keeter, *What Americans Know about Politics and Why It Matters*.

5. See Wood and Oliver, "Toward a More Reliable Implementation of Ideology in Measures of Public Opinion."

6. For the canonical assessment, see Converse, "The Nature of Belief Systems in Mass Publics."

7. Dahl, *Who Governs?*, 22.

8. Converse, "The Nature of Belief Systems in Mass Publics."

9. This draws from Converse's classic work on belief systems; ibid. Or, as Noel recently put it, ideology is "a shared set of preferences . . . a system of constrained beliefs. . . . Constraint is the key element—what one believes on one issue predicts what one believes on others. Ideology therefore structures people's issue positions": Noel, *Political Ideologies and Political Parties in America*, 14.

10. Wood and Oliver, "Toward a More Reliable Implementation of Ideology in Measures of Public Opinion." For a good discussion of the state of the public opinion literature, see Carmines and D'Amico, "The New Look in Political Ideology Research."

11. Brooks, "The Republicans' Incompetent Caucus."

12. As former Republican presidential candidate Pat Buchanan says, "Our culture is superior because our religion is Christianity and that makes men free." Buchanan made this statement in a speech to the Christian Coalition in 1993 after his failed primary challenge of president H. W. Bush in 1992 (and his [in]famous

"Culture War" speech at the Republican National Convention that year): "Christian Group Keeping to Right." For an extended and thoughtful treatment of the Culture Wars and Buchanan's role in the battles, among others, see Hartman, *A War for the Soul of America*.

13. Salient examples here would be Epstein, *The Classical Liberal Constitution*, and denizens of the Cato Institute, a libertarian think tank founded by Charles Koch in 1977. Lichtblau, "Cato Institute and Koch Brothers Reach Agreement."

14. See, for example, Dreher, "Individualism and Conservatism."

15. William F. Buckley and his colleagues at *National Review* deserve the lion's share of the credit for intellectually bringing together these strands under the project of "fusionism." Glenn and Teles, "Studying the Role of Conservatives in American Political Development," 13.

16. Paul, "From Jesus' Socialism to Capitalistic Christianity." Additionally, see the following passages in the Bible as a starting point: Acts 2:44, 45, 4:32–37; Matt. 6:24, 19:21, 25:31–46; Rom. 13:1–7; Luke 14:13, 14; and Tim. 6:10. For example: "You cannot serve both God and money" (Matt. 6:24); "For the love of money is the root of all kinds of evil" (Tim. 6:10).

17. The four values are denoted with the following questions. (1) Status quo orientation: "Traditional ideas are better because they have withstood the test of time"; "People were better off in the old days when they knew just how they were supposed to act." (2) Laissez-faire economics: "The single best thing government can do is to leave the free market economy alone"; "There are too many costly and useless regulations on American business." (3) Christian tradition: "America was founded as a Christian nation, and religion should be a bigger part of public life"; "Government policies should be based solely on scientific evidence and not on spiritual beliefs." (4) Rugged individualism: "In order to help the poor, the federal government should cut funds for welfare programs and let volunteers take up the slack"; "One basic responsibility of government is to ensure that all its citizens have a minimum level of food and shelter."

18. See Feldman, "Structure and Consistency in Public Opinion"; Page and Shapiro, *The Rational Public*.

19. There is a correlation coefficient of .34 between the moral traditionalism and free market conservatism scales for liberals. For conservatives and moderates, these correlations are less than .06.

20. For example, conservatives are three times more likely than moderates or liberals to say they are conservative, orthodox, or evangelical in their religious beliefs: 55 percent of conservatives identify as evangelical Protestant, while only 13 percent of liberals do; 34 percent of conservatives identify as orthodox Christian, while only 16 percent of liberals do (the numbers for Mormons are even more disparate: 61 to 9 percent, respectively). "Religious Landscape Study" (study).

21. Ellis and Stimson, *Ideology in America*, 133.

22. When political scientists want to measure someone's liberalness or conservativeness, for example, they often tally up all their opinions on an assortment of issues, including everything from taxes and foreign aid to abortion and the environment. See Ansolabehere, Rodden, and Snyder, "The Strength of Issues."

23. The originators of this concept are Carmines and Stimson, "The Two Faces of Issue Voting."

24. In reviewing data from the American National Elections Studies, we find that the percentage of respondents answering Don't Know varies a great deal by the question. Respondents were far more likely to answer Don't Know on questions about whether the government should guarantee jobs and income, provide health insurance, or ensure school integration, all matters that are highly complex. Respondents were far less likely to say Don't Know about issues such as equal roles for women, aid to blacks, or whether they trust government officials to do what's right.

25. For the leading scholar on this, see Druckman, "Political Preference Formation."

26. Zaller, *The Nature and Origins of Mass Opinion*. Recent research has reinforced that partisans—those who tend to be better informed and more likely to enjoy higher levels of education—engage in motivated reasoning even when provided with objective measures such as the unemployment rate or the deficit. See, for example, Schaffner and Roche, "Misinformation and Motivated Reasoning"; Bartels, "Beyond the Running Tally."

27. On core values and public opinion, see Feldman, "Structure and Consistency in Public Opinion."

28. Many of these differences are attributable to the lower education and income levels of fundamentalists. On religion and education level, see Pew Research Center's extensive report on religion in America, "Religious Landscape Study"; on the homepage, click on Education under the "Topics and Questions" section. Once these factors are controlled, fundamentalism ceases to be an effective predictor of policy opinion.

29. We asked respondents five separate questions about major ACA provisions. These included (1) whether they agreed that health insurers should not be able to deny coverage to applicants based on preexisting conditions (89 percent agreeing); (2) whether young people should be able to stay on their parents' health plans until they are twenty-six years old (70 percent agreeing); (3) whether all Americans must obtain health insurance or pay a tax penalty (33 percent agreeing); (4) whether we should increase prescription benefits for senior citizens (64 percent agreeing); and (5) whether Medicaid should be expanded for people living only slightly above the poverty line (85 percent agreeing).

30. This item was based on whether the respondent rejected at least three provisions within the ACA.

31. Interestingly, the one provision of the ACA that does evoke a pattern similar to the question about Obamacare as a whole is the question of the insurance

mandate. Not only is this overwhelmingly the least popular aspect of the ACA (only a third of Americans support this as a policy), but opposition increases most precipitously among Intuitionists. Unlike general ideas about increasing health coverage for the elderly or the poor, the idea of the government mandating that citizens purchase health insurance is most objectionable to Intuitionists, regardless of their ideological leanings. Although data from the Kaiser Family Foundation Health Polls suggest that few Americans object to Obamacare specifically because of the mandate, clearly the idea of the government forcing Americans to obtain health insurance or otherwise pay a fine is something that speaks especially strongly to Intuitionists. Given the high premium they place on their intuitions, we suspect that this aspect of health policy reform speaks to some latent view.

32. "Views of Gun Control" (survey).

33. Bartels, "Constituency Opinion and Congressional Policy Making"; McCright and Dunlap, "The Politicization of Climate Change and Polarization in the American Public's Views of Global Warming, 2001–2010."

34. For the immigration question, respondents were given three choices for responding to the statement "We need to deal with the problem of illegal immigrants in the United States by . . .": (1) allowing unauthorized immigrants who have been in the United States for five years and broken no other laws to apply for official resident status (37 percent); (2) allowing some unauthorized immigrants to stay here temporarily and hold three-year work permits (26 percent); or (3) deporting all unauthorized immigrants and strengthening border security (37 percent). For the gun rights questions, respondents were asked how much they agree with the statement "Citizens should be able to carry sidearms in restaurants and shopping malls if they have a permit." Forty-five percent favor open-carry permits. For defense spending, respondents were asked, "With regard to our military, we need to . . ." and then given five choices ranging from "greatly cut defense spending" to "greatly increase defense spending." Thirty-five percent favored either modestly increasing or greatly increasing this spending.

35. For the global warming question, respondents were given three choices for finishing the sentence "Global warming is . . .": (1) not a problem we can or should try to solve (14 percent); (2) a minor problem we can solve by increasing fuel efficiency and renewable energy (36 percent); (3) a major crisis that the government immediately needs to address by reducing carbon dioxide emissions (50 percent). The gun rights statement was a five-point Likert scale with Strongly Disagree coded as 0 and Strongly Agree coded as 1.

36. For abortion, respondents were given four choices for ending the sentence "Abortion should be . . .": (1) legal in all circumstances (23 percent); (2) legal in most circumstances (25 percent); (3) only legal in cases of rape or incest (34 percent); (4) always illegal (18 percent). For this variable, the responses were coded on a four-point scale ranging from 0 (legal in all circumstances) to 1 (always illegal). For marijuana legalization, the respondents were asked to finish the sentence "The

federal government should . . ." (1) legalize marijuana for recreational use as they have in Alaska, Colorado, Oregon, and Alaska (65 percent); (2) keep the current federal laws prohibiting the sale and possession of marijuana (35 percent). Figure 4.7 lists the percentage that wants to keep the current law. For physician-assisted suicide, respondents were asked to finish the sentence "Doctors should . . ." with either (1) be able to help patients end their own life if they are suffering from a terminal disease (65 percent); (2) always try to keep their patients alive no matter what (35 percent). Those opposed to physician-assisted suicide are coded as 1, and the percentages for each category are depicted in the figure.

37. For a compilation of various religious groups' stance on abortion, see "Religious Groups' Official Positions on Abortion" (survey).

38. Conversely, if we were to supplement the Intuitionism scale with items measuring adherence to fundamentalist beliefs, such as biblical inerrancy or end-time prophecy, the effects would be even greater and would far outstrip those of ideology. In other words, by holding fundamentalist religious views constant, we are making a much more conservative estimate.

39. For two of these issues, respondents were asked how much they agree or disagree with the following three statements: "The government should provide tax breaks for people who homeschool their children" and "Eliminating gluten from your diet will make you healthier." For this figure, we report the percentage who agree. For the GMO policy, respondents were asked to choose between answering "The Federal government should . . ." (1) ban Genetically Modified Foods (GMOs); (2) not outlaw GMOs. The vaccine question was "Schools have . . ." (1) no right to tell parents whether to vaccinate their children; (2) a responsibility to ensure that all children are vaccinated.

40. Kunzman, *Write These Laws on Your Children*.

41. A 2015 survey from NSF International, a Michigan public health advocacy group, found that only 35 percent of Americans knew what gluten is (though large numbers had "heard of" it). "Confusion about Gluten-Free Foods and Identifying Them at the Grocery Store" (survey).

Chapter Five

1. As late as 2015, 24 percent of Americans were willing to say there was a "different explanation" for the terrorist attack on September 11, 2001. "60 Minutes/ Vanity Fair Poll" (survey).

2. Oliver and Wood, "Conspiracy Theories and the Paranoid Styles(s) of Mass Opinions."

3. Rahn and Oliver, "Trump Voters Aren't Authoritarians."

4. On taxes, see Bernstein, "The Flat Tax Falls Flat for Good Reasons." On flying, see Ball, "How Safe if Air Travel Really?" On swimming pools and handguns, see Levitt, "Pools More Dangerous than Guns."

5. Glueck, "Cruz Throws a Little Populism at Trump"; Lowry, "Ben Carson, the Superior Outsider"; Rubin, "What Kind of Populism?"

6. See, for example, Bonokowski and Gidron, "The Populist Style in American Politics"; Hawkins, "Is Chavez Populist?; Lee, "The Populist Chameleon"; Gerteis and Goolsby, "Nationalism in America"; Mudde, "The Populist Zeitgeist"; Jansen, "Populist Mobilization"; Kazin, *The Populist Persuasion*; Goodwyn, *The Populist Moment*.

7. On populists' rhetorical devices, see Canovan, "Trust the People!"; Hawkins, "Is Chavez Populist?"; Lee, The Populist Chameleon"; Moffitt and Tormey, "Rethinking Populism"; Stanley, "The Thin Ideology of Populism."

8. On Trump's populist rhetoric during the 2016 primaries, see Oliver and Rahn, "Rise of the Trumpenvolk."

9. See, for example, Moffitt and Tormey, "Rethinking Populism"; Canovan, "Trust the People!"; Albertazzi and McDonnell, "Introduction."

10. Arditi, "Populism as an Internal Periphery of Democratic Politics," 75.

11. As quoted in Johnson, "Donald Trump's Vision of Doom and Despair in America."

12. Oliver and Rahn, "Rise of the Trumpenvolk."

13. Sometimes populist politicians also align themselves with socialist principles, as with Venezuela's Hugo Chavez or Bolivia's Evo Morales. But frequently, they exist as competing political forces. In Europe, for example, anti-immigrant populist movements often are at odds with leftist socialists. Similarly, in the United States, Bernie Sanders often went to great lengths to differentiate his "democratic socialism" from the nativist, populist appeals of Donald Trump.

14. Fenster, *Conspiracy Theories*.

15. On Revolutionary-era pamphleteering, see Bailyn, *The Ideological Origins of the American Revolution*. On senator Joseph McCarthy, see Oshinsky, *A Conspiracy So Immense*.

16. Goldberg, *Enemies Within*.

17. Hofstadter, *The Paranoid Style in American Politics*.

18. Maduro stated, "We have the intuition that our commander Chavez was poisoned by dark forces that wanted him out of the way": quoted in Cawthorne, "Venezuela to Probe Chavez Cancer Poisoning Accusation."

19. Fenster, *Conspiracy Theories*.

20. "2016 Democratic Popular Vote" (survey).

21. We construct our measure of populism by first running a principal component analysis of twelve questions meant to gauge populist features. These four all had loadings above .64. Based on the principal component analysis, we constructed a factor score for this dimension.

22. Compared with "Ordinary people can really use the help of experts for understanding complicated things like health and science."

23. The populism scale is a simple additive scale of each of the three factor scores. Because the factor scores were calculated from a rotated factor analysis, each of the

dimensions is uncorrelated with the other. The mean value for each factor scale is 0, with a standard deviation of 1. The populism score has a mean of 0 and a standard deviation of 1.7.

24. Respondents were asked, "Among all candidates in both parties, who would be your first choice?"

25. To briefly explain the figure, each of the scales is situated so that its mean value for the entire sample is 0. What the figure illustrates is the distance from the total sample of the average score for each candidate's supporters.

26. We also ran the scales without the more partisan birther and truther conspiracy theories, and the results were largely unchanged.

27. Responses to each item were coded −2 for Strongly Disagree, −1 for Disagree, 0 for Neither Disagree nor Agree, 1 for Agree, 2 for Strongly Agree. People who agree with more conspiracy theories in total than disagree with them have positive scores; those who disagree more have negative scores; and those who neither agree nor disagree tend to score close to 0.

28. The conspiracism scale has a .47 correlation coefficient with the populism scale, a .48 correlation coefficient with the political populism scale, a .36 correlation coefficient with the cultural populism scale, and a −.03 correlation coefficient with the national affiliation scale.

29. The partial correlations are correlation coefficients that control for the effects of education, age, gender, and ideology. In other words, these are the correlations between the two variables that first control for these other, potentially cofounding variables.

30. Respondents can give answers ranging from Strongly Agree to Strongly Disagree. These items are scaled so that responses of Neither are coded as 0 and recoded so that antitax sentiments have a positive score.

31. For interpretive ease, we divided the sample into simple quintiles along each of the populism and conspiracism scales. The strong relationships depicted here are also evident in multivariate analyses that control for education, age, ideology, and gender.

32. Gass, "The 9 Worst Predictions about Trump's Rise to the Top."

33. Cohen et al., *The Party Decides*; see also Bawn et al., "A Theory of Political Parties."

34. Oliver and Rahn, "Rise of the Trumpenvolk."

35. "Donald Trump's Argument for America" (video).

Chapter Six

1. In deemphasizing the religious motivation behind these terror attacks, President Obama was in fact following the precedent set by his Republican predecessor, and trying to counter Islamist attempts to stoke a cultural war between observant Muslims and Western nations.

2. Schuman, *Racial Attitudes in America.*

3. Mendelberg, *The Race Card.*

4. Wrangham and Glowacki, "Intergroup Aggression in Chimpanzees and War in Nomadic Hunter-Gatherers."

5. Knauft et al., "Violence and Sociality in Human Evolution (and Comments and Replies)."

6. As quoted in Kinder and Kam, *Us against Them,* 5. The term *ethnocentrism* was first coined over a century ago by one of the founders of American social science, William Graham Sumner. Looking to explain how societies operated, Sumner noticed that people tended to divide the world into social groups, especially in relation to their own. He labeled this tendency ethnocentrism.

7. Ibid.

8. See LeVine and Campbell, *Ethnocentrism.* See also Kinder and Kam, *Us against Them,* for a summary of research.

9. Nor are these relationships a result of aggregating these votes and undocumented populations at a coarse geographical unit like a state. The same relationships persist even when using individual survey responses from the 2016 Cooperative Congressional Election Study, predicting presidential vote choice and political preferences for immigration policy, with undocumented immigrant population estimates measured at the county level. In each case, living in counties having more undocumented immigrants made respondents less inclined to vote for Trump, and more opposed to harsh immigration policy response, even after controlling for age, race, education, income, and partisanship. Nor is there some special electoral advantage available to a racial populist in those states disproportionately composed of unauthorized Mexican residents. If it was the case that Trump's appeals for racial reckoning had a special resonance with those voters experiencing the day-to-day anxieties from competition with Mexican nationals for jobs and public goods, we should observe a strong positive relationship. Instead, states disproportionately composed of Mexican nationals moved away from Trump, relative to 2012.

10. These range from the traumas of childhood, as described in *The Authoritarian Personality* (see chapter 3), to notions of genetic predispositions. For our research, we choose to build on the work of Kinder and Kam, Henri Tajfel's social identity theory, and Gordon Allport's book, *The Nature of Prejudice.*

11. Harnad, "To Cognize Is to Categorize."

12. Park and Judd, "Rethinking the Link between Categorization and Prejudice within the Social Cognition Perspective"; Brown, *Prejudice.*

13. For some of the earliest work on this, see Tajfel, "Social Identity and Intergroup Behaviour"; Fein and Spencer, "Prejudice as Self-Image Maintenance," 31. See also Tajfel, *Social Identity and Intergroup Relations.*

14. See Brown, "Social Identity Theory"; Abrams and Hogg, "Comments on the Motivational Status of Self Esteem in Social Identity and Intergroup Discrimination."

15. Lippmann, *Public Opinion,* 1:43.

16. Brewer and Brown, "Intergroup Relations."

17. Lippmann, *Public Opinion*, 1:45.

18. Swift, "Putin's Image Rises in US, Mostly among Republicans" (survey).

19. Smith, *Civic Ideals*.

20. For a recent overview, see Tesler, *Post-Racial or Most-Racial?*

21. But while such scales are often described as a general ethnocentrism scale, they really only apply to white ethnocentrism, since they focus on stereotypes that historically have been directed at African Americans, Latinos, and other minorities.

22. The data for this chapter were gathered in an online sample recruited by the survey firm Qualtrics in the days between the sixth and twelfth of December 2016. This survey had the fortuitous advantage of being conducted in the immediate aftermath of the presidential election—Democratic respondents were unusually anxious about the policy implications of President Trump's unexpected electoral victory, and the deeply nationalistic tenor of the election was still ringing in survey respondents' ears. Consistent with our previous surveys, we estimated survey weights using ranking to make the survey's margins reflect the adult population on race, income, gender, education, and partisanship.

23. In simple terms, we take the average of the difference between white respondents' evaluation of their group and their evaluation of some other group, averaging across groups and evaluative dimensions; i indexes traits (intelligent, hardworking, and peaceful) and j indexes nonwhite groups (Asians, Hispanics, Muslims, and blacks). In intuitive terms, E measures the extent to which a white respondent thinks that whites are more intelligent, hardworking, and peaceful, on average, than other racial/ethnic and religious groups.

There are two methodological consequences of our adopting the Kinder-Kam formulation of ethnocentrism. First, it assumes a constant effect of respondents' negative evaluation of separate groups—that is, preferences for whites over Asians or Muslims provide the same contribution to a respondent's specific E estimate. Second, it provides a constant effect of ethnocentrism from different evaluative attributes—impressions that some minority is less intelligent, or less hardworking, provide identical effects to a respondent's E estimate. Kinder and Kam defend this simplification with the claim that exploratory factor analysis suggests that a more complicated estimating procedure, allowing separate effects for particular groups and attributes, would provide a comparable estimate of overall ethnocentrism. This is *decidedly not* the case with our data and clusters. Intuitionists are particularly inclined to regard both Muslims and blacks as less hardworking and peaceful, with far smaller group differences for other combinations of groups and attributes. While we retain the simpler Kinder-Kam formulation in our chapter to maximize the comparability of our estimates, this decision causes us to underestimate the true relationship between cluster membership and ethnocentrism.

24. The conspiracy scale comes from a factor score generated by responses to questions about conspiracies concerning Wall Street, the Food and Drug Adminis-

tration, the attacks of 9/11, and Barack Obama's citizenship, and whether a secret cabal controls the world. See chapter 5 for specific item descriptions.

25. To make the coefficients legible, all variables are scaled so that their maximum value is 1 and their minimum value is 0.

26. The December 2016 survey was taken four weeks after Donald Trump's election as president. This event had a profound effect on the pessimism scale, especially the items predicting recession, terrorist attacks, and war with China and Russia. Whereas in previous surveys the pessimism scale had a robust correlation with the symbolic thinking and apprehension scales, in this survey the correlation disappeared. Moreover, the pessimism scale no longer correlated with many of the magical thinking items. This suggests that our use of the pessimism scale in earlier surveys was somewhat time bound, but also susceptible to political shocks. For the December 2016 survey, we excluded it from the Intuitionism scale. This meant that the Intuitionism scale in this survey is also less precise; for example, it is less accurate than the pessimism scale in the previous four surveys at predicting supernatural beliefs or conspiracy beliefs.

27. Coates, *Between the World and Me*; Oliver, *The Paradoxes of Integration*.

28. These items are adapted from the 2016 American National Election Study.

29. Tichenor, *Dividing Lines*.

30. As cited in Pei, "The Paradoxes of American Nationalism."

31. Baum and Nau, "Foreign Policy Views and US Standing in the World" (paper).

32. The importance question was on a seven-point sliding scale, ranging from Not Important at All to Extremely Important; the flag-flying question was on a five-point scale ranging from Never (32 percent) to Every Day (16 percent).

33. The questions: "Too many people coming across the US border are criminals or cheats"; "We need to deal with the problem of illegal immigrants in the United States by deporting all unauthorized immigrants and strengthening border security"; "On the whole, immigrants . . . are a burden on our country, taking jobs, housing, and public benefits/strengthen our country with their hard work and talents"; "For ordinary Americans, free-trade agreements like NAFTA or the Pacific Trade deal . . . cause more harm than benefits/have equal harm and benefits/cause more benefits than harm."

Chapter Seven

1. Haelle, "First Confirmed U.S. Measles Death in More than a Decade."

2. Omer et al., "Vaccine Refusal, Mandatory Immunization, and the Risks of Vaccine-Preventable Diseases."

3. Diphtheria, polio, measles, smallpox, and rubella killed nearly 650,000 people annually, on average, over the course of the twentieth century. See Mooney, "Why Does the Vaccine/Autism Controversy Live On?"

4. Stern and Markel, "The History of Vaccines and Immunization."

5. Newport, "In U.S., Percentage Saying Vaccines Are Vital Dips Slightly" (survey).

6. Fox, "Americans Spend $30 Billion a Year on Alternative Medicine."

7. See the National Center for Complementary and Integrative Health and the National Center for Health Statistics' study "The Use of Complementary and Alternative Medicine in the United States," which details alternative medicine use in the United States.

8. This is generally described as the fight-or-flight response. See Cannon's seminal works *Wisdom of the Body* and *Bodily Changes in Pain, Hunger, Fear, and Rage.*

9. Roth, *The Long Evolution of Brains and Minds.*

10. Kolata, "A Medical Mystery of the Best Kind."

11. Ingraham, "There's Never Been a Safer Time to Be a Kid in America."

12. To see a brief recounting of the Tuskegee syphilis experiment, see "U.S. Public Health Service Syphilis Study at Tuskegee" (reference work).

13. Prasad and Cifu, *Ending Medical Reversal.* Also by Prasad and Cifu, see Prasad, Cifu, and Ioannidis, "Reversals of Established Medical Practices: Evidence to Abandon Ship"; Prasad et al., "A Decade of Reversal."

14. For Edward Jenner's smallpox vaccine, see Riedel, "Edward Jenner and the History of Smallpox and Vaccination." For herd immunity, see Fine, "Herd Immunity."

15. Pitcairn, *Vaccination,* 9–10.

16. See Canadian Paediatric Society, "Autistic Spectrum Disorder," 393–95. Also see "Vaccine Safety" (study).

17. A California mother's personal communication to the authors.

18. See "Autism Spectrum Disorder": "Young children with ASD can usually be reliably diagnosed by age two."

19. Wakefield is a British doctor who in 1998 published a fraudulent research paper in the British medical journal *Lancet* purporting to show a link between the MMR vaccine and autism. He was later barred from practicing medicine in the United Kingdom.

20. See the survey by Funk, "5 Key Findings on What Americans and Scientists Think about Science."

21. See Jalonick, "Obama Signs Bill Requiring Labeling of GMO Foods."

22. See "What's Wrong with Genetic Engineering?"; our italics.

23. Feltman, "This Weird Worm Is a Surprisingly Close Cousin of Ours."

24. Blancke, "Why People Oppose GMOs Even Though Science Says They Are Safe."

25. Gelman, "Psychological Essentialism in Children."

26. Repp, "Biotech Pollution."

27. See Brown, "Human Universals, Human Nature and Human Culture"; Meyer-Rochow, "Food Taboos."

28. Harris, *Good to Eat.*

29. Simoons, *Eat Not This Flesh.*

30. Gribble, "Food Chemistry and Chemophobia."

31. Abelson, "Testing for Carcinogens with Rodents."

32. Mosby, "'That Won-Ton Soup Headache.'"

33. "Within days of the cyclamate ban, consumer advocate Ralph Nader warned Congress that monosodium glutamate (MSG), an additive in baby food, was harmful to infants." Mazur, *True Warnings and False Alarms*, 25.

34. "Questions and Answers on Monosodium Glutamate (MSG)."

35. Obayashi and Nagamura, "Does Monosodium Glutamate Really Cause Headache?," 54.

36. Levinovitz, *The Gluten Lie*.

37. See Vani Hari's website at http://foodbabe.com.

38. Francl, "Are Corporations Putting Feathers in Your Food?"

39. "Frequently Asked Questions on Azodicarbonamide (ADA)."

40. For an excellent description of the diet plan formula, see Gladwell, "The Pima Paradox."

41. Ibid.

42. "What Is Celiac Disease?" (reference work).

43. Levinovitz, *The Gluten Lie*.

44. Brown, "Human Universals, Human Nature and Human Culture."

45. "Americans Spent $33.9 Billion Out-of-Pocket on Complementary and Alternative Medicine."

46. As Marcia Angell and Jerome Kassirer note, "What most sets alternative medicine apart, in our view, is that it has not been scientifically tested and its advocates largely deny the need for such testing." Angell and Kassirer, "Alternative Medicine," 840.

47. Chopra, "Medicine's Great Divide."

48. While it is a common trope that placebo tests are often as efficacious as real medicine, the empirical evidence is lacking. Comparisons of samples given a placebo with samples given no medical treatment show the same rates of healing. See Hróbjartsson and Gøtzsche, "Is the Placebo Powerless?"

49. Refer to "Homeopathy."

50. For an example of magical correspondence, see Wigington, "Magical Correspondence Tables" (reference work).

51. Wang, "Dandelion Health Benefits" (reference work).

52. As Dr. Paul Offit notes, "They've spent $374,000 of taxpayer money to find out that inhaling lemon and lavender scents doesn't promote wound healing; $390,000 to find out that ancient Indian remedies don't control Type 2 diabetes; $446,000 to find that magnetic mattresses don't treat arthritis; $283,000 to discover that magnets don't treat migraine headaches; $406,000 to determine that coffee enemas don't cure pancreatic cancer; and $1.8 million to find out that prayer doesn't cure AIDS or brain tumors or improve healing after breast reconstruction surgery." Offit, *Do You Believe in Magic?*, 13.

53. Marshall, "The Politics of Alternative Medicine."

54. The 2013 data come from a nationally representative, online survey sample of 1,351 adults that was collected in August and September of 2013 by Internet market research company YouGov. The 2015 data come from a nationally representative, online survey sample of 1,275 adults that was generated by Survey Sampling International. Both surveys were weighted to provide a representative sample of the population.

55. The strength of this association may be partly related to the content of the conspiracy theories in question. In the January 2015 survey, the conspiracy theories included questions about FDA, vaccines, and the health effects of cell phone use.

Chapter Eight

1. McLaughlin, "No, This Is Not How We Got Trump."

2. Frank, "Donald Trump Is Moving to the White House, and Liberals Put Him There."

3. Plumer, "What a Liberal Sociologist Learned from Spending Five Years in Trump's America."

4. Lerner, "Stop Shaming Trump Supporters."

5. It is important to also recognize some structural factors behind Trump's victories. In the primary election, Trump benefited from unprecedented media coverage and a divided opposition. In the general election, most voters who supported Trump did so because they were Republicans and he was the Republican nominee. The hatred that many Trump voters expressed toward the "liberal media" was simply an echo of a theme common to conservative media over the past three decades. In other words, much of Trump's success can be attributed to structural factors that had little to do with him.

6. Gerth and Mills, *From Max Weber*.

7. Ahlstrohm, *A Religious History of the American*.

8. Ellwood, *The Fifties Spiritual Marketplace*.

9. Thomas, *Religion and the Decline of Magic*.

10. Trussler and Soroka, "Consumer Demand for Cynical and Negative News Frames."

11. Liu, Huang, and Brown, "Information and Risk Perception."

12. Prior, *Post-broadcast Democracy*.

13. Ladd, *Why Americans Hate the Media and How It Matters*, 70, 167.

14. "The Rising Cost of Not Going to College" (survey).

15. Hamilton, "The Growth of Homeschooling" (survey).

16. Gallup polls in the mid-1950s showed that 98 percent of Americans said they believed in God. Johnson, "See How Americans' Belief in God Has Changed over 70 Years" (survey).

17. Membership in these churches has dropped from 28 percent of the population in the 1970s, to under 15 percent today. "America's Changing Religious Landscape" (survey).

18. Hout and Smith, "Fewer Americans Affiliate with Organized Religions, Belief and Practice Unchanged" (survey).

19. Winsemann, "Does More Educated Really = Less Religious?" (survey).

20. "Chapter 3: Demographic Profiles of Religious Groups" (study).

21. "Trust in Government: 1958–2015" (survey).

22. "Confidence in Institutions" (survey).

23. Perhaps the most famous exemplar of this was Alexis de Tocqueville.

24. "Introduction: Searching for a Golden Age."

25. Starr, *The Social Transformation of American Medicine*.

26. For example, in his influential book, *The End of Ideology*, sociologist Daniel Bell observed that "in the Western world . . . there is a rough consensus among intellectuals on political issues: the acceptance of a Welfare State; the desirability of decentralized power; a system of mixed economy and of political pluralism . . . the ideological age has ended." Bell, *The End of Ideology*, 402–3. Historian Arthur Schlesinger Jr.'s *The Vital Center* called for a liberal democracy marked by "empiricism and gradualism" as opposed to grand ideological theories. Schlesinger, *The Vital Center*, 254. Louis Hartz remarked, "We have made the Enlightenment work in spite of itself, and surely it is time we ceased to be frightened of the mechanisms we have derived to do so." As quoted in Purcell, *Democratic Theory*, 258.

27. On pluralism and "elite" theory, see, respectively, Dahl, *Who Governs?*; Mills, *The Power Elite*; on the median voter theorem and its inability to explain empirical reality, see Hacker and Pierson, "After the 'Master Theory'"; on the Enlightenment and liberal consensus, see Marsden, *The Twilight of the American Establishment*; Hodgson, *America in Our Time*.

28. Skowronek and Engel, introduction to Skowronek, Engel, and Ackerman, *The Progressives' Century*, 9.

29. Ibid.; Daniel Carpenter, *The Forging of Bureaucratic Autonomy*.

30. Grisinger, "The (Long) Administrative Century," 360; Carpenter, "Completing the Constitution." As Carpenter demonstrates, many of these federal reforms were predated by state-level regulatory efforts.

31. Gerstle, "The Protean Character of American Liberalism," 1048.

32. Hans Noel has persuasively argued that the New Deal's policy prescriptions can be traced back to the ideas argued for a generation earlier in progressive magazines such as the *New Republic*. Noel, *Political Parties and Political Ideologies in America*. Other useful perspectives include Katznelson, *Fear Itself*; Kornhauser, *Debating the American State*; Cowie, *The Great Exception*; Rodgers, *Atlantic Crossings*, 415.

33. Brinkley, *The End of Reform*, 37–38.

34. Katznelson, *Fear Itself*, 252.

35. Kornhauser, *Debating the American State*, 16, 30–31, 32.

36. Schickler, *Racial Realignment*.

37. Following Gunnar Myrdal's social scientific opus on race relations, *The American Dilemma*, liberals began to devise theories to "treat" racism as an irrational psychological problem. Tesler, *Post-Racial or Most-Racial?*; Kinder and Kam, *Us against Them*; Achen and Bartels, *Democracy for Realists*.

38. Schickler, *Racial Realignment*.

39. Wall, *Inventing the "American Way,"* 78–79, 90–91.

40. Hart, *Forged Consensus*.

41. As George Nash, one of the first chroniclers of the conservative movement and still one of the most cited authors on the subject, wrote, "If *National Review* (or something like it) had not been founded, there would probably have been no cohesive intellectual force on the Right in the 1960s and 1970s . . . the history of reflective conservatism in America after 1955 is the history of the individuals who collaborated in . . . the magazine William F. Buckley, Jr. founded." Nash, *The Conservative Intellectual Movement in America since 1945*, 153. On the enduring importance of Nash's work, see Burns, "In Retrospect." On this point, see also Noel, *Political Ideologies and Political Parties in America*, 5–6.

42. "The Magazine's Credenda," 6; emphases added. A few years prior, Buckley had published an attack on American higher education and liberal elites; see *God and Man at Yale*.

43. In her best-selling 1964 book, *A Choice Not an Echo*, Schlafly sought to "translate" conservative ideas for the grass roots. Crichtlow, *Phyllis Schlafly and Grassroots Conservatism*, 41.

44. As quoted in Critchlow, *Phyllis Schlafly and Grassroots Conservatism*, 75. It is perhaps ironic that even though the conservative movement was preoccupied by the "satanic utopianism" of communism, Buckley styled himself an "intellectual revolutionary," and conservatives explicitly mimicked the tactics of Lenin in taking over the Republican Party in 1964. Kabaservice, *Rule and Ruin*, 16, 49–52.

45. Schlafly, *A Choice Not an Echo*, 25–26, 76, 86, 115.

46. Kazin, *The Populist Persuasion*.

47. On Father Coughlin, see Tull, *Father Coughlin and the New Deal*, 231–32.

48. As Michael Kazin explains, "In the Wheeling, [West Virginia] speech that launched [McCarthy], he accused 'the bright young men who are born with silver spoons in their mouth' of 'selling this nation out.' Later, he would revel in denouncing 'parlor pinks and parlor punks' and ridiculed famous adversaries with epithets like 'Alger—I mean Adlai' (Stevenson) and 'the elegant and alien [Dean] Acheson—Russian as to heart, British as to manner.'" Kazin, *The Populist Persuasion*, 185.

49. The cultural populists' distaste for educated elites was evident even during the New Deal. As historian Michael Avery Sutton recounts: A "poor country minister" called on President Roosevelt to "clean out a lot of them Harvard boys . . .

that some way have squirmed into Washington and pretty nearly ruined the your whole administration." This incensed Presbyterian minister from Fort Lauderdale, Florida, advised Roosevelt, "Mr. President, you have never had to work for a living. For that reason you are impractical, but being from Ha'v'd you don't know it." Sutton, *American Apocalypse*, 238.

50. Wallace, *Stand Up for America*, 86, 87.

51. As quoted in Perlstein, *Nixonland*, 224.

52. As quoted in Cowie, "Nixon's Class Struggle" 264.

53. Kristol, *Two Cheers for Capitalism*, 15. Irving Kristol was not the first to talk of a "new class"; one of the intellectual debts Kristol had was James Burnham's *The Managerial Revolution* (1941), which has played a role in the current intellectual defenses of "Trumpism" (i.e., the idea that American elites and democracy have failed us).

54. Continetti, "Crisis of the Conservative Intellectual."

55. William Rusher, the publisher of *National Review*, formulated his complaint against this group of elites in his influential 1975 book *The Making of the New Majority Party*.

56. As quoted in Perlstein, *Nixonland*, 438.

57. In the 1970s, many books appeared with titles like *Don't Blame the People: How the News Media Uses Bias, Distortion, and Censorship to Manipulate Public Opinion*; *The News Twisters*; and *The Left-Leaning Antenna: Political Bias in Television*.

58. As quoted in West, *The Rise and Fall of the Media Establishment*, 104.

59. Ladd, *Why Americans Hate the Media and How It Matters*, 79. On Limbaugh, see Jamieson and Cappella, *Echo Chamber*; Berry and Sobieraj, *The Outrage Industry*, 13, 21. To be sure, there is outrage media that caters to the Left, but it is diminutive in comparison. Ibid., 98–99. Notably, Berry and Sobieraj's research showed "outrage media" to be "virtually absent" as late as 1975.

60. Ladd, *Why Americans Hate the Media and How It Matters*, 70. Today, Rush Limbaugh draws 14.75 million weekly listeners; Sean Hannity, the second-most popular conservative talk radio host, has a weekly audience of 14 million. Santhanam, Mitchell, and Olmstead, "Audio: By the Numbers" (survey). Limbaugh has been sympathetic to Trump this election cycle, while Hannity has made his support for Trump clear. On Limbaugh and Trump, see Friedersdorf, "Rush Limbaugh Is Cheating on Conservatism with Donald Trump"; on Hannity and Trump, see Rutenberg, "Sean Hannity Turns Adviser in the Service of Donald Trump."

61. Levundusky, *How Partisan Media Polarize America*.

62. Illing, "Why This Conservative Radio Host Quit after Trump's Victory."

63. Critchlow, *Phyllis Schlafly and Grassroots Conservatism*, 18.

64. Jerry Falwell warned, "If we don't succeed in winning the hearts and minds of ordinary Americans, then propaganda of the 'freeze-niks' and the 'better red than dead' crowd will soon come to dominate public thought. Once this happens

the Soviets will take our freedom from us—it's that simple and that final!" As quoted in Winters, *God's Right Hand*, 202.

65. Francis Schaeffer emerged as the dominant intellectual force in fundamentalism. His 1976 tome *How Should We Then Live? The Rise and Decline of Western Thought and Culture* was hugely influential among fundamentalists—Jerry Falwell credited Schaffer with his turn to political activism, especially in regard to abortion. Schaeffer, *A Christian Manifesto*, 20. On Falwell's relationship with Schaeffer, see Williams, *God's Own Party*.

66. While it is a mistake to trace the rise of fundamentalism solely to the secularization of society and the culture wars post-1960s, it is undeniable that the Christian Right social movement fully flowered in the late 1970s. See Schlozman, *When Social Movements Anchor Parties*, chaps. 4, 8.

67. Reagan's radio interview as quoted in Williams, *God's Own Party*, 124. While one can debate whether Reagan was a "true" Christian, at the very least he knew how to talk to his target audience; in the 1970s, the Christian Right moved from a preoccupation with communism to "secular humanism." Bean, *The Politics of Evangelical Identity*, 33. For Reagan's quote on teaching creationism, see Lewis, "Abroad at Home." The "Evil Empire" speech was given on March 9, 1983; see under "March 9, 1983" in the bibliography.

68. Ever since 1974, the General Social Survey has been asking Protestant respondents whether they were "Fundamentalist, Moderate, or Liberal" in their religious views in addition to their religious denomination and their ideology. This figure illustrates the deviation from the national average for four religious categories: fundamentalist Protestants, mainline Protestants, Catholics, and people with no religious affiliation.

69. French, "The Price I've Paid for Opposing Donald Trump."

70. Sykes, "Charlie Sykes on Where the Right Went Wrong."

71. "Evangelicals Rally to Trump, Religious 'Nones' Back Clinton" (survey).

72. Continetti, "Crisis of the Conservative Intellectual."

73. Freeman, *The Closing of the Western Mind*, 61.

74. Huntington, *American Politics*.

75. Festinger, *A Theory of Cognitive Dissonance*, 2:86.

76. Cramer, *The Politics of Resentment*.

77. Crwys-Williams, *In the Words of Nelson Mandela*, 14.

78. Maibach, "Communicating Effectively about Climate and Health," 1.

79. Ansolabehere and Konisky, *Cheap and Clean*.

Bibliography

Books

Abramowitz, Alan I. *The Disappearing Center: Engaged Citizens, Polarization, and American Democracy*. New Haven, CT: Yale University Press, 2010.

Achen, Christopher H., and Larry M. Bartels. *Democracy for Realists: Why Elections Do Not Produce Responsive Government*. Princeton, NJ: Princeton University Press, 2016.

Adorno, Theodor W., Else Frenkel-Brunswik, Daniel J. Levinson, and R. Nevitt Sanford. *The Authoritarian Personality*. New York: W. W. Norton, 1993 [1950].

Ahlstrohm, Sidney E. *A Religious History of the American*. New Haven, CT: Yale University Press, 1972.

Albertson, Bethany, and Shana Kushner Gadarian. *Anxious Politics: Democratic Citizenship in a Threatening World*. New York: Cambridge University Press, 2015.

Allport, Gordon. *The Nature of Prejudice*. Cambridge, MA: Addison-Wesley, 1954.

Altemeyer, Bob. *Right-Wing Authoritarianism*. Manitoba: University of Manitoba Press, 1981.

Ansolabehere, Stephen, and David M. Konisky. *Cheap and Clean: How Americans Think about Energy in the Age of Global Warming*. Cambridge, MA: MIT Press, 2014.

Baddeley, Alan D. *Human Memory: Theory and Practice*. Midsomer Norton, UK: Psychology Press, 1997.

Bailyn, Bernard. *The Ideological Origins of the American Revolution*. Cambridge, MA: Belknap Press of Harvard University Press, 1967.

Bean, Lydia. *The Politics of Evangelical Identity: Local Churches and Partisan Divides in the United States and Canada*. Princeton, NJ: Princeton University Press, 2014.

Bell, Daniel. *The End of Ideology: On the Exhaustion of Political Ideas in the 1950s*. Glencoe, IL: Free Press, 1960.

Berelson, Bernard R., Paul F. Lazarsfeld, and William N. McPhee. *Voting: A Study of Opinion Formation in a Presidential Campaign.* Chicago: University of Chicago Press, 1954.

Berry, Jeffrey M., and Sarah Sobieraj. *The Outrage Industry: Political Opinion Media and the New Incivility.* New York: Oxford University Press, 2014.

Bettelheim, Bruno. *The Uses of Enchantment: The Meaning and Importance of Fairy Tales.* New York: Alfred A. Knopf, 1975.

Biss, Eula. *On Immunity: An Inoculation.* Minneapolis: Graywolf Press, 2014.

Boyer, Pascal. *Religion Explained: The Evolutionary Origins of Religious Thoughts.* New York: Basic Books, 2001.

Brinkley, Alan. *The End of Reform: New Deal Liberalism in Recession and War.* New York: Vintage, 1995.

Brown, Rupert. *Prejudice: Its Social Psychology.* Cambridge, MA: Blackwell, 1995.

Buckley, William F., Jr. *God and Man at Yale: The Superstition of "American Freedom."* Chicago: Regnery, 1951.

Burnham, James. *The Managerial Revolution: What Is Happening in the World.* New York: John Day, 1941.

Cannon, Walter B. *Bodily Changes in Pain, Hunger, Fear, and Rage.* New York: Appleton-Century-Crofts, 1929.

———. *Wisdom of the Body.* New York: W. W. Norton, 1932.

Carpenter, Daniel. *The Forging of Bureaucratic Autonomy: Reputations, Networks, and Policy Innovation in Executive Agencies, 1862–1928.* Princeton, NJ: Princeton University Press, 2001.

Carson, Rachel. *Silent Spring.* Boston: Houghton Mifflin Harcourt, 2002.

Carsten, Frances Ludwig. *The Rise of Fascism.* 2nd ed. Berkeley: University of California Press, 1982 [1967].

Cirino, Robert. *Don't Blame the People: How the News Media Use Bias, Distortion and Censorship to Manipulate Public Opinion.* Los Altos, CA: Diversity Press, 1971.

Coates, Ta-Nehisi. *Between the World and Me.* New York: Spiegel and Grau, 2015.

Cohen, Marty, David Karol, Hans Noel, and John Zaller. *The Party Decides: Presidential Nominations before and after Reform.* Chicago: University of Chicago Press, 2008.

Cowie, Jefferson. *The Great Exception: The New Deal and the Limits of American Politics.* Princeton, NJ: Princeton University Press, 2016.

Cramer, Katherine J. *The Politics of Resentment: Rural Consciousness in Wisconsin and the Rise of Scott Walker.* University of Chicago Press, 2016.

Crichtlow, Donald T. *Phyllis Schlafly and Grassroots Conservatism: A Woman's Crusade.* Princeton, NJ: Princeton University Press, 2005.

Crwys-Williams, Jennifer, ed. *In the Words of Nelson Mandela.* New York: Bloomsbury USA, 2011.

Dahl, Robert A. *Who Governs? Democracy and Power in an American City*. New Haven, CT: Yale University Press, 1961.

Damasio, Antonio R. *Descartes' Error: Emotion, Reason, and the Human Brain*. New York: Penguin Putnam, 1994.

Delli Carpini, Michael, and Scott Keeter. *What Americans Know about Politics and Why It Matters*. New Haven, CT: Yale University Press, 1996.

Dobson, James. *Dare to Discipline*. Rev. ed. Wheaton, IL: Tyndale House, 2014.

Douglas, Mary. *Purity and Danger: An Analysis of the Concepts of Pollution and Taboo*. New York: Routledge, 2003 [1966].

Druckman, James N., and Lawrence R. Jacobs. *Who Governs? Presidents, Public Opinion, and Manipulation*. Chicago: University of Chicago Press, 2015.

Ellis, Christopher, and James A. Stimson. *Ideology in America*. New York: Cambridge University Press, 2012.

Ellwood, Robert S. *The Fifties Spiritual Marketplace: American Religion in a Decade of Conflict*. New Brunswick, NJ: Rutgers University Press, 1997.

Epstein, Richard A. *The Classical Liberal Constitution*. Cambridge, MA: Harvard University Press, 2014.

Evans, Dylan, and Pierre Cruse, eds. *Emotion, Evolution, and Rationality*. Oxford: Oxford University Press.

Fenster, Mark. *Conspiracy Theories: Secrecy and Power in American Culture*. 2nd ed. Minneapolis: University of Minnesota Press, 2008.

Festinger, Leon. *A Theory of Cognitive Dissonance*. Vol. 1. Palo Alto, CA: Stanford University Press, 1957.

———. *A Theory of Cognitive Dissonance*. Vol. 2. Palo Alto, CA: Stanford University Press, 1962.

Fiorina, Morris P., Samuel J. Abrams, and Jeremy C. Pope. *Culture War? The Myth of a Polarized America*. 2nd ed. New York: Pearson Longman, 2006.

———. *Culture War? The Myth of a Polarized America*. 3rd ed. New York: Longman, 2009.

Frazer, James G. *The Golden Bough: A Study in Magic and Religion*. 3rd ed. London: Macmillan, 1990 [1890].

———. *The Golden Bough: A Study in Magic and Religion*. Abridged ed. Mineola, NY: Dover, 2002.

Freeman, Charles. *The Closing of the Western Mind: The Rise of Faith and the Fall of Reason*. New York: Vintage, 2007 [2002].

Gerth, Hans H., and C. Wright Mills, eds. *From Max Weber*. New York: Oxford University Press, 1946.

Gilens, Martin. *Why Americans Hate Welfare: Race, Media, and the Politics of Antipoverty Policy*. Chicago: University of Chicago Press, 1999.

Gilovich, Thomas, Dale W. Griffin, and Daniel Kahneman, eds. *Heuristics and Biases: The Psychology of Intuitive Judgment*. New York: Cambridge University Press, 2002.

Goldberg, Robert A. *Enemies Within: The Culture of Conspiracy in Modern America*. New Haven, CT: Yale University Press, 2001.

Goodwyn, Lawrence. *The Populist Moment*. Oxford: Oxford University Press, 1978.

Guthrie, Stewart. *Faces in the Clouds: A New Theory of Religion*. New York: Oxford University Press, 1995.

Harris, Marvin. *Good to Eat: Riddles of Food and Culture*. Long Grove, IL: Waveland Press, 1998.

Hart, David M. *Forged Consensus: Science, Technology, and Economic Policy in the United States, 1921–1953*. Princeton, NJ: Princeton University Press, 1998.

Hartman, Andrew. *A War for the Soul of America: A History of the Culture Wars*. Chicago: University of Chicago Press, 2015.

Hartz, Louis. *The Liberal Tradition in America*. Boston: Houghton Mifflin Harcourt, 1991.

Hatemi, Peter K., and Rose McDermott. *Man Is by Nature a Political Animal: Evolution, Biology, and Politics*. Chicago: University of Chicago Press, 2011.

Hetherington, Marc J., and Jonathan D. Weiler. *Authoritarianism and Polarization in American Politics*. New York: Cambridge University Press, 2009.

Hibbing, John R., Kevin B. Smith, and John R. Alford. *Predisposed: Liberals, Conservatives, and the Biology of Political Differences*. Abingdon, UK: Routledge, 2013.

Hodgson, Godfrey. *America in Our Time: From World War II to Nixon—What Happened and Why*. Princeton, NJ: Princeton University Press, 1978.

Hofstadter, Richard. *The Paranoid Style in American Politics*. New York: Vintage, 2008 [1965].

Hume, David. *A Treatise of Human Nature*. North Chelmsford, MA: Courier, 2003 [1739].

Huntington, Samuel P. *American Politics: The Promise of Disharmony*. Cambridge, MA: Harvard University Press, 1981.

Jacobs, Lawrence R., and Robert Y. Shapiro. *Politicians Don't Pander: Political Manipulation and the Loss of Democratic Responsiveness*. Chicago: University of Chicago Press, 2000.

Jamieson, Kathleen Hall, and Joseph N. Cappella. *Echo Chamber: Rush Limbaugh and the Conservative Media Establishment*. New York: Oxford University Press, 2008.

Jung, Carl Gustav, and Marie-Luise Von Franz. *Man and His Symbols*. New York: Dell, 1968.

Kabaservice, Geoffrey. *Rule and Ruin: The Downfall of Moderation and the Destruction of the Republican Party, from Eisenhower to the Tea Party*. New York: Oxford University Press, 2012.

Kahneman, Daniel. *Thinking, Fast and Slow*. New York: Farrar, Straus and Giroux, 2011.

Katznelson, Ira. *Fear Itself: The New Deal and the Origins of Our Time*. New York: Liveright, 2013.

Kazin, Michael. *The Populist Persuasion: An American History*. Rev. ed. Ithaca, NY: Cornell University Press, 1998.

Keeley, Joseph K. *The Left-Leaning Antenna: Political Bias in Television*. New Rochelle, DE: Arlington House, 1971.

Kinder, Donald R., and Cindy D. Kam. *Us against Them: Ethnocentric Foundations of American Opinion*. Chicago: University of Chicago Press, 2009.

Kinder, Donald R., and Lynn M. Sanders. *Divided by Color: Racial Politics and Democratic Ideals*. Chicago: University of Chicago Press, 1996.

Kornhauser, Anne. *Debating the American State: Liberal Anxieties and the New Leviathan, 1930–1970*. Philadelphia: University of Pennsylvania Press, 2015.

Kristol, Irving. *Two Cheers for Capitalism*. New York: Basic Books, 1978.

Kunzman, Robert. *Write These Laws on Your Children: Inside the World of Christian Conservative Homeschooling*. Boston: Beacon Press, 2009.

Ladd, Jonathan M. *Why Americans Hate the Media and How It Matters*. Princeton, NJ: Princeton University Press, 2011.

Lakoff, George, and Mark Johnson. *Metaphors We Live By*. 2nd ed. Chicago: University of Chicago Press, 2003.

Lee, Taeku. *Mobilizing Public Opinion: Black Insurgency and Racial Attitudes in the Civil Rights Era*. Chicago: University of Chicago Press, 2002.

Lenz, Gabriel. *Follow the Leader? How Voters Respond to Politicians' Policies and Performance*. Chicago: University of Chicago Press, 2012.

LeVine, Robert A., and Donald T. Campbell. *Ethnocentrism: Theories of Conflict, Ethnic Attitudes, and Group Behavior*. New York: John Wiley and Sons, 1972.

Levinovitz, Alan. *The Gluten Lies: And Other Myths about What You Eat*. New York: Regan Arts, 2015.

Levundusky, Matthew. *How Partisan Media Polarize America*. Chicago: University of Chicago Press, 2013.

———. *The Partisan Sort: How Liberals Became Democrats and Conservatives Became Republicans*. Chicago: University of Chicago Press, 2009.

Lewis-Beck, Michael S., William G. Jacoby, Helmut Norpoth, and Herbert F. Weisberg. *The American Voter Revisited*. Ann Arbor: University of Michigan Press, 2008.

Lippmann, Walter. *Public Opinion*. Vol. 1. Piscataway, NJ: Transaction, 1946.

Lodge, Milton, and Charles S. Taber. *The Rationalizing Voter*. New York: Cambridge University Press, 2013.

Luhrmann, Tanya M. *When God Talks Back: Understanding the American Evangelical Relationship with God*. New York: Vintage Books, 2012.

Malinkowski, Bronislaw. *Magic, Science, and Religion and Other Essays*. Garden City, NY: Doubleday, 1948.

Marcus, George E. *The Sentimental Citizen: Emotion in Democratic Politics*. University Park: Pennsylvania State University, 2002.

Marcus, George E., W. Russell Neuman, and Michael MacKuen. *Affective Intelligence and Political Judgment*. Chicago: University of Chicago Press, 2000.

Marsden, George M. *Fundamentalism and American Culture*. New York: Oxford University Press, 2006.

———. *The Twilight of the American Establishment: The 1950s and the Crisis of Liberal Belief*. New York: Basic Books, 2014.

———. *Understanding Fundamentalism and Evangelicalism*. Grand Rapids, MI: Eerdmans, 1991.

Marty, Martin E., and R. Scott Appleby, eds. *Fundamentalisms Observed*. Chicago: University of Chicago Press, 1991.

Mazur, Allan. *True Warnings and False Alarms: Evaluating Fears about the Health Risks of Technology, 1948–1971*. Washington, DC: Resources for the Future, 2004.

McCarty, Nolan, Keith T. Poole, and Howard Rosenthal. *Polarized America: The Dance of Ideology and Unequal Riches*. Cambridge, MA: MIT Press, 2006.

Mendelberg, Tali. *The Race Card: Campaign Strategy, Implicit Messages, and the Norm of Equality*. Princeton, NJ: Princeton University Press, 2001.

Mills, C. Wright. *The Power Elite*. New York: Oxford University Press, 1956.

Morone, James A. *Hellfire Nation: The Politics of Sin in American History*. New Haven, CT: Yale University Press, 2003.

Mueller, John, and Mark G. Stewart. *Terror, Security, and Money*. New York: Oxford University Press, 2011.

Myrdal, Gunnar. *An American Dilemma: The Negro Problem and Modern Democracy*. 2 vols. New York: Harper and Row, 1944.

Nash, George. *The Conservative Intellectual Movement since 1945*. New York: Basic Books, 1976.

Neuman, W. Russell, George E. Marcus, Ann N. Crigler, and Michael MacKuen, eds. *The Affect Effect: Dynamics of Emotion in Political Thinking and Behavior*. Chicago: University of Chicago Press, 2007.

Noel, Hans. *Political Ideologies and Political Parties in America*. New York: Cambridge University Press, 2014.

Norenzayan, Ara. *Big Gods: How Religion Transformed Cooperation and Conflict*. Princeton, NJ: Princeton University Press, 2015.

Nussbaum, Martha C. *Upheavals of Thought: The Intelligence of Emotions*. New York: Cambridge University Press, 2001.

Offit, Paul A. *Do You Believe in Magic? The Sense and Nonsense of Alternative Medicine*. New York: HarperCollins, 2013.

Oliver, J. Eric. *The Paradoxes of Integration: Race, Neighborhood, and Civic Life in Multiethnic America*. Chicago: University of Chicago Press, 2010.

Oshinsky, David M. *A Conspiracy So Immense: The World of Joseph McCarthy*. New York: Free Press, 1983.

Page, Benjamin I., and Robert Y. Shapiro. *The Rational Public: Fifty Years of Trends in Americans' Policy Preferences*. Chicago: University of Chicago Press, 1992.

Pankseep, Jaak. *Affective Neuroscience: The Foundations of Human and Animal Emotions*. New York: Oxford University Press, 2004.

Perlstein, Rick. *Nixonland: The Rise of a President and the Fracturing of America*. New York: Scribner, 2009.

Piaget, Jean. *The Child's Conception of Space*. London: Routledge and Kegan Paul, 1956 [1948].

———. *The Child's Conception of the World*. London: Routledge and Kegan Paul, 1960 [1926].

———. *The Moral Judgment of the Child*. London: Routledge and Kegan Paul, 1965 [1932].

———. *The Origins of Intelligence in Children*. New York: International Universities Press, 1952.

Pinker, Steven. *The Blank Slate: The Modern Denial of Human Nature*. New York: Viking, 2002.

Pitcairn, John. *Vaccination*. Philadelphia: Anti-Vaccination League of Pennsylvania, 1907.

Polkinghorne, John. *Testing Scripture: A Scientist Explores the Bible*. Grand Rapids, MI: Brazos Press, 2011.

Prasad, Vinay, and Adam Cifu. *Ending Medical Reversal: Improving Outcomes, Saving Lives*. Baltimore: Johns Hopkins University Press, 2015.

Prior, Markus. *Post-broadcast Democracy: How Media Choice Increases Inequality in Political Involvement and Polarizes Elections*. New York: Cambridge University Press, 2007.

Purcell, Edward A., Jr. *Democratic Theory: Scientific Naturalism and the Problem of Value*. Lexington: University Press of Kentucky, 1973.

Robertson, Pat. *The New World Order*. Boston: G. K. Hall, 1992.

Rodgers, Daniel T. *Atlantic Crossings: Social Politics in a Progressive Age*. Cambridge, MA: Harvard University Press, 2000.

Roth, Gerhard. *The Long Evolution of Brains and Minds*. Berlin: Springer, 2013.

Rusher, William A. *The Making of the New Majority Party*. New York: Sheed and Ward, 1975.

Sandeen, Ernest R. *The Roots of Fundamentalism*. Chicago: University of Chicago Press, 1970.

Schaeffer, Francis A. *A Christian Manifesto*. Westchester, IL: Crossway Books, 1981.

———. *How Should We Then Live? The Rise and Decline of Western Thought and Culture*. Westchester, IL: Crossway Books, 1976.

Schickler, Eric. *Racial Realignment: The Transformation of American Liberalism, 1932–1965*. Princeton, NJ: Princeton University Press, 2016.

Schlafly, Phyllis. *A Choice Not an Echo: The Inside Story of How American Presidents Are Chosen*. Alton, IL: Pere Marquette Press, 1964.

Schlesinger, Arthur, Jr. *The Vital Center: The Politics of Freedom*. New York: Houghton Mifflin, 1949.

Schlozman, Daniel. *When Social Movements Anchor Parties: Electoral Alignments in American History*. Princeton, NJ: Princeton University Press, 2015.

Scholzman, Kay Lehman, Sidney Verba, and Henry E. Brady. *The Unheavenly Chorus: Unequal Political Voice and the Broken Promise of American Democracy*. Princeton, NJ: Princeton University Press, 2012.

Schuman, Howard. *Racial Attitudes in America: Trends and Interpretations*. Cambridge, MA: Harvard University Press, 1997.

Sehat, David. *The Myth of American Religious Freedom*. New York: Oxford University Press, 2010.

Sernagor, Evelyne, Stephen Eglen, Bill Harris, and Rachel Wong, eds. *Retinal Development*. New York: Cambridge University Press, 2006.

Shermer, Michael. *Why People Believe Weird Things: Pseudoscience, Superstition, and Other Confusion of Our Time*. New York: Henry Holt, 2002.

Shtulman, Andrew. *Scienceblind: Why Our Intuitive Theories about the World Are So Often Wrong*. New York: Basic Books, 2017.

Simoons, Frederick J. *Eat Not This Flesh: Food Avoidances from Prehistory to the Present*. Madison: University of Wisconsin Press, 1961.

Skowronek, Stephen, Stephen Engel, and Bruce Ackerman, eds. *The Progressives' Century: Political Reform, Constitutional Government, and the Modern American State*. New Haven, CT: Yale University Press, 2016.

Smith, Rogers M. *Civic Ideals: Conflicting Visions of Citizenship in US History*. New Haven, CT: Yale University Press, 1999.

Sniderman, Paul M., Richard A. Brody, and Philip Tetlock. *Reasoning and Choice: Explorations in Political Psychology*. New York: Cambridge University Press, 1993.

Starr, Paul. *The Social Transformation of American Medicine*. New York: Basic Books, 1982.

Styers, Randall. *Making Magic: Religion, Magic, and Science in the Modern World*. New York: Oxford University Press, 2004.

Subbotsky, Eugene. *Magic and the Mind: Mechanisms, Functions, and Development of Magical Thinking and Behavior*. New York: Oxford University Press, 2010.

Sutton, Matthew A. *American Apocalypse: A History of Modern Evangelicalism*. Cambridge, MA: Harvard University Press, 2014.

Tajfel, Henri, ed. *Social Identity and Intergroup Relations*. New York: Cambridge University Press, 2010.

Tesler, Michael. *Post-Racial or Most-Racial? Race and Politics in the Obama Era*. Chicago: University of Chicago Press, 2016.

Tetlock, Philip. *Expert Political Judgment: How Good Is It? How Can We Know?* Princeton, NJ: Princeton University Press, 2005.

Thomas, Keith. *Religion and the Decline of Magic: Studies in Popular Beliefs in Sixteenth and Seventeenth-Century England*. London: Penguin UK, 2003.

Tichenor, Daniel J. *Dividing Lines: The Politics of Immigration Control in America*. Princeton, NJ: Princeton University Press, 2009.

Torrey, Reuben A. et al., eds. *The Fundamentals: The Famous Sourcebook of Foundational Biblical Truths*. Updated by Charles L. Feinberg et al. Grand Rapids, MI: Kregel Publications, 1990.

Tripp, Ted, and David Powlison. *Shepherding a Child's Heart*. Wapwallopen, PA: Shepherd Press, 2011.

Tull, Charles J. *Father Coughlin and the New Deal*. Syracuse, NY: Syracuse University Press, 1965.

Vyse, Stuart. *Believing in Magic: The Psychology of Superstition*. 2nd ed. New York: Oxford University Press, 2014.

Wall, Wendy L. *Inventing the "American Way": The Politics of Consensus from the New Deal to the Civil Rights Movement*. New York: Oxford University Press, 2008.

Wallace, George C. *Stand Up for America*. Garden City, NY: Doubleday, 1976.

West, Darrell M. *The Rise and Fall of the Media Establishment*. Boston: Bedford/St. Martin's, 2001.

Williams, Daniel K. *God's Own Party: The Making of the Christian Right*. New York: Oxford University Press, 2012.

Winters, Sean M. *God's Right Hand: How Jerry Falwell Made God a Republican and Baptized the American Right*. New York: HarperCollins, 2012.

Zaller, John. *The Nature and Origins of Mass Opinion*. New York: Cambridge University Press, 1992.

Zusne, Leonard, and Warren H. Jones. *Anomalisitic Psychology: A Study of Magical Thinking*. New York: Psychology Press, 1989.

Articles and Chapters

Abelson, Philip. "Testing for Carcinogens with Rodents." *Science* 249, no. 4975 (1990): 1357.

Abramowitz, Alan I., and Steven Webster. "The Rise of Negative Partisanship and the Nationalization of U.S. Elections in the 21st Century." *Electoral Studies* 41, no. 1 (2016): 12–22.

Abrams, Dominic, and Michael A. Hogg. "Comments on the Motivational Status of Self-Esteem in Social Identity and Intergroup Discrimination." *European Journal of Social Psychology* 18, no. 4 (1988): 317–34.

Albertazzi, Daniele, and Duncan McDonnell. "Introduction: The Sceptre and the Spectre." In *Twenty-First Century Populism: The Spectre of Western European Democracy*, edited by Daniele Albertazzi and Duncan McDonnell, 1–11. New York: Palgrave Macmillan, 2008.

"Americans Spent $33.9 Billion Out-of-Pocket on Complementary and Alternative Medicine." National Center for Complementary and Integrative Health, last modified February 20, 2013. https://nccih.nih.gov/news/2009/073009.htm.

Angell, Marcia, and Jerome Kassirer. "Alternative Medicine—the Risks of Untested and Unregulated Remedies." *New England Journal of Medicine* 339, no. 12 (1998): 839–41.

Ansolabehere, Stephen, Jonathan Rodden, and James M. Snyder. "The Strength of Issues: Using Multiple Measures to Gauge Preference Stability, Ideological Constraint, and Issue Voting." *American Political Science Review* 102, no. 2 (2008): 215–32.

Arditi, Benjamin. "Populism as an Internal Periphery of Democratic Politics." In *Populism and the Mirror of Democracy*, edited by Francisco Panizza, 72–117. New York: Verso Press, 2005.

Ascher, Marcia, and Robert Ascher. "Ethnomathematics." *History of Science* 24, no. 2 (1986): 125–44.

"Autism Spectrum Disorder." National Institute of Mental Health, October 2016. http://www.nimh.nih.gov/health/topics/autism-spectrum-disorders-asd/index.shtml.

Ball, James. "How Safe Is Air Travel Really?" *Guardian* (Manchester), July 24, 2014.

Bar-Hillel, Maya. "The Base-Rate Fallacy in Probability Judgments." *Acta Psychologica* 44 (1980): 211–33.

Baron-Cohen, Simon. "Theory of Mind in Normal Development and Autism." *Prisme* 34 (2001): 174–83.

Bartels, Larry M. "Beyond the Running Tally: Partisan Bias in Political Perceptions." *Political Behavior* 24, no. 2 (2002): 117–50.

———. "Constituency Opinion and Congressional Policy Making: The Reagan Defense Buildup." *American Political Science Review* 85, no. 2 (1991): 457–74.

Bawn, Kathleen, Martin Cohen, David Karol, Seth Masket, Hans Noel, and John Zaller. "A Theory of Political Parties: Groups, Policy Demands and Nominations in American Politics." *Perspectives on Politics* 10, no. 3 (2012): 571–97.

Bechara, Antoine. "The Role of Emotion in Decision-Making: Evidence from Neurological Patients with Orbitofrontal Damage." *Brain and Cognition* 55, no. 1 (2004): 30–40.

Berenbaum, Howard, Matthew Boden, and John P. Baker. "Emotional Salience, Emotional Awareness, Peculiar Beliefs, and Magical Thinking." *Emotion* 9, no. 2 (2009): 197–205.

Bernstein, Jared. "The Flat Tax Falls Flat for Good Reasons." PostEverything, *Washington Post*, May 26, 2015. https://www.washingtonpost.com/posteverything/wp/2015/05/26/the-flat-tax-falls-flat-for-good-reasons.

Berzonsky, Michael D. "The Role of Familiarity in Children's Explanations of Physical Causality." *Child Development* 42, no. 3 (1971): 705–15.

Blancke, Stefaan. "Why People Oppose GMOs Even Though Science Says They Are Safe." *Scientific American*, August 18, 2015. http://www.scientificamerican. com/article/why-people-oppose-gmos-even-though-science-says-they-are-safe.

Bloom, Paul. "To Urgh Is Human." *Guardian* (Manchester), July 21, 2004. https:// www.theguardian.com/science/2004/jul/22/research.science4.

Bonokowski, Bart, and Noam Gidron. "The Populist Style in American Politics: Presidential Campaign Rhetoric, 1952–1996." *Social Forces* 94, no. 4 (2016): 1593–1621.

Boyles, Salynn. "Phiten Necklaces: Baseball Boost or Myth?" CBS News, October 16, 2008. http://www.cbsnews.com/news/phiten-necklace-baseball-boost-or-myth.

Brader, Ted. "Striking a Responsive Chord: How Political Ads Motivate and Persuade Voters by Appealing to Emotions." *American Journal of Political Science* 49, no. 2 (2005): 388–405.

Breslau, Joshua. "Mental Disorders and Subsequent Educational Attainment in a US National Sample." *Journal of Psychiatric Research* 42, no. 9 (2008): 708–16.

Brewer, Marilynn B., and Rupert Brown. "Intergroup Relations." In *The Handbook of Social Psychology*, edited by Daniel Todd Gilbert, Susan T. Fiske, and Gardner Lindzey, 78–92. Boston: McGraw-Hill, 1998.

Brooks, David. "The Republicans' Incompetent Caucus." *New York Times*, October 13, 2015.

Brown, Donald E. "Human Universals, Human Nature and Human Culture." *Dœdalus* 133, no. 4 (2006): 47–54.

Brown, Rupert. "Social Identity Theory: Past Achievements, Current Problems, and Future Challenges." *European Journal of Social Psychology* 30, no. 6 (2000): 745–78.

Brugger, Peter, and Roger E. Graves. "Testing vs. Believing Hypotheses: Magical Ideation in the Judgment of Contingencies." *Cognitive Neuropsychiatry* 2, no. 4 (1957): 251–72.

Burns, Jennifer. "In Retrospect: George Nash's *The Conservative Intellectual Movement since 1945*." *Reviews in American History* 32, no. 3 (2004): 447–62.

Butler, Gillian, and Andrew Mathews. "Cognitive Processes in Anxiety." *Advances in Behaviour Research and Therapy* 5, no. 1 (1983): 51–62.

Cacioppo, John T., and Richard E. Petty. "The Elaboration Likelihood Model of Persuasion." *Advances in Consumer Research* 11 (1984): 673–75.

———. "The Need for Cognition." *Journal of Personality and Social Psychology* 42, no. 1 (1982): 116–31.

Cacioppo, John T., Richard E. Petty, Jeffrey A. Feinstein, and W. Blair G. Jarvis. "Dispositional Differences in Cognitive Motivation: The Life and Times of Individuals Varying in Need for Cognition." *Psychological Bulletin* 1996, no. 2 (1996): 197–253.

Calin-Jageman, Robert, and Tracy L. Caldwell. "Replication of the Superstition and Performance Study by Damisch, Stoberock, and Mussweiler (2010)." *Social Psychology* 45, no. 3 (2014): 239–45.

Canadian Paediatric Society. "Autistic Spectrum Disorder: No Causal Relationship with Vaccines." *Paediatrics and Child Health* 12, no. 5 (2007): 393–95.

Canovan, Margaret. "Trust the People! Populism and the Two Faces of Democracy." *Political Studies* 47, no. 1 (1999): 2–16.

Carmines, Edward G., and Nicholas J. D'Amico. "The New Look in Political Ideology Research." *Annual Review of Political Science* 18 (2015): 205–16.

Carmines, Edward G., and James A. Stimson. "The Two Faces of Issue Voting." *American Political Science Review* 74, no. 1 (1980): 78–91.

Carpenter, Daniel. "Completing the Constitution: Progressive-Era Economic Regulation and the Political Perfection of Article I, Section 8." In *The Progressives' Century: Political Reform, Constitutional Government, and the Modern American State*, edited by Stephen Skowronek, Stephen Engel, and Bruce Ackerman, 291–315. New Haven, CT: Yale University Press, 2016.

Cawthorne, Andrew. "Venezuela to Probe Chavez Cancer Poisoning Accusation." Reuters, March 12, 2013. http://www.reuters.com/article/us-venezuela-election/venezuela-to-probe-chavez-cancer-poisoning-accusation-idUBRE92B0MM20130313.

"Chicago Statement on Biblical Inerrancy." *Journal of the Evangelical Theological Society* 21, no. 4 (1978): 289–96.

"Christian Group Keeping to Right." *New York Times*, September 12, 1993.

Chong, Dennis, and James N. Druckman. "Dynamic Public Opinion: Communication Effects over Time." *American Political Science Review* 104, no. 4 (2010): 663–80.

———. "Framing Theory." *Annual Review of Political Science* 10 (2007): 103–26.

Chopra, Deepak. "Medicine's Great Divide—the View from the Alternative Side." *AMA Journal of Ethics* 13, no 6 (2011): 394–98.

Chumley, Cheryl K. "4 in 10 American Adults: We're Living in the End Times." *Washington Times*, September 12, 2013. http://www.washingtontimes.com/news/2013/sep/12/4-in10-american-adults-were-living-end-times.

Cohn, Nate. "Polarization Is Dividing American Society, Not Just Politics." The Upshot, *New York Times*, June 12, 2014. http://www.nytimes.com/2014/06/12/upshot/polarization-is-dividing-american-society-not-just-politics.html?_r=0.

Continetti, Matthew. "Crisis of the Conservative Intellectual." *Washington Free Beacon*, October 21, 2016. http://freebeacon.com/columns/crisis-conservative-intellectual.

Converse, Phillip. "The Nature of Belief Systems in Mass Publics." In *Ideology and Discontent*, edited by David E. Apter, 206–61. Glencoe, IL: Free Press, 1964.

Cowie, Jefferson. "Nixon's Class Struggle: Romancing the New Right Worker, 1969–1973." *Journal of Labor History* 43, no. 2 (2002): 257–83.

Cunningham-Parmeter, Keith. "Alien Language: Immigration Metaphors and the Jurisprudence of Otherness." *Fordham Law Review* 79, no. 4 (2010): 1545–98.

Dag, Ihsan. "The Relationship among Paranormal Beliefs, Locus of Control and Psychopathology in a Turkish College Sample." *Personality and Individual Difference* 26, no. 4 (1999): 723–37.

Damisch, Lysann, Barbara Stoberock, and Thomas Mussweiler. "Keep Your Fingers Crossed! How Superstition Improves Performance." *Psychological Science* 21, no. 7 (2010): 1014–20.

Davis, Mark H. "Measuring Individual Differences in Empathy: Evidence for a Multidimensional Approach." *Journal of Personality and Social Psychology* 44, no. 1 (1983): 113–26.

Dilliplane, Susanna. "Activation, Confirmation, or Reinforcement? The Impact of Partisan News Exposure on Vote Choice." *American Journal of Political Science* 58, no. 1 (2014): 79–94.

Dockrill, Peter. "Dogs May Look Ashamed, but They Don't Feel Guilt." Science Alert, August 24, 2015. http://www.sciencealert.com/dogs-may-look-ashamed-but -they-don-t-feel-guilt-experts-say.

Domke, David, Mark D. Watts, Dhavan V. Shah, and David P. Fan. "The Politics of Conservative Elites and the 'Liberal Media' Argument." *Journal of Communication* 49, no. 4 (1999): 35–58.

Dreher, Rod. "Individualism and Conservativism." *American Conservative*, August 31, 2012. http://www.theamericanconservative.com/dreher/individualism-and -conservatism.

Druckman, James N. "Political Preference Formation: Competition, Deliberation, and the (Ir)relevance of Framing Effects." *Annual Political Science Review* 98, no. 4 (2004): 671–86.

———. "Priming the Vote: Campaign Effects in a U.S. Senate Election." *Political Psychology* 25, no. 4 (2004): 577–94.

Duckitt, John. "Authoritarianism and Group Identification: A New View of an Old Construct." *Political Psychology* 10, no. 1 (1989): 63–84.

Egan, Patrick J., and Megan Mullin. "Local Weather and Climate Concern." *Nature Climate Change* 4 (2014): 89–90.

Epley, Nicholas, Adam Waytz, and John T. Cacioppo. "On Seeing Human: A Three-Factor Theory of Anthropomorphism." *Psychological Review* 114, no. 4 (2007): 864–86.

Eskridge, William N., Jr. "Body Politics: *Lawrence v. Texas* and the Constitution of Disgust and Contagion." *Florida Law Review* 57, no. 5 (2005): 1011–64.

Evans, Gary W., and Rochelle C. Cassells. "Childhood Poverty, Cumulative Risk Exposure, and Mental Health in Emerging Adults." *Clinical Psychological Science* 2, no. 3 (2014): 287–96.

Faulkner, Jason, Mark Schaller, Justin H. Park, and Lesley A. Duncan. "Evolved Disease-Avoidance Mechanisms and Contemporary Xenophobic Attitudes." *Group Processes and Intergroup Relations* 7, no. 4 (2004): 333–53.

Fein, Steven, and Steven J. Spencer. "Prejudice as Self-Image Maintenance: Affirming the Self through Derogating Others." *Journal of Personality and Social Psychology* 73, no. 1 (1997): 31–44.

Feldman, Stanley. "Structure and Consistency in Public Opinion: The Role of Core Beliefs and Values." *American Journal of Political Science* 32, no. 2 (1988): 416–40.

Feldman, Stanley, and Karen Stenner. "Perceived Threat and Authoritarianism." *Political Psychology* 18, no. 4 (1997): 741–70.

Feltman, Rachel. "This Weird Worm Is a Surprisingly Close Cousin of Ours." *Washington Post*, November 19, 2015.

Fine, Paul E. M. "Herd Immunity: History, Theory, Practice." *Epidemiologic Reviews* 15, no. 2 (1993): 265–302.

Fox, Maggie. "Americans Spend $30 Billion a Year on Alternative Medicine." NBC News, June 22, 2016. http://www.nbcnews.com/health/health-news/americans-spend-30-billion-year-alternative-medicine-n596976.

Francl, Michelle M. "Are Corporations Putting Feathers in Your Food?" *Slate*, February 18, 2015. http://www.slate.com/articles/health_and_science/science/2015/02/food_babe_book_and_blog_claims_beaver_ass_coal_tar_and_yoga_mat_in_your.html.

Frank, Thomas. "Donald Trump Is Moving to the White House, and Liberals Put Him There." Opinion, *Guardian* (Manchester), November 9, 2016. https://www.theguardian.com/commentisfree/2016/nov/09/donald-trump-white-house-hillary-clinton-liberals.

French, David. "The Price I've Paid for Opposing Donald Trump." *National Review*, October 21, 2016. http://www.nationalreview.com/article/441319/donald-trump-alt-right-internet-abuse-never-trump-movement.

"Frequently Asked Questions on Azodicarbonamide (ADA)," U.S. Food and Drug Administration, April 25, 2016. http://www.fda.gov/Food/IngredientsPackagingLabeling/FoodAdditivesIngredients/ucm387497.htm.

Friedersdorf, Conor. "Rush Limbaugh Is Cheating on Conservatism with Donald Trump." *Atlantic*, January 14, 2016. https://www.theatlantic.com/politics/archive/2016/01/why-rush-limbaugh-is-cheating-on-conservatism-with-donald-trump/424083/.

Gaines, Brian J., James H. Kuklinski, Paul J. Quirk, Buddy Peyton, and Jay Verkuilen. "Same Facts, Different Interpretations: Partisan Motivation and Opinion on Iraq." *Journal of Politics* 69, no. 4 (2007): 957–74.

Gass, Nick. "The 9 Worst Predictions about Trump's Rise to the Top." *Politico*, May 4, 2016. http://www.politico.com/story/2016/05/trump-pundits-wrong-predictions-222789.

Gelman, Susan A. "Psychological Essentialism in Children." *Trends in Cognitive Science* 8, no. 9 (2004): 404–9.

Gerber, Alan S., and Gregory A. Huber. "Partisanship, Political Control, and Economic Assessments." *American Journal of Political Science* 54, no. 1 (2010): 153–73.

Gerstle, Gary. "The Protean Character of American Liberalism." *American Historical Review* 99, no. 4 (1994): 1044–73.

Gerteis, Joseph, and Alyssa Goolsby. "Nationalism in America: The Case of the Populist Movement." *Theory and Society* 34, no. 2 (2005): 197–225.

Gigerenzer, Gerd, and Wolfgang Gaissmaier. "Heuristic Decision Making." *Annual Review of Psychology* 62 (2011): 451–82.

Gladwell, Malcolm. "The Pima Paradox." *New Yorker*, February 2, 1998.

Glenn, Brian J., and Steven M. Teles. "Studying the Role of Conservatives in American Political Development." In *Conservatism and American Political Development*, edited by Brian J. Glenn and Steven M. Teles, 3–20. New York: Oxford University Press, 2009.

Glueck, Katie. "Cruz Throws a Little Populism at Trump." *Grand Old Primary* (blog), *Politico*, February 28, 2016. http://www.politico.com/blogs/2016-gop-primary-live -updates-and-results/2016/02/ted-cruz-donald-trump-super-tuesday-219935.

Gmelch, George. "Superstition and Ritual in American Baseball." *Elysian Fields Quarterly* 11, no. 3 (1992): 25–36.

Goldberg, Jeffrey. "Were There Dinosaurs on Noah's Ark?" *Atlantic*, October 2014. https://www.theatlantic.com/magazine/archive/2014/10/the-genesis-code /379341/.

Green, Emma. "You Can't Educate People into Believing in Evolution." *Atlantic*, November 23, 2014. http://www.theatlantic.com/national/archive/2014/11/you -cant-educate-people-into-believing-in-evolution/382983/.

Gribble, Gordon. "Food Chemistry and Chemophobia." *Food Security* 5, no. 2 (2013): 177–87.

Grisinger, Joanna. "The (Long) Administrative Century." In *The Progressives' Century: Political Reform, Constitutional Government, and the Modern American State*, edited by Stephen Skowronek, Stephen Engel, and Bruce Ackerman, 360–81. New Haven, CT: Yale University Press, 2016.

Hacker, Jacob S., and Paul Pierson. "After the 'Master Theory': Downs, Schattschneider, and the Rebirth of Policy-Focused Analysis." *Perspectives on Politics* 12, no. 2 (2014): 643–62.

Haelle, Tara. "First Confirmed U.S. Measles Death in More Than a Decade." *Forbes*, July 2, 2015. http://www.forbes.com/sites/tarahaelle/2015/07/02/first-u-s-measles -death-in-more-than-a-decade/#3295e02e1918.

Haidt, Jonathan, and Sam Abrams. "The Top 10 Reasons American Politics Are So Broken." *Wonkblog,Washington Post*, January7,2015.https://www.washingtonpost .com/news/wonk/wp/2015/01/07/the-top-10-reasons-american-politics-are -worse-than-ever.

Haidt, Jonathan, Clark McCauley, and Paul Rozin. "Individual Differences in Sensitivity to Disgust: A Scale Sampling Seven Domains of Disgust Elicitors." *Personality and Individual Differences* 16 (1994): 701–13.

Harnad, Stevan. "To Cognize Is to Categorize: Cognition Is Categorization." In *Handbook of Categorization in Cognitive Science*, edited by Henri Cohen and Claire Lefebvre, 20–45. 2nd ed. Cambridge, MA: Elsevier, 2017.

Hawkins, Kirk A. "Is Chaves Populist? Measuring Populist Discourse in Comparative Perspective." *Comparative Political Studies* 42, no. 8 (2009): 1040–67.

Hirstein, William, and Vilayanur S. Ramachandran. "Capgras Syndrome: A Novel
  Probe for Understanding the Neural Representation of the Identity and Famil-
  iarity of Persons." *Proceedings of the Royal Society of London B: Biological
  Sciences* 264, no. 1380 (1997): 437–44.
"Homeopathy." National Center for Complementary and Integrative Health,
  April 4, 2016. https://nccih.nih.gov/health/homeopathy.
Hróbjartsson, Asbjørn, and Peter C. Gøtzsche. "Is the Placebo Powerless?—an
  Analysis of Clinical Trials Comparing Placebo with No Treatment." *New En-
  gland Journal of Medicine* 344 (2001): 1594–1602.
Hudson, Christopher G. "Socioeconomic Status and Mental Illness: Tests of Social
  Causation and Selection Hypotheses." *American Journal of Orthopsychiatry* 75,
  no. 1 (2005): 3–18.
Illing, Sean. "Why This Conservative Radio Host Quit after Trump's Victory." *Vox*,
  January 3, 2017. http://www.vox.com/conversations/2017/1/3/14103136/donald
  -trump-conservative-media-talk-radio-john-ziegler-rush-limbaugh.
Ingraham, Christopher. "There's Never Been a Safer Time to Be a Kid in America."
  Wonkblog, Washington Post, April 14, 2015. https://www.washingtonpost.com/news
  /wonk/wp/2015/04/14/theres-never-been-a-safer-time-to-be-a-kid-in-america.
"Introduction: Searching for a Golden Age." 1998. America's Golden Age of Med-
  icine?, website of the History and Sociology of Science Department, University
  of Pennsylvania. http://ccat.sas.upenn.edu/goldenage/intro/intro.htm.
Jalonick, Mary Clare. "Obama Signs Bill Requiring Labeling of GMO Foods."
  Washington Post, July 29, 2016. https://www.washingtonpost.com/lifestyle/food
  /obama-signs-bill-requiring-labeling-of-gmo-foods/2016/07/29/1f071d66-55d2
  -11e6-b652-315ae5d4d4dd_story.html.
Jansen, Robert S. "Populist Mobilization: A New Theoretical Approach to Populism." *Sociological Theory* 29, no. 2 (2011): 75–96.
Johnson, Jenna. "Donald Trump's Vision of Doom and Despair in America." *Washing-
  ton Post*, July 21, 2016. https://www.washingtonpost.com/politics/donald-trumps
  -message-of-doom-and-despair-in-america/2016/07/21/8afe4cae-3f22-11e6-80bc
  -d06711fd2125_story.html?utm_term=.9f1d5252e5a5.
Kahneman, Daniel, Jack L. Knetsch, and Richard H. Thaler. "Anomalies: The
  Endowment Effect, Loss Aversion, and Status Quo Bias." *Journal of Economic
  Perspectives* 5, no. 1 (1991): 193–206.
Kahneman, Daniel, and Dan Lovallo. "Delusions of Success: How Optimism Un-
  dermines Executives' Decisions." *Harvard Business Review* 81 (2003): 56–63.
Keleman, Deborah. "Are Children 'Intuitive Theists'? Reasoning about Purpose
  and Design in Nature." *Psychological Science* 15, no. 5 (2004): 295–301.
———. "Function, Goals, and Intention: Children's Teleological Reasoning about
  Objects." *Trends in Cognitive Science* 3, no. 12 (1999): 461–68.
———. "The Scope of Teleological Thinking in Preschool Children." *Cognition* 70,
  no. 3 (1999): 241–72.

Keleman, Deborah, Joshua Rottman, and Rebecca Seston. "Professional Physical Scientists Display Tenacious Teleological Tendencies: Purpose-Based Reasoning as a Cognitive Default." *Journal of Experimental Psychology: General* 142, no. 4 (2013): 1074–83.

Klaczynski, Paul. "There's Something about Obesity: Culture, Contagion, Rationality, and Children's Responses to Drinks 'Created' by Obese Children." *Journal of Experimental Child Psychology* 99, no. 1 (2008): 58–74.

Kolata, Gina. "A Medical Mystery of the Best Kind: Major Diseases Are in Decline." The Upshot, *New York Times*, July 8, 2016. https://www.nytimes.com /2016/07/10/upshot/a-medical-mystery-of-the-best-kind-major-diseases-are-in -decline.html.

Knauft, Bruce M., Thomas S. Abler, Laura Betzig, Christopher Boehm, Robert Knox Dentan, Thomas M. Kiefer, Keither F. Otterbein, John Paddock, and Lars Rodseth. "Violence and Sociality in Human Evolution (and Comments and Replies)." *Current Anthropology* 32, no. 4 (1991): 391–428.

Kuran, Timur, and Cass R. Sunstein. "Availability Cascades and Risk Regulation." *Stanford Law Review* 51 (1999): 683–768.

"Labor Force Statistics from the Current Population Study." United States Department of Labor, 2015. http://www.bls.gov/cps/cpsaat11.htm.

Ladd, Jonathan, and Gabriel S. Lenz. "Reassessing the Role of Anxiety in Vote Choice." *Political Psychology* 29, no. 2 (2008): 275–96.

Layman, Geoffrey C. "Party Polarization in American Politics: Characteristics, Causes, and Consequences." *Annual Review of Political Science* 9 (2006): 83–110.

Lee, Michael J. "The Populist Chameleon: The People's Party, Huey Long, George Wallace, and the Populist Argumentative Frame." *Quarterly Journal of Speech* 92, no. 4 (2006): 355–78.

Lerner, Michael. "Stop Shaming Trump Supporters." Opinion, What Happened on Election Day, *New York Times*, November 9, 2016. https://www.nytimes .com/interactive/projects/cp/opinion/election-night-2016/stop-shaming-trump -supporters.

Levitt, Steven D. "Pools More Dangerous Than Guns." *Chicago Sun-Times*, July 28, 2001.

Lewis, Anthony. "Abroad at Home: Religion and Politics." *New York Times*, September 18, 1980.

Lichtblau, Eric. "Cato Institute and Koch Brothers Reach Agreement." *The Caucus* (blog), *New York Times*, June 25, 2012. http://thecaucus.blogs.nytimes.com /2012/06/25/cato-institute-and-koch-brothers-reach-agreement.

Lieberman, Matthew D. "Intuition: Social Cognitive Neuroscience Approach." *Psychological Bulletin* 126, no. 1 (2000): 109–37.

Lippman, Daniel, Darren Samuelsohn, and Isaac Arnsdorf. "Trump's Week of Errors, Exaggerations and Flat-Out Falsehoods." *Politico*, March 13, 2016. http://

www.politico.com/magazine/story/2016/03/trump-fact-check-errors-exaggera
tions-falsehoods-213730.

Liu, Shiping, Ju-Chin Huang, and Gregory L. Brown. "Information and Risk Perception: A Dynamic Adjustment Process." *Risk Analysis* 18, no. 6 (1998): 689–99.

Lowry, Rich. "Ben Carson, the Superior Outsider." *Politico*, September 2, 2015. http:// www.politico.com/magazine/story/2015/09/ben-carson-the-superior-outsider -213291.

Luo, Michael. "On Abortion, It's the Bible of Ambiguity." *New York Times*, November 13, 2005.

"The Magazine's Credenda." *National Review*, November 19, 1955.

Maibach, Edward. "Communicating Effectively about Climate and Health." September 19, 2015. http://www.psr.org/assets/summit/session-12-communicating .pdf.

Marcus, George E. "The Psychology of Emotion and Politics." In *Oxford Handbook of Political Psychology,* edited by Leonie Huddy, David Sears, and Robert Jervis, 183–221. New York: Oxford University Press, 2003.

Marks, Gary, and Norman Miller. "Ten Years of Research on the False-Consensus Effect: An Empirical and Theoretical Review." *Psychological Bulletin* 102, no. 1 (1987): 72–90.

Marshall, Eliot. "The Politics of Alternative Medicine." *Science* 265, no. 5181 (1994): 2000–2002.

Mayer, John D., and Glenn Geher. "Emotional Intelligence and the Identification of Emotion." *Intelligence* 22, no. 2 (1996): 89–113.

McCright, Aaron M., and Riley E. Dunlap. "The Politicization of Climate Change and Polarization in the American Public's Views of Global Warming, 2001– 2010." *Sociological Quarterly* 52, no. 2 (2011): 155–94.

McLaughlin, Dan. "No, This Is Not How We Got Trump." *National Review*, June 28, 2016. http://www.nationalreview.com/article/437219/donald-trump-not-product -republican-obama-criticism.

McLeod, Jane D., and Michael J. Shanahan. "Trajectories of Poverty and Children's Mental Health." *Journal of Health and Social Behavior* 37 (1996): 207–20.

Meyer-Rochow, Victor B. "Food Taboos: Their Origins and Purposes." *Journal of Ethnobiology and Ethnomedicine* 5, no. 1 (2009): 18.

Moffitt, Benjamin, and Simon Tormey. "Rethinking Populism: Politics, Mediatisation and Political Style." *Political Studies* 62, no. 2 (2014): 381–97.

Mooney, Chris. "Why Does the Vaccine/Autism Controversy Live On?" *Discover* (June 2009), http://discovermagazine.com/2009/jun/06-why-does-vaccine-autism -controversy-live-on.

Mosby, Ian. "'That Won-Ton Soup Headache': The Chinese Restaurant Syndrome, MSG and the Making of American Food, 1968–1980." *Social History of Medicine* 22, no. 1 (2009): 133–51.

Mudde, Cas. "The Populist Zeitgeist." *Government and Opposition* 39, no. 4 (2004): 542–63.

Nickerson, Raymond S. "Confirmation Bias: A Ubiquitous Phenomenon in Many Guises." *Review of General Psychology* 2, no. 2 (1998): 175–220.

Nyhan, Brendan, and Jason Reifler. "Displacing Misinformation about Events: An Experimental Test of Causal Corrections." *Journal of Experimental Political Science* 2, no. 1 (2015): 81–93.

———. "Does Correcting Myths about the Flu Vaccine Work? An Experimental Evaluation of the Effects of Corrective Information." *Vaccine* 33, no. 3 (2015): 459–64.

———. "When Corrections Fail: The Persistence of Political Misperceptions." *Political Behavior* 32, no. 2 (2010): 303–30.

Obayashi, Yoko, and Yoichi Nagamura. "Does Monosodium Glutamate Really Cause Headache? A Systematic Review of Human Studies." *Journal of Headache and Pain* 17 (2016): 54.

Oliver, J. Eric, and Wendy M. Rahn. "Rise of the Trumpenvolk: Populism in the 2016 Election." *Annals of the American Academy of Political and Social Science* 667, no. 1 (2016): 189–206.

Oliver, J. Eric, and Thomas Wood. "Conspiracy Theories and the Paranoid Style(s) of Mass Opinions." *American Journal of Political Science* 58, no. 4 (2014): 952–66.

Oliver, J. Eric, Thomas Wood, and Alexandra Bass. "*Liberellas* versus *Konservateeves*: Social Status, Ideology, and Birth Names in the United States." *Political Behavior* 38, no. 1 (2016): 55–81.

Omer, Saad B., Daniel A. Salmon, Walter A. Orenstein, M. Patricia deHart, and Neal Halsey. "Vaccine Refusal, Mandatory Immunization, and the Risks of Vaccine-Preventable Diseases." *New England Journal of Medicine* 360 (May 2009): 1981–88.

Orwell, George. "In Front of Your Nose." In *The Collected Essays, Journalism and Letters of George Orwell*, bk. 4, *In Front of Your Nose, 1945–1950*, edited by Sonia Orwell and Ian Angus, 124. Harmondsworth, UK: Penguin, 1970.

Panksepp, Jaak. "Affective Consciousness: Core Emotional Feelings in Animals and Humans." *Consciousness and Cognition* 14, no. 1 (2005): 30–80.

Park, Bernadette, and Charles M. Judd. "Rethinking the Link between Categorization and Prejudice within the Social Cognition Perspective." *Personality and Social Psychology Review* 9, no. 2 (2005): 108–30.

Parker-Pope, Tara. "Most Believe God Gets Involved." *New York Times*, March 10, 2010. http://well.blogs.nytimes.com/2010/03/10/most-believe-god-gets-involved/?_r=0.

Paul, Gregory. "From Jesus' Socialism to Capitalistic Christianity." *Washington Post*, August 12, 2011.

Pei, Minxin. "The Paradoxes of American Nationalism." *Foreign Policy*, November 2, 2009. http://foreignpolicy.com/2009/11/02/the-paradoxes-of-american-nationalism.

Pham, Michel Tuan. "Emotion and Rationality: A Critical Review and Interpretation of Empirical Evidence." *Review of General Psychology* 11, no. 2 (2007): 155–78.

Plumer, Brad. "What a Liberal Sociologist Learned from Spending Five Years in Trump's America." *Vox*, October 25, 2016. https://www.vox.com/2016/9/6/128 03636/arlie-hochschild-strangers-land-louisiana-trump.

Prasad, Vinay, Adam Cifu, and John P. A. Ioannidis. "Reversals of Established Medical Practices: Evidence to Abandon Ship." *Journal of the American Medical Association* 307, no. 1 (2012): 37–38.

Prasad, Vinay, Andrae Vandross, Caitlin Toomey, Michael Cheung, Jason Rho, Steven Quinn, Satish J. Chacko, et al. "A Decade of Reversal: An Analysis of 146 Contradicted Medical Practices." *Mayo Clinic Proceedings* 88, no. 8 (2013): 790–98.

Premack, David, and Guy Woodruff. "Does the Chimpanzee Have a Theory of Mind?" *Behavioral and Brain Sciences* 4 (1978): 515–26.

"Questions and Answers on Monosodium Glutamate (MSG)." U.S. Food and Drug Administration, November 19, 2012. http://www.fda.gov/Food/IngredientsPack agingLabeling/FoodAdditivesIngredients/ucm328728.htm.

Rahn, Wendy, and Eric Oliver. "Trump Voters Aren't Authoritarians." *Washington Post*, March 9, 2016. https://www.washingtonpost.com/news/monkey-cage /wp/2016/03/09/trumps-voters-arent-authoritarians-new-research-says-so-what -are-they.

Ratner, Rebecca K., and Kenneth C. Herbst. "When Good Decisions Have Bad Outcomes: The Impact of Affect on Switching Behavior." *Organizational Behavior and Human Decision Processes* 96, no. 1 (2005): 23–37.

Repp, Richard A. "Biotech Pollution: Assessing Liability for Genetically Modified Crop Production and Genetic Drift." *Idaho Law Review* 36, no. 3 (1999–2000): 585–620.

Riedel, Stefan. "Edward Jenner and the History of Smallpox and Vaccination." *Baylor University Medical Center Proceedings* 18, no. 1 (2005): 21–25.

Rozin, Paul, Jonathan Haidt, and Clark R. McCauley. "Disgust: The Body and Soul Emotion." In *Handbook of Cognition and Emotion*, edited by Tim Dalgleish and Mick J. Power, 429–45. Chichester, UK: John Wiley and Sons, 1999.

Rozin, Paul, Laura Lowery, Sumio Imada, and Jonathan Haidt. "The CAD Triad Hypothesis: A Mapping between Three Moral Emotions (Contempt, Anger, Disgust) and Three Moral Codes (Community, Autonomy, Divinity)." *Journal of Personality and Social Psychology* 76, no. 4 (1999): 574–86.

Rozin, Paul, and Carol Nemeroff. "Sympathetic Magical Thinking: The Contagion and Similarity 'Heuristics.'" In *Heuristics and Biases: The Psychology of Intuitive Judgment*, edited by Thomas Gilovich, Dale W. Griffin, and Daniel Kahneman, 201–16. New York: Cambridge University Press, 2002.

Rozin, Paul, Linda Millman, and Carol Nemeroff. "Operation of the Laws of Sympathetic Magic in Disgust and Other Domains." *Journal of Personality and Social Psychology* 50, no. 4 (1986): 703–12.

Rubin, Jennifer. "What Kind of Populism?" *Washington Post*, June 14, 2015.

Rutenberg, Jim. "Sean Hannity Turns Adviser in the Service of Donald Trump." *New York Times*, August 21, 2016.

Salovey, Peter, and John D. Mayer. "Emotional Intelligence." *Imagination, Cognition, and Personality* 9, no. 3 (1990): 185–211.

Schaffner, Brian F., and Cameron Roche. "Misinformation and Motivated Reasoning: Responses to Economic News in a Politicized Environment." *Public Opinion Quarterly* 81, no. 1 (2016): 86–110.

Schnall, Simone, Jonathan Haidt, Gerard L. Clore, and Alexander H. Jordan. "Disgust as Embodied Moral Judgment." *Personality and Social Psychology Bulletin* 34, no. 8 (2008): 1096–1109.

Schultz, Wolfram, Peter Dayan, and P. R. Montague. "A Neural Substrate of Prediction and Reward." *Science* 275, no 5306 (1997): 1593–99.

Schwarz, Norbert, Fritz Strack, Denis Hilton, and Gabi Naderer. "Base Rates, Representativeness, and the Logic of Conversation: The Contextual Relevance of 'Irrelevant' Information." *Social Cognition* 9 (1991): 67–84.

Sears, David O. "Symbolic Politics." In *Explorations in Political Psychology*, edited by Shanto Iyengar and William J McGuire, 113–49. Durham, NC: Duke University Press, 1993.

Shellnutt, Kate, and Hannah Anderson. "The Divine Rise of Multilevel Marketing." *Christianity Today*, November 23, 2015. http://www.christianitytoday .com/ct/2015/december/divine-rise-of-multilevel-marketing-christians-mlm .html.

Simon, Herbert. "Rationality as Process and Product of Thought." *American Economic Review* 68, no. 2 (1978): 1–16.

Skowronek, Stephen, and Stephen Engel. Introduction to *The Progressives' Century: Political Reform, Constitutional Government, and the Modern American State*, edited by Stephen Skowronek, Stephen Engel, and Bruce Ackerman, 1–24. New Haven, CT: Yale University Press, 2016.

Smidt, Corwin D. "Polarization and the Decline of the American Floating Voter." *American Journal of Political Science* 61, no. 2 (2017): 365–81.

Smith, Ben, and Byron Tau. "Birtherism: Where It All Began." *Politico*, April 22, 2011. http://www.politico.com/story/2011/04/birtherism-where-it-all-began-053563.

Stanley, Ben. "The Thin Ideology of Populism." *Journal of Political Ideologies* 13, no. 1 (2008): 95–110.

Steensland, Brian, Lynn D. Robinson, W. Bradford Wilcox, Jerry Z. Park, Mark D. Regnerus, and Robert D. Woodberry. "The Measure of American Religion: Toward Improving the State of the Art." *Social Forces* 79, no. 1 (2000): 291–318.

Stern, Alexandra, and Howard Markel. "The History of Vaccines and Immunization: Familiar Patterns, New Challenges." *Health Affairs* 24, no. 3 (2005): 611–21.

Sykes, Charles. "Charlie Sykes on Where the Right Went Wrong." *New York Times*, December 15, 2016.

Tajfel, Henri. "Social Identity and Intergroup Behaviour." *Social Science Information* 13, no. 2 (1974): 65–93.

———. "Social Psychology of Intergroup Relations." *Annual Review of Psychology* 33, no. 1 (1982): 1–39.

Tobacyk, Jerome, and Gary Milford. "Belief in Paranormal Phenomena: Assessment, Instrumental Development and Implications for Personality Functioning." *Journal of Personality and Social Psychology* 44, no. 5 (1983): 1029–37.

Trussler, Marc, and Stuart Soroka. "Consumer Demand for Cynical and Negative News Frames." *International Journal of Press/Politics* 19, no. 3 (2014): 360–79.

Tversky, Amos, and Daniel Kahneman. "Belief in the Law of Small Numbers." *Psychological Bulletin* 76 (1971): 105–10.

———. "Extensional versus Intuitive Reasoning: The Conjunction Fallacy in Probability Judgment." *Psychological Review* 90 (1983): 293–315.

———. "Judgment under Uncertainty: Heuristics and Biases." *Science* 185 (1974): 1123–31.

Valentino, Nicholas A., Ted Brader, and Ashley E. Jardina. "Immigration Opposition among U.S. Whites: General Ethnocentrism or Media Priming of Attitudes about Latinos?" *Political Psychology* 34, no. 2 (2013): 149–66.

Wadsworth, Martha E., Tali Raviv, Christine Reinhard, Brian Wolff, Catherine DeCarlo Santiago, and Lindsey Einhorn. "An Indirect Effects Model of the Association between Poverty and Child Functioning: The Role of Children's Poverty-Related Stress." *Journal of Loss and Trauma: International Perspectives on Stress and Coping* 13, nos. 2–3 (2008): 156–85.

Wen, Tiffanie. "Why Do People Believe in Ghosts?" *Atlantic*, September 5, 2014. http://www.theatlantic.com/health/archive/2014/09/why-do-people-believe -in-ghosts/379072.

"What's Wrong with Genetic Engineering?" Greenpeace International, http://www .greenpeace.org/international/en/campaigns/agriculture/problem/genetic -engineering, accessed December 6, 2017.

Whitehouse, Harvey. "Cognitive Foundations of Religiosity." In *Mind and Religion: Psychological and Cognitive Foundations of Religiosity*, edited by Harvey Whitehouse and Robert N. McCavley, 223–51. Walnut Creek, CA: Alta Mira, 2005.

Wolfe, Alan. "The Authoritarian Personality Revisited." *Chronicle of Higher Education* 52, no. 7 (2005): B12–B13.

Wolfradt, Uwe. "Dissociative Experience, Train Anxiety and Paranormal Beliefs." *Personality and Individual Differences* 23, no. 1 (1997): 15–19.

Wood, Thomas, and J. Eric Oliver. "Toward a More Reliable Implementation of Ideology in Measures of Public Opinion." *Public Opinion Quarterly* 76, no. 4 (2012): 636–62.

Wrangham, Richard W., and Luke Glowacki. "Intergroup Aggression in Chimpanzees and War in Nomadic Hunter-Gatherers." *Human Nature* 23, no. 1 (2012): 5–29.

Surveys and Other Sources

"America's Changing Religious Landscape." Pew Research Center, May 12, 2015. http://www.pewforum.org/2015/05/12/americas-changing-religious-landscape/.

American National Election Study. 2016. http://www.icpsr.umich.edu/icpsrweb/ICPSR/studies/36390.

Baum, Matthew, and Henry R. Nau. "Foreign Policy Views and US Standing in the World." HKS Faculty Research Working Paper Series RWP09-028. Cambridge, MA: John F. Kennedy School of Government, Harvard University, 2009. https://dash.harvard.edu/bitstream/handle/1/4448880/Baum%20Foreign%20Policy%20Views.pdf.

"Chapter 3: Demographic Profiles of Religious Groups." Pew Research Center, May 12, 2015. http://www.pewforum.org/2015/05/12/chapter-3-demographic-pro files-of-religious-groups.

Chase, Chris. "10 of Baseball's Greatest Fan Superstitions, Ranked by Effectiveness." Fox Sports, October 20, 2016. http://www.foxsports.com/mlb/gallery/mlb -baseball-superstitions-fans-rally-caps-ranked-101116.

"Confidence in Institutions." Gallup, 2017. http://www.gallup.com/poll/1597/con fidence-institutions.aspx.

"Confusion about Gluten-Free Foods and Identifying Them at the Grocery Store." NSF International, December 16, 2015. http://www.nsf.org/newsroom /nsf-survey-finds-us-consumers-struggle-to-define-identify-gluten.

"Donald Trump's Argument for America." Team Trump on YouTube, 2:00. Posted November 6, 2016. https://www.youtube.com/watch?v=vST61W4bGm8.

"Evangelicals Rally to Trump, Religious 'Nones' Back Clinton." Pew Research Center, July 13, 2016. http://www.pewforum.org/2016/07/13/evangelicals-rally-to-trump -religious-nones-back-clinton/.

Funk, Cary. "5 Key Findings on What Americans and Scientists Think about Science." Pew Research Center, January 29, 2015. http://www.pewresearch.org /fact-tank/2015/01/29/5-key-findings-science.

Gallup News. "Confidence in Institutions." http://news.gallup.com/poll/1597/confi dence-institutions.aspx, accessed December 6, 2017.

Hamilton, Amelia. "The Growth of Homeschooling." Watchdog.org, December 18, 2015. http://watchdog.org/252358/the-growth-of-homeschooling.

Hari, Vani. Food Babe website. http://foodbabe.com.

Hout, Michael, and Tom W. Smith. "Fewer Americans Affiliate with Organized Religions, Belief and Practice Unchanged: Key Findings from the 2014 General Social Survey." NORC, University of Chicago, March 2015. http://www.norc .org/PDFs/GSS%20Reports/GSS_Religion_2014.pdf.

Johnson, David. "See How Americans' Belief in God Has Changed over 70 Years." *Time*, April 7, 2016. http://time.com/4283975/god-belief-religion-americans.

Lipman, Ellen E., and Michael H. Boyle. *Linking Poverty and Mental Health: A Lifespan View*. Ontario: Provincial Centre of Excellence for Child and Youth Mental Health at CHEO, September 2008.

Lodge, Milton, and Charles S. Taber. "The Rationalizing Voter: Unconscious Thoughts in Political Information Processing." December 21, 2007. Social Science Research Network, http://papers.ssrn.com/sol3/papers.cfm?abstract_id=1077972.

"March 8, 1983: 'Evil Empire' Speech." Miller Center, University of Virginia, https://millercenter.org/the-presidency/presidential-speeches/march-8-1983 -evil-empire-speech.

Masci, David. "For Darwin Day, 6 Facts about the Evolution Debate." Pew Research Center, February 10, 2017. http://www.pewresearch.org/fact-tank/2016/02/12 /darwin-day/.

Moore, David W. "Three in Four Americans Believe in Paranormal." Gallup, June 16, 2005. http://www.gallup.com/poll/16915/three-four-americans-believe-paranormal .aspx.

Moore, Peter. "Over 40% of Americans Believe Humans and Dinosaurs Shared the Planet." YouGov, June 18, 2015. https://today.yougov.com/news/2015/06/18 /jurassic-world.

Newport, Frank. "In U.S., 42% Believe Creationist Views of Human Origins." Gallup, June 2, 2014. http://www.gallup.com/poll/170822/believe-creationist -view-human-origins.aspx.

———. "In U.S., Percentage Saying Vaccines Are Vital Dips Slightly." Gallup, March 6, 2015. http://www.gallup.com/poll/181844/percentage-saying-vaccines -vital-dips-slightly.aspx.

———. "In U.S., 77% Identify as Christian." Gallup, December 24, 2012. http:// www.gallup.com/poll/159548/identify-christian.aspx.

———. "Most Americans Still Believe in God." Gallup, June 29, 2016. http://www .gallup.com/poll/193271/americans-believe-god.aspx.

"Religious Groups' Official Positions on Abortion." Pew Research Center, January 16, 2013. http://www.pewforum.org/2013/01/16/religious-groups-official-positions-on -abortion.

"Religious Landscape Study." Pew Research Center, 2014. http://www.pewforum .org/religious-landscape-study.

"The Rising Cost of Not Going to College." Pew Research Center, February 11, 2014. http://www.pewsocialtrends.org/2014/02/11/the-rising-cost-of-not-going-to -college.

Santhanam, Laura, Amy Mitchell, and Kenny Olmstead. "Audio: By the Numbers." Pew Research Center's Project for Excellence in Journalism: The State of the News Media 2013. http://www.stateofthemedia.org/2013/audio-digital-drives -listener-experience/audio-by-the-numbers.

"Scientists and Beliefs about Human Evolution." Pew Research Center, February 11, 2016. http://www.pewresearch.org/fact-tank/2016/02/12/darwin-day.

Shani, Danielle. "Knowing Your Colors: Can Knowledge Correct for Partisan Bias in Political Perceptions?" Paper presented at the Annual Meeting of the Midwest Political Science Association, Chicago, April 4, 2006.

"64% Believe Jesus Christ Rose from the Dead." Rasmussen Reports, March 29, 2013. http://www.rasmussenreports.com/public_content/lifestyle/holidays/march _2013/64_believe_jesus_christ_rose_from_the_dead.

"60 Minutes/Vanity Fair Poll: Conspiracy Theories." CBS News, May 6, 2015. http://www.cbsnews.com/news/60-minutes-vanity-fair-poll-conspiracy.

Smith, Tom W., Peter Marsden, Michael Hout, and Jibum Kim. *General Social Surveys, 1972–2014*; machine-readable data file. Principal investigator, Tom W. Smith; co-principal investigator, Peter V. Marsden; co-principal investigator, Michael Hout. Sponsored by the National Science Foundation. Chicago: National Opinion Research Center at the University of Chicago [producer]; Storrs, CT: Roper Center for Public Opinion Research, University of Connecticut [distributor], 2015.

"Sprit and Power—a 10-Country Survey of Pentecostals." Pew Research Center, October 5, 2006. http://www.pewforum.org/2006/10/05/spirit-and-power.

Sussell, Jesse, and James A. Thomson. "Are Changing Constituencies Driving Rising Polarization in the U.S. House of Representatives?" Santa Monica, CA: RAND Corporation, 2015. https://books.google.com/books?hl=en&lr=&id =pXD_BgAAQBAJ&oi=fnd&pg=PR1&ots=02xplVAfoq&sig=glxhPivElJsV nvfAha76s2P9RVA#v=onepage&q&f=false.

Swift, Art. "Putin's Image Rises in US, Mostly among Republicans." Gallup, February 21, 2017. http://www.gallup.com/poll/204191/putin-image-rises-mostly-among -republicans.aspx.

"Trust in Government: 1958–2015." Pew Research Center, November 23, 2015. http://www.people-press.org/2015/11/23/1-trust-in-government-1958-2015/.

"2016 Democratic Popular Vote." Real Clear Politics, 2016. http://www.realclear politics.com/epolls/2016/president/democratic_vote_count.html.

"U.S. Public Health Service Syphilis Study at Tuskegee." Centers for Disease Control and Prevention, December 8, 2016. https://www.cdc.gov/tuskegee/timeline .htm.

"The Use of Complementary and Alternative Medicine in the United States." National Center for Complementary and Integrative Health, March 22, 2016. https://nccih.nih.gov/research/statistics/2007/camsurvey_fs1.htm.

"Vaccine Safety." Centers for Disease Control and Prevention, November 23, 2015. http://www.cdc.gov/vaccinesafety/concerns/autism.html.

"Views of Gun Control—a Detailed Demographic Breakdown." Pew Research Center, January 13, 2011. http://www.pewresearch.org/2011/01/13/views-of-gun -control-a-detailed-demographic-breakdown/.

Wang, Kim. "Dandelion Health Benefits." NaturalRemedies.org. http://www.natural
    remedies.org/dandelion, accessed December 6, 2017.

"What Is Celiac Disease?" Celiac Disease Foundation. https://celiac.org/celiac
    -disease/understanding-celiac-disease-2/what-is-celiac-disease.

Wigington, Patti. "Magical Correspondence Tables," ThoughtCo, June 26, 2016;
    updated March 23, 2017. http://paganwiccan.about.com/od/spellworkfolkmagic
    /tp/Magical-Correspondence-Tables.htm.

Winsemann, Albert L. "Does More Educated Really = Less Religious?" Gallup,
    February 4, 2003. http://www.gallup.com/poll/7729/does-more-educated-really
    -less-religious.aspx.

Index

stereotypes, 12, 17, 23, 130, 134–39, 224n21
Stimson, Jim, 91, 198, 218n23
stress, 17, 19, 36, 62, 67, 70–72
supernatural beliefs, 9, 11, 32, 36, 39, 41, 50–53, 55–59, 62–65, 72–73, 93, 150–51, 209n7, 211n20, 214n19
superstitions, xi, xiii, 3, 6, 16–18, 25, 35–37, 40–41, 173, 175, 191–92
suspicion, 2, 128, 143, 154, 166, 169–70, 186
symbolic thinking scale, 46–48, 210n12, 210n13
symbols, 3–4, 8, 11, 28–29, 38, 45–48, 54, 57, 61–63, 65, 105–6, 125, 127, 143, 146

Taber, Charles S., 24–25
Tajfel, Henri, 223n10, 223n13
taxes, xi, 12–13, 89, 96–99, 110, 124–25, 173, 183, 218n22, 218n29, 220n39, 220n4
terrorism, 9, 11, 23, 34, 43–44, 107, 110, 114, 125, 129, 150, 175–76, 195, 220n1, 225n26
Tesler, Michael, 224n20, 230n37
Tetlock, Phillip, 202n11
thinking: positive, 57–58, 165, 211n34; symbolic, 40, 48, 56, 62, 225n26
threats, 16, 19, 63–64, 74, 78, 101–2, 105, 110, 131, 149–50, 173, 176, 190, 192–93, 195

Trump, Donald, xi–xiii, 12–13, 106–9, 111–13, 115–17, 119, 123, 125–30, 132–33, 169–73, 190–94, 221n8, 221n13, 228n5, 231n60
trust, 12, 60–61, 117–18, 131, 179, 187, 194
truthers, 107, 109, 111, 113, 115, 117, 119–21, 123, 125, 127, 190
Tuskegee syphilis experiment, 151, 226n12
Tversky, Amos, 20–21, 26, 203n23, 205n16, 205n18

uncertainty, 7, 17–20, 23, 42, 54, 68, 105, 134, 158, 166, 174, 195, 205n15

vaccines, xi–xiii, 1–2, 10, 12–13, 15, 31, 103–4, 148–51, 153–55, 163, 165–70, 220n39, 225n3, 226n14, 226n19, 228n55
values, core, 3, 37, 88, 94, 218n27
Verba, Sidney, 210n18

Weiler, Jonathan, 74
white ethnocentrism, 137–42, 147, 224n21
white people, 13, 136, 138–42, 147, 186, 224n23
Williams, Daniel K., 232n65, 232n67